# BANGLADESH

Relatively little is known or understood about Bangladesh by outsiders. Since its hard-won independence from Pakistan in 1971, it has been ravaged by economic and environmental disasters. Only recently has the country begun to emerge as a fragile, but functioning, parliamentary democracy, relatively self-sufficient in food production and with an economy that has been consistently achieving growth. The story of Bangladesh, told through the pages of this concise and readable book, is a truly remarkable one. By delving into its past, and through an analysis of the economic, political and social changes that have taken place over the last twenty years, the book explains how Bangladesh is becoming of increasing interest to the international community as a portal into some of the key issues of our age: the way globalisation affects the world's poorer countries, the long-term effects of the international development industry, the potential risks to people and environment from climate change and the political challenges facing modern Muslim-majority nations. In this way the book offers an important corrective to the view of Bangladesh as a failed state and also sheds light on the lives of a new generation of its citizens.

David Lewis is a Professor of Social Policy at the London School of Economics and Political Science. His publications include, with Nazneen Kanji, *Non-Governmental Organisations and Development* (2009) and *The Management of Non-Governmental Development Organizations: Second Edition* (2006).

For Nazneen

T

# Bangladesh

## Politics, Economy and Civil Society

**DAVID LEWIS**

London School of Economics and Political Science

CAMBRIDGE
UNIVERSITY PRESS

CAMBRIDGE UNIVERSITY PRESS
Cambridge, New York, Melbourne, Madrid, Cape Town,
Singapore, São Paulo, Delhi, Tokyo, Mexico City

Cambridge University Press
32 Avenue of the Americas, New York, NY 10013-2473, USA

www.cambridge.org
Information on this title: www.cambridge.org/9780521713771

First published 2011

Printed in the United States of America

*A catalog record for this publication is available from the British Library.*

*Library of Congress Cataloging in Publication data*
Lewis, David, 1960–
Bangladesh : politics, economy and civil society / David Lewis.
p.   cm.
Includes bibliographical references and index.
ISBN 978-0-521-88612-3 (hardback) – ISBN 978-0-521-71377-1 (pbk.)
1. Bangladesh – Politics and government – 1971–   2. Bangladesh – Economic conditions.
3. Bangladesh – Social conditions.   I. Title.
DS395.5.L49   2011
954.9205–dc22       2011008211

ISBN 978-0-521-88612-3 Hardback
ISBN 978-0-521-71377-1 Paperback

# Contents

*Maps*                                                                    *page* vii

*Abbreviations*                                                               ix

*Acknowledgements*                                                           xiii

1   Introduction                                                              1

    Approaching Bangladesh in the Literature                                 6

2   A State in the Making                                                    12

    Bangladeshi Society                                                      13
    Bangladesh and the International Aid System                              35
    Conclusion: The Current Picture                                         39

3   Towards Bangladesh                                                       41

    Precolonial Bengal                                                       42
    Conclusion: Past and Present                                            73

4   State, Politics and Institutions                                        75

    Governing Bangladesh (1): From Nation-building to the
        Military Era                                                         76
    Governing Bangladesh (2): From Democratic Renewal to
        "Illiberal Democracy"                                               90
    Understanding the State, Politics and "Illiberal Democracy"             97
    Conclusion: The Patron State                                           107

5   Nongovernmental Actors and Civil Society                               109

    Nonstate Actors in Historical Perspective: Religion, Charity and
        Resistance                                                         111

The Modern Nongovernmental Organisation Sector          113
The Idea of Civil Society                               125
Conclusion: Creativity and Contradiction               134

6   Economic Development and Transformation             136

The Formal Economy since 1971                           137
Bangladesh in the International Economy (1): The Rise of
    Nontraditional Exports                              148
Bangladesh in the International Economy (2): Global and
    Regional Issues                                     153
Poverty and Economic Change                             158
Conclusion: Cautious Optimism?                          165

7   Population, Natural Resources and Environment       167

Natural Resources and Ecology                           168
Population                                              179
Migration and Refugees                                  182
Well-Being and Capabilities                             188
Conclusion: People, Nature and Resources                195

8   Conclusion                                          197

Dilemmas in an Age of Neoliberalism                     198
Wider Issues                                            200

*Glossary of Bengali Terms*                             207
*Bibliography*                                          211
*Index*                                                 225

# Maps

1  Bangladesh in regional context                                              *page* 18
2  Map of Bangladesh                                                                141
3  Bangladesh as a riparian country: combined catchment area
   of the Ganges–Brahmaputra–Meghna river systems                               169

# Abbreviations

| | |
|---|---|
| ACC | Anti-Corruption Commission |
| ADAB | Association of Development Agencies in Bangladesh |
| ADB | Asian Development Bank |
| ADP | Annual Development Plan |
| AL | Awami League |
| ASA | Association for Social Advancement (NGO) |
| BAKSAL | Bangladesh Peasants and Workers Awami League |
| BDR | Bangladesh Rifles, now Border Guard Bangladesh |
| BNP | Bangladesh Nationalist Party |
| BOSC | Basti Basheer Odhikar Surakha Committee |
| BRAC | Bridging Resources Across Communities (NGO) (formerly Bangladesh Rural Advancement Committee) |
| BRDB | Bangladesh Rural Development Board |
| BRIC | Brazil, Russia, India, China |
| CFPR | Challenging Frontiers of Poverty Programme (BRAC) |
| CHT | Chittagong Hill Tracts |
| CSP | Civil Service of Pakistan |
| CUP | Coalition of the Urban Poor |
| DFID | Department for International Development (UK) |
| EIU | Economist Intelligence Unit |
| EPI | Expanded Programme of Immunization |
| EPZ | Export processing zone |
| EU | European Union |
| FAP | Flood Action Plan |
| FBCCI | Federation of Bangladesh Chambers of Commerce and Industry |
| FNB | Federation of NGOs in Bangladesh |
| FYP | Five Year Plan |

| | |
|---|---|
| GDP | Gross domestic product |
| GK | Gonoshasthya Kendra (NGO) |
| GNCC | GO-NGO Consultative Council |
| GNP | Gross national product |
| GSS | Gono Shahajjo Sangstha |
| HACCP | Hazard Analysis Critical Control Point |
| HDI | Human development index |
| HEED | Health, Education and Economic Development |
| HFWC | Health and Family Welfare Centre |
| HNPSP | Health, Nutrition and Population Sector Programme |
| HPSP | Health and Population Sector Programme |
| HYV | High-yielding variety |
| ICS | Indian Civil Service |
| IDPAA | Institute for Development Policy Analysis and Advocacy |
| IPCC | Inter-Governmental Panel on Climate Change |
| IRDP | Integrated rural development projects |
| IRRI | International Rice Research Institute |
| IUCN | World Conservation Union |
| JCD | Jatiyabadi Chhatra Dal, BNP student wing |
| JI | Jama'at-i-Islami Party |
| JMB | Ja'amatul Mujaheedin Bangladesh |
| JSD | Jatiya Samajtantrik Dal Party |
| KPP | Krishak Proja Party |
| KSP | Krishak Sramik Party |
| MDGs | Millennium Development Goals |
| MDTF | Multi-Donor Trust Fund |
| MFA | Multi-Fibre Arrangement |
| MJF | Manusher Jonno Foundation |
| MLA | Martial Law Administrator |
| MP | Member of Parliament |
| NAP | National Awami Party |
| NAPA | National Adaptation Plan of Action |
| NBC | National Broadcasting Company (US) |
| NGO | Nongovernmental organization |
| NIP | New Industrial Policy |
| NK | Nijera Kori (NGO) |
| NWFP | North-West Frontier Province |
| OIC | Organization of the Islamic Conference |
| PCJSS | Parbatya Chattagram Janasaghati Samity |
| PKSF | Palli Karma-Sahayak Foundation |

| | |
|---|---|
| PRSP | Poverty Reduction Strategy Paper |
| RAB | Rapid Action Battalion |
| RIP | Revised Industrial Policy |
| SAARC | South Asian Association for Regional Cooperation |
| TI | Transparency International |
| TUP | Targeting the Ultra-Poor (BRAC) |
| UMP | United Muslim Party |
| UN | United Nations |
| UNDP | UN Development Programme |
| UNO | *Upazila* Nirbahi Officer |
| UP | Union *parishad* |
| USAID | U.S. Agency for International Development |
| USC | Union Sub-Centre |
| V-AID | Village Agricultural Industrial Development |
| VAT | Value-added tax |
| VGD | Vulnerable Group Development |
| WHO | UN World Health Organization |
| WTO | World Trade Organization |

# Acknowledgements

During my work on Bangladesh over the past two decades, a great many people have helped and inspired me. They are too numerous to thank individually. However, I would like to single out Shapan Adnan, Shaheen Anam, Jessica Ayers, Harry Blair, Joseph Devine, Colette Chabbott, Sharad Chari, Ben Crow, Jude Fernando, Katy Gardner, Marion Glaser, Richard Holloway, Abul Hossain, Naomi Hossain, B. K. Jahangir, Tom-Felix Jöhnk, Naila Kabeer, Mafruza Khan, Sam Landell-Mills, Allister McGregor, Imran Matin, S. M. Nurul Alam, Iftekhar Sayeed, Hakan Seckinelgin, Dina Siddiqi, M. Shameem Siddiqi, Babar Sobhan, Bo and Sylvia Sundstrom, Sarah White, Geof Wood and Sushila Zeitlyn for special thanks. I remain indebted to Salauddin Mahaboob, who first properly introduced me to the country all those years ago. Nazneen Kanji carefully read and commented on my earliest chapter drafts, and gave me the confidence to continue. Later Abul Hossain, Katy Gardner and S. M. Nurul Alam each gave very useful comments on the manuscript. I would also like to thank David Ludden for support and ideas during the process of producing the book, as well as thank two anonymous referees. I am very grateful for the assistance of Shapar Selim, Nahid Kamal, Sarah Karim and Rajib Ahmed Chowdhury who provided me with documents from Bangladesh at short notice. Sarah Lewis provided very helpful and detailed editorial comments, and Christine A. T. Dunn did an excellent job with the final copyediting. Finally, I wish to thank Marigold Acland for commissioning the book and for encouragement throughout the writing process.

# Introduction

On December 13, 2010, the streets of Dhaka were once again convulsed by demonstrations and a strike by the nation's garment workers. Workers blocked the highways and roads with barricades and picketed outside factories, demanding that the government implement a new minimum wage of US$43 per month, which was supposed to have come into effect in November. At least three protesters lost their lives in clashes with police, and dozens more were injured in the violence that followed. Similar protests had taken place earlier in June and July of that year and were the latest in a history of regular garment-worker mobilizations that dated back to the early 1990s. Bangladesh's ready-made garment industry is worth $15 billion annually, accounts for more than three-quarters of its exports and services a wide range of well-known Western clothing companies that include Gap, Marks and Spencer and Walmart. A typical garment worker is a young woman recently arrived from a rural village and who lives in rented slum housing near a factory or an export processing zone (EPZ), where she works as a machinist and earns approximately $1.50 a day. The garment workplace brings her face to face with the contradictions and complexity of a globalised economy: the factory may be Korean-owned, the fabric from Taiwan, the yarn from India and the packaging materials from China, yet the garments that she manufactures will each carry a "made in Bangladesh" label. Located within a remote, weakly regulated outpost of the global capitalist economy, and increasingly dependent on a precarious and exploitative international division of labour, these garment workers are typical of many people in Bangladesh. They try to build a livelihood through working to secure whatever income can be managed from the market, struggling for justice from the state and attempting to organise themselves within a civil society in order to protect their interests.

The aim of this book is to provide a concise, up-to-date overview of the politics, economy and civil society of Bangladesh in a way that makes sense of the achievements and contradictions faced by Bangladesh and its people in a changing world. It is intended as an introductory text for general readers, students and teachers and does not assume prior knowledge of its subject. It aims to move beyond the level of description to dig more deeply under the surface of issues than a traditional textbook might allow. It seeks to engage with current debates and at times challenge received wisdom. The book presents the key background and a wide range of factual information, but the reader should also note that this is also a personal interpretative essay that inevitably reflects my research interests over the past twenty-five years in the broad field of development studies and my own personal positioning as a Western outsider.

Understanding Bangladesh's politics, economy and civil society requires covering a considerable amount of historical and political ground in order to identify the main themes. Processes of change and development have been contradictory, with transformation accompanied by a recurrent set of tensions. In the economic sphere, since the 1980s the mainstream international development donor community has pushed heavily for the liberalisation and privatisation of Bangladesh's economy. Although this agenda has been driven through in many areas of the economy, in others it is still resisted through the actions of citizens and government. Nevertheless, a level of relative peace and social stability has been secured in Bangladesh (at least compared with most of South Asia), and during the past decade, there has also been consistent economic growth and renewed interest in discoveries of potentially exploitable natural resources. In the social and political spheres, there are longstanding tensions between religious and secular Bangladeshi identities, recurring periods of unease between majority Bengali Muslims and other minority Bangladeshi communities, and an increasingly grid-locked set of national political institutions. These problems have increasingly led many internal and external observers to characterise Bangladesh as a regularly "failing" state.

Formerly East Pakistan, Bangladesh emerged as an independent nation in 1971, after a prolonged two-decade struggle for autonomy that culminated in a nine-month war with the Pakistan army and, eventually, in the military intervention of India. A "least developed country" according to UN categorisation, Bangladesh is predominantly rural in character, has a population estimated at around 162 million, a per capita annual income of $369 and an economy that has long been heavily foreign-aid dependent. Bangladesh has seen periods of authoritarian military rule as well as two decades of unstable electoral democracy, and is still widely seen today as suffering from severe problems of governance and high levels of corruption. It has long been a country central to the aid industry, and has become particularly known for the extensiveness of its nongovernmental organisation (NGO) sector that some have identified with a wider "civil society." The sector nevertheless has far longer roots that go back to the wider social movements and associational life that have regularly engaged its citizens in local and national struggles.

Apart from Willem Van Schendel's *A History of Bangladesh* (2009), which this book aims to complement, and Rounaq Jahan's (2001) edited book *Bangladesh: Promise and Performance*, now more than a decade old and therefore rather out of date, there is no such introductory book currently available to an international readership. This absence provides an obstacle to students requiring an introductory academic text and to people who may visit Bangladesh for an increasing variety of reasons – conducting business, seeing family, undertaking development work or simply exploring a country that has so far escaped the mainstream tourist market. This shortage of basic literature might at first appear a surprising omission. Yet one of the paradoxes of Bangladesh is that, despite its dramatic emergence as a nation that reshaped the postcolonial order in South Asia, its status as an archetypal "developing" country and its widely dispersed migrant communities, it remains relatively unknown compared with the rest of the region.

Although Bangladesh is a country that is just four decades old, as the eastern part of the region of Bengal it has a long and varied history – as India's commercial centre during the seventeenth and eighteenth centuries, as a key acquisition of the British Empire and later as part of the new postcolonial state of Pakistan. Since 1971 Bangladesh has undergone significant political and economic changes. These include numerous coup d'états that produced two long periods of authoritarian military governments, a series of popular mass protest movements that culminated in the *gono andolon*, or "people power," overthrow of the final military regime of General H. M. Ershad in 1990 and the establishment in 1991 of a fragile, though still functioning, system of parliamentary democracy. This system remains in place despite the imposition in January 2007 of an unelected military-backed caretaker government for a two-year period. This was eventually followed by democratic elections that returned for a second term Sheikh Hasina Wazed, leader of the Awami League (AL) political party founded by her father, Sheikh Mujibur Rahman, known popularly as "the father of the nation," or *bangabandhu,* "friend of Bengal." Nor has Bangladesh's economy stood still during four decades of political turbulence. A heavy reliance on foreign aid was gradually displaced during the 1990s by the growth of overseas remittances from migrant workers as the country's main source of foreign exchange, and its historical reliance on jute exports was replaced by two new nontraditional exports in the form of ready-made garments and frozen shrimps.

Despite a population that is comparable in size to that of Pakistan, and extensive communities of global migrants of Bangladeshi origin present in the Gulf States, Europe, North America and India, Bangladesh and Bangladeshis receive surprisingly little attention within the Western media. It has been of limited geopolitical interest to Western nations compared with Pakistan and largely overshadowed by India in the Western imagination. In the United Kingdom, Bangladesh is rarely featured in the news, except every few years when pictures of severe flooding or cyclone damage briefly make the headlines. During the writing of this book, I would often log on to the South Asia section of the BBC News Web site and find information about Bangladesh to be strangely absent. It was almost as if important events were only to be found taking place in India, Pakistan, Sri Lanka and Nepal, just as within the academic field of South Asian studies, research and teaching also remains dominated by a far larger volume of work devoted to India and Pakistan. An important aim of this book is to argue the case for Bangladesh's importance, not only for its inhabitants and neighbours but also for the wider global community as a whole. There are four main elements to this argument.

First, Bangladesh's position within the ongoing expansion and integration of the global capitalist economy is changing. Although Bangladesh in recent decades has mainly been viewed as only as a source of cheap labour within the international economic system, which is epitomised by the rapid growth of its garment industry, new concerns over energy scarcity at the global level mean that it is attracting increased attention as the location for potentially valuable natural resources. It has long been known that there are gas and coal reserves in the region, but only recently have rising international energy prices led foreign companies to begin systematic exploration activity in Bangladesh, and the sector has been opened up to limited foreign investment. In 2007, for example, the Bibyana gas field in Sylhet began production as part of a joint venture between the U.S.-based Chevron company and the state Petrobangla agency. There has been considerable domestic opposition to the exploitation of natural resources by foreign capital, and energy has now become a highly charged political issue.

Second, Bangladesh remains an important focus for the international development industry. It has long attracted high levels of aid and been a testing ground for development ideas and approaches. Recently, Bangladesh has gained international respect as a country that has made significant progress towards at least some of the Millennium Development Goals (MDGs) developed by the United Nations, which focuses on meeting targets by 2015 for, among other things, poverty eradication, reduction of child mortality, improved maternal health and primary education. Bangladesh's extensive NGO sector increasingly commands international media attention. Some of the leaders of these NGOs have been acclaimed as development visionaries or "social entrepreneurs," counterpointed against an increasingly pessimistic popular view of a struggling international development industry compromised by lack of competence and wasted aid resources. Today, Bangladesh is internationally known as the homeland of 2006 Nobel Prize winner Professor Mohammed Yunus, founder of the pioneering microfinance organisation Grameen Bank and now active as a global propagator of new ideas about the transformational power of "social business." Another increasingly well-known figure is Sir Fazle H. Abed, knighted in 2010 in the United Kingdom in recognition of his work with BRAC, the organisation he founded shortly after Bangladesh's Liberation War, which has grown into one of the world's leading development organisations.

Third, as the third most populous Muslim majority country in the world, Bangladesh has gained a new profile in the post-9/11 era. Within the policy climate of the so-called war on terror – the term coined by George W. Bush that emerged during the 2000s – this status provided it with a new strategic importance within U.S. foreign policy and led to several high-profile visits by key leaders such as Hillary Clinton. This carried with it a counternarrative of concern that Bangladesh was under an additional threat alongside more familiar problems of poverty and humanitarian disasters, in which its continuing governance problems could prove fertile for breeding international terrorism and threaten its status as a moderate Muslim majority country. The book *Bangladesh: The Next Afghanistan?* (2005) by Indian journalist Hiranmay Karlekar highlights growing and increasingly paranoid concerns being voiced in some quarters within India. Yet despite these moral panics, Bangladesh continues to serve as an important antidote to Samuel Huntingdon's (1993) warning of a so-called clash of civilisations between the east and the west. It has come to be seen as an example of a moderate majority Muslim democratic country and is often favourably contrasted with Pakistan because it has maintained a reputation as a relatively tolerant society. A distinctive Bengali Muslim identity has been forged within a post-colonial secular nationalist setting. This identity has been informed by the struggle to preserve the richness of the Bengali language and culture, within a context that has been conditioned over thousands of years by religious influences that have included Sufi, Hindu and Buddhist traditions.

Fourth, the issue of climate change has now catapulted Bangladesh into the international environmental debates. A predominantly flat deltaic country prone to regular flooding, even the smallest of sea-level rises could have severe consequences for millions of its inhabitants. This is leading to increasing global concern, as climate change climbs higher up the international agenda. There have always been disaster stories in the mainstream media whenever Bangladesh is affected, as it regularly is, by the severe floods and destructive cyclones that cause massive loss of life and human suffering (Novak 1993). It is now also portrayed as being on the frontline of climate change, at the heart of a new crisis narrative that warns of "a country underwater" and the creation of what some people have begun calling "climate change refugees." For the first time, with climate change, Bangladesh's problems are being felt also as part of "our" problems in the west. Typical of this often-breathless tone of reporting was Ian Williams's (2009) National Broadcasting Company (NBC) Worldblog report:

More than half of Bangladesh is less than 20 feet above sea level. Experts say it faces a double threat: rising sea levels as a result of the melting ice caps and glaciers, and more extreme weather, like cyclones and heavy rain. Taken together this could generate more climate change refugees than anywhere else on earth.

In an increasingly globalised world, perhaps the problems of "poor" countries such as Bangladesh are beginning to feel much closer to people in the wealthy countries than they had once seemed before.

## Approaching Bangladesh in the Literature

Much of what has been, and continues to be, written about Bangladesh is heavily slanted towards particular viewpoints and perspectives. Boundaries around knowledge production are acute, and these hamper understanding in different ways. Academic researchers working within or on South Asia confine themselves within certain disciplinary or geographical perspectives. For example, historians have tended to focus on the prepartition period and social scientists have concerned themselves with the present. Partition in 1947 did not only mean the imposition of new borders and movements of people across boundaries, as Mahbubar Rahman and Willem Van Schendel (2004: 209) remind us, but also the creation of divisions within academic communities studying India, Pakistan and Bangladesh. Many scholars still restrict their work to issues of citizenship, nation and development only within the modern borders of South Asia. Since 1947, tensions between the new states have limited the exchange of ideas among the subcontinent's scholars. This narrowing of focus was reproduced among foreign researchers studying South Asia, many of whom opt to study just one postpartition country. Research on Bangladesh, beyond that focusing specifically on "development," has also tended to be subsumed within the wider "Indianist" study of Bengal.

Aid issues have long loomed large in what has been written about Bangladesh, and much of the writing that is produced originates from within the "aid industry," even today. The Norwegian economist Just Faaland and J. R. Parkinson (1976) famously described Bangladesh as a "test case for development," while leading Bangladeshi economist Rehman Sobhan wrote the influential book *The Crisis of External Dependence* (1982). Seen as an archetypal "developing" country, people learn about contemporary Bangladesh mainly from the reports of agencies such as the World Bank regarding issues such as poverty and economic growth or from NGOs such as Transparency International (TI). TI's *Corruption Perceptions Index* consistently ranks Bangladesh as a poor performer within the international league tables of "good governance." Geoffrey Wood, another longstanding researcher on Bangladesh, entitled a collection of writings *Bangladesh: Whose Ideas, Whose Interests?* (1994) in recognition of the way that the outside influence of foreign-aid interests has helped to shape Bangladesh's institutions, policies and even its ideas.

Finally, historical writing on Bangladesh has also been strongly shaped by nationalist visions of various kinds. These include the British colonial viewpoint of prepartition Bengal, the ideas of those who advocated the unified Islamic nation of Pakistan with its western and eastern "wings" and those scholars who went on to write Bangladesh's history as a newly independent nation. Each of these narratives are useful in providing insight into the various ways that Bangladesh is experienced and imagined today, but the picture can often appear obscured by what may, at times, seem to be overgeneralised themes of progress, modernisation and heroism. There are as yet far fewer historical accounts of the "subaltern" kind constructed in Bangladesh than are found in India, where generalised narratives and assumed cultural continuities have been challenged and broken apart since the 1980s, revealing the more fragmented and multiple stories of less visible social groups, identities and classes.

### Structure of the Book

Following from this introduction, Chapter 2 introduces the structure of Bangladesh's society in terms of class, gender and religion, and provides some basic data on population, social indicators, gross domestic product

(GDP), main productive sectors and exports. It also contextualises Bangladesh within the international economy and the international aid system. Chapter 3 offers a brief historical overview that serves to contextualise an analysis of the state and economy since 1971. It begins with a discussion of precolonial Bengal and the role of the East India Company in securing the region as part of the British Empire, and then considers the post-1947 experience when Bangladesh existed as East Pakistan, before describing the processes of internal colonisation and resistance that led to the outbreak of civil war in 1971.

In Chapter 4 we focus on the state, analysing the development of Bangladesh's political structures and institutions and the tensions and transformations that have taken place within political actors and processes since 1971. It begins with a review of the nation-building work that followed the Liberation War victory under the leadership of Sheikh Mujibur Rahman (known as Mujib), which was based on the secular nationalist principles that had labelled Islamic political parties as collaborators with the Pakistani army. It goes on to trace the disillusionment that followed as Mujib's increasingly rigid and repressive regime failed to capitalise on the momentum of independence, the rise to power of General Ziaur Rahman and the new military politics that continued until the restoration of democracy in 1991. The main achievements of the elected governments (two Bangladesh Nationalist Party [BNP] and two AL) that followed the "people power" movement of 1990 are discussed, alongside the gridlocked politics that have come to characterise government-opposition party relationships. The focus in Chapter 5 is on the nongovernmental sector in Bangladesh. The comparative weakness of the state in Bangladesh has facilitated and been perpetuated by the emergence of a range of powerful nonstate actors. This chapter analyses this nongovernmental sector in all its diversity, from its earliest origins in various traditions of social movement in Bengal, and later in the efforts of international agencies to support development and relief after the 1971 war and a succession of natural disasters that followed, to the evolution of sophisticated and large-scale NGOs. Chapter 6 discusses the economy, which has undergone considerable change since independence in terms of production and trade. This change includes the rise of nontraditional industrial exports, such as ready-made garments and intensive irrigation-led agriculture. It also requires an understanding of important shifts in economic governance, namely the gradual move away from 1970s-style centralised state planning towards a partially liberalised economy.

In Chapter 7 we review the relationship between political and economic change and broader demographic and environmental factors. With a population of more than 160 million, people remain – along with water – one of the country's key assets. The challenge of bringing down high levels of population growth has long been a key priority among government policy makers and international development agencies. Chapter 8 concludes, drawing together the main discussions of the earlier chapters in order to assess the current state of democracy and economy in Bangladesh in an age of neoliberalism. It will argue that Bangladesh is at a crossroads of sorts, and faces a number of pressing dilemmas. First, it confronts the challenge of reinvigorating its democratic institutions in order to build a more inclusive politics, while safeguarding its institutions from the risks brought by growing forms of intolerance and uncivil society. Second, it needs to build on its recent economic growth in such a way that the trend of accelerating inequality is kept in check and benefits are harnessed for its still-large rural population and not just the urban middle classes. Third, Bangladesh will need to manage effectively a new strategic context of the so-called war on terror that it now finds itself in, with domestic and international implications.

Overall, the book is informed by a political economy approach to understanding Bangladesh's society and institutions. The term *political economy* can carry at least two different meanings. Adam Smith used the term in *The Wealth of Nations* (1776; repr. 1970), emphasising the role of the state as one of creating optimum conditions for wealth production, but subsequent liberal economists went on to emphasise the power of the "invisible hand" of markets over politics. Today, their descendants, the neoclassical economists, tend to use the term *political economy* far more narrowly to refer to the interrelationships between economic and political factors in the formation of public policies. This approach has influenced much of what passes for political economy analysis in relation to Bangladesh within international development policy frameworks, such as the UK Department for International Development's (DFID's) "drivers of change" approach to "governance" reform during the early 2000s or, more recently, the World Bank's interest in "problem-driven governance and political economy analysis" (World Bank 2009). Although these ideas may have some practical utility and influence, their analytical value is limited because the emphasis is primarily on the formulation of development policies and the ways these may be constrained or facilitated by the social and political context. Radical traditions of political economy have instead come to refer to the ways that the historical interplay of class relations and power organise and are organised by the economy (Hoogvelt 2001). Influenced by Marxist theory, this approach to political economy calls for an analysis of the structural factors that affect social and political change and draws attention to the underlying dynamics of economic and political power. In relation to Bangladesh, such an analysis requires us to focus on the narrative of East Bengal's economic exploitation by the British colonial regime within the wider process of India's incorporation during the nineteenth century into a global economy based on capitalist development, the creation of a transformed system of small-scale agricultural commodity producers growing cash crops for the market and the continuing exploitation of surplus value from rural labour under the Pakistan regime during the postcolonial era (McGuire 2009).

A radical political economy perspective aims to provide a more unified view of the power relationships and interests that underpin processes of political action and economic activity and of the underlying structural factors that facilitate and constrain processes of social transformation at local, national and international levels. Although accessing the wealth of material and ideas that many development donor documents may contain, the approach taken here is to address the dominant development discourses about Bangladesh's economics and politics from a critical perspective. At the same time, the heavy emphasis within some forms of radical political economy on macrolevel structural explanations runs the risk of overgeneralisation and also needs to be approached with caution. For example, McGuire's (2009: 25) claim that Bangladesh's "position has hardly changed since it claimed nationhood in 1971" may carry some elements of a general truth, but it fails to do justice to the economic and social transformations that have taken place. A fine-grained approach characterises much of Sobhan's (2004) work, who argues, for example, that the deep-rooted problems of "malgovernance" from which the country has long suffered – such as endemic corruption, poor quality administration and a lack of law and order – require analysis through structural historical analysis, while recognising that change, with positive and negative consequences for different sections of society, has taken place.

The historical approach taken in this book has been influenced by Frederick Cooper's (2002) idea of "the past of the present," with which he argues that an investigation of the past helps us not only to understand the present better but also perhaps to imagine the future. Bangladesh's present and future cannot easily be understood without reference to Bengal's earlier conquest by the Mughals and later by the British, and to the anticolonial struggles that led first to the formation of Pakistan and later to the liberation of Bangladesh. But at the same time we need to resist the notion that the past determines the shape of the present, and we also need to remain sensitive to the fact that history does not unfold in terms of the clearly demarcated periods often described in textbooks.

Some caveats are nevertheless required. In taking the state, market and civil society as the organising framework, some may correctly argue that a tripartite conceptual distinction of institutions risks oversimplification. It is used here as a framing device that provides a useful way into a complex subject matter, but the intention is not to suggest that these are separate or discrete "sectors" in the ways that some academics and policy makers sometimes imply. The boundaries between these institutional fields are often unclear and permeable, structured by the vertical relationships of patronage and kinship. These relationships blur the line between public and private interests and resources, making simple models of "good governance" propagated by some donors out of step with everyday reality in Bangladesh (Lewis 2010). Furthermore, in the end liberal pluralist democratic models require that all three sectors are adequately conceptualised in relation to each other, rather than viewed in isolation. For example, development donors tend to see the reduction of the scale of the state and the public sector as a key objective in promoting liberal democracy. But a strong state is still needed to ensure that a market economy operates effectively or to oversee the privatisation of inefficient state assets in ways that ensure that additional wealth is not simply transferred to elites who further concentrate their power. If government is reduced, this may weaken the very institutions that support the reproduction of the workforce or help in basic ways to reduce the vulnerability of the poor. As Cooper (2002: 202–3) argues,

We need to think more subtly than the opposition of state and market or of a dichotomy between state and civil society. . . . Rejecting the state in the name of civil society or the market is likely to be no more effective than assuming that the state can solve all problems in the name of the people.

Although the primarily focus of the book is on the population and institutions within the territorial unit of Bangladesh, it is also important to recognise that Bangladesh needs to be understood beyond its limits as a geographically bounded nation-state. Bangladesh past and present is the continuing and still changing result of the global and local interplay between populations, institutions and power. Issues of foreign aid, religion, ecology and migration take us well beyond the country's borders.

## 2

## A State in the Making

Bangladesh is a comparatively new nation that is still in the process of taking shape – hence, it remains a "state in the making." It became an independent country on December 16, 1971, when, after a violent liberation struggle, it seceded from Pakistan. Under the hastily drawn up arrangements for the partition of British India in 1947, a homeland for Indian Muslims had been created with two wings, known as West Pakistan and East Pakistan, that were separated by more than twelve hundred miles of Indian territory. East Pakistan, populated mainly by Muslim Bengalis, quickly became the subordinate partner in the new country and faced internal economic exploitation and clumsy attempts to impose Urdu as the national language of Pakistan. National elections in 1970 gave the Eastern wing a majority of assembly delegates, and after a vicious West Pakistani military clampdown, the nationalist resistance movement eventually secured victory. Events during this period of the country's formation have been vividly brought to life in Tahmima Anam's novel *A Golden Age* (2007). During the conflict, the Pakistan army is believed to have killed more than a million Bengalis in a systematic genocide designed to bring the renegade province back under control. With large numbers of refugees pouring across the border into West Bengal, Bangladeshi forces were also aided by the Indian army because India saw an important political opportunity to secure the breakup of Pakistan.

During the four decades that followed what was a tumultuous episode in twentieth-century postcolonial history, Bangladesh has continued to evolve and change. The country has faced serious problems throughout its history: from the terrible cost in human lives inflicted by the Pakistan army during its bloody inception, extensive and pervasive poverty, and environmental vulnerability, to a continuing set of problems relating to political instability and poor governance. Yet Bangladesh has also made considerable progress during this time, challenging those who prophesied that the new state would be unviable. Bangladesh has shown the world that it has been able to expand its food production substantially, develop important new export industries such as ready-made garments and shrimp, improve areas of its health-care and education social sectors through concerted government action and point the way to new potential solutions to global poverty problems through the innovative work of some of its NGOs. It is precisely because of the scale of problems that Bangladesh has experienced, and the resilence and creativity that this has instilled in its people, that many now see the country as a "laboratory for innovative solutions in the developing world" (Beit 2011).

## Bangladeshi Society

Bangladesh contains a population, estimated at about 162 million people, located within a land area of 57,000 square miles, which is not much larger than that of England. This makes Bangladesh the most densely populated country in the world, outside of the small city states of Singapore or Hong Kong. The majority of the population lives in rural areas, where land is productive but scarce and the overall ecology is extremely fragile. Although the majority of the population is Bengali Muslims, there are significant Hindu, Christian and Animist minorities that, it is estimated, make up approximately 15 percent of the population.

Bangladesh is a riverine, or riparian, state, located within a lowland alluvial plain that forms the lower part of the massive river-delta area formed by the confluence of the great Ganges, Brahmaputra and Meghna river systems. These rivers flow down from the Himalayas through the Indian subcontinent into the area that is now Bangladesh, merging within its borders before flowing southwards into the Bay of Bengal. For thousands of years, the country's position within this highly fertile deltaic ecosystem has attracted people to an area offering high levels of agricultural productivity. At the same time, its location makes it highly vulnerable to natural disasters with destructive cyclones, perpetual land erosion from river and sea and floods that routinely cover one-fifth of the land and, during a bad year, may engulf two-thirds of the entire country.

When it emerged as an independent country, Bangladesh was a pre-dominantly rural society populated by peasant smallholders. The previous feudal order fell apart after partition compelled many of those who had formed part of what was a predominantly Hindu zamindar landlord class to leave for India, and their lands were taken over or redistributed by the government. A national bourgeoisie had not been allowed to emerge in East

Pakistan because the small number of elite families that dominated the few industries that had existed had been non-Bengalis. These families had duly returned to Pakistan after the Liberation War, and it was a similar story with the bureaucracy and the army. Crucial to the emergence of Bangladesh as an independent country had been the rise of what Jahan (1972) termed a "vernacular elite" in the east, drawn mainly from Bengali-speaking, provincial, lower middle-class families. This group contrasted with the traditional ruling "national" elite, composed of a mainly urban Calcutta-based cosmopolitan class, and the rise of the AL reflected the growing influence of this new vernacular elite.

After 1971, the small new political class that began to emerge was drawn primarily from the party leaders and activists around Sheikh Mujibur Rahman who had challenged the dominance of what was sometimes termed the "Punjabi bureaucracy" that had ruled Pakistan. At the same time, a new military elite also emerged, led by AL political appointees and some of the few Bengali officers who had held rank in the Pakistan armed forces. This elite built up the new Bangladeshi army partly from the ranks of former freedom fighters (although many of this group quickly grew disillusioned by what they saw as a subsequent neglect of their interests by the new government) and partly from former Bengali soldiers in the Pakistan army. The latter had been imprisoned by the West Pakistani authorities and had not taken part in the Liberation War. Many of them resented being under the authority of this new and, in their view, inexperienced ruling elite (Barua 1978).

For the bulk of its population, access to land has been the key structural asset that has mainly defined social class. Most of the countryside was "minifundist" in character, that is, with the majority of people building livelihoods as smallholder farmers, and there were few of the large landlord-run estates found in many other areas of the subcontinent (Wood 1976). Yet rural Bangladesh was far from being an idyllic picture of small-farm peasant life because landholding was highly unequal. Ramkrishna Mukherjee's seminal study *Six Villages of Bengal* (1971), conducted during the early 1940s, had earlier emphasised land ownership as the key to economic differentiation between households. By the 1970s, large sections of the rural population owned little or no agricultural land of their own. Some worked as sharecroppers or leased in small plots, while many others were forced to labour on other people's land or undertake paid employment as day labourers or rickshaw pullers (Hartmann and Boyce 1983). By the 1980s, landholding census data indicated that at least half of Bangladesh's rural households were now identified as "functionally landless," meaning that what small landholdings they once may have owned had now been lost, either through forced or distress sale, or fragmented into largely unviable units through the endless process of subdivision that is required by family inheritance norms (Jannuzi and Peach 1980).

Women's rural labour has been central to agricultural production, particularly in the postharvest processing activities because Muslim women's access to public space in particular is restricted by *purdah* norms, even though these norms are far from fixed and are constantly under negotiation (White 1992). Women have traditionally remained largely excluded from formal labour markets, with many supplementing household income by undertaking domestic work in better-off households. Since the 1980s, female migration to urban areas has grown steadily, particularly in relation to the extensive large-scale export garment sector. The new opportunities provided for women by the garment industry and other areas of the labour market have helped contribute to an increased female presence in the labour force and to bringing about a major shift in the economic and social position of women. Women are more mobile, with a stronger presence in public space and a higher level of representation in formal paid labour (Rozario 2002). The challenge to social norms has not been without resistance. Previously rare phenomena of dowry inflation, dowry deaths and acid-throwing attacks on women have become more frequent in recent years, even though, as Dina Siddiqi (1998) argues, no straightforward causal link can necessarily be assumed.

As a result of the declining economic opportunities afforded to most rural households from agriculture, Bangladesh began to urbanise rapidly from the 1980s onwards, a process driven more by the poverty and hardship of life in the rural areas than by genuine industrialised labour-market opportunities. The result has been that this increasing rural-to-urban migration has led to the creation of large groups of "floating" workers who do not have permanent employment in the industrial sector and who try to build fragile, multistranded livelihood strategies in the cities and the many informal settlements. The one important exception is the rise of the ready-made garment industries of Dhaka and Chittagong, and one of the most visible changes in the urban environment is that more than a million female workers are now employed in the ready-made garment sector.

Bangladesh's middle class is growing, but this area of social transformation has not yet received much attention from researchers, and it would be fair to say that very little is really known about its numbers, character or diversity. The relatively small but well-established educated vernacular elite that dominated after the Liberation War through its power base within the bureaucracy, the universities and older businesses, with its international connections and Western education and with its largely secular nationalist ideas, had been influential during the country's emergence during the 1960s and 1970s. This elite has increasingly been challenged by new middle-class entrants often with different priorities, values and ideas. In the rural areas, upwardly mobile households have broadened their livelihoods from agricultural trade and services into the rural nonfarm economy. This has fed into the growth of a new section of urban middle class that since the 1990s has consolidated its economic base from the boom in construction and in the manufacture and retailing of pharmaceuticals and other industries. This group is less well educated and more pragmatic, ready to make more opportunistic compromises with religious political interests, and often far less wedded to the secular Bengali nationalist tradition, which helps underpin the support base of the centre-right BNP. Its values signalled a rejection of the refined Kolkata *bhadralok* tradition and the vernacular elite, in favour of brash and assertive nouveau riche values and a new respect for the street-level politics of the *mustaan* (Van Schendel 2009). From the 1990s, this new "business" group with roots in urban and rural areas has – in broad terms at least, because the realities are more complex and nuanced – emerged as another central key element within the post-Liberation power structure dominated by the military, senior bureaucracy and political leadership (Blair 2001).

The postcolonial state in Bangladesh has been dominated by different middle-class groups and factions, though none have delivered much in the way of positive economic or social change for the bulk of the population (Alam 1995). Furthermore, despite the state's heavy dependence on foreign assistance, neither the older elites nor the newer middle classes utilised aid in ways that could build domestic productive capacity. A range of important prerequisite conditions for domestic capital formation such as land reform, infrastructure and the creation of an internal market have not been secured in the decades that followed independence, with the result that Bangladesh conspicuously failed to build an indigenous industrial bourgeoisie in the four decades after 1971. The national and local economy has remained largely in the control of a petit-bourgeois "rentier" class that has not made productive investment a priority. More recently, a range of first-generation businesses have gained a national profile in the form of "business group" conglomerates, of which Beximco is the largest. Beximco is active in many sectors including pharmaceuticals, textiles, ceramics, financial services and the media, and was recently reported to be the largest bank-loan defaulter in the country (Liton and Hasan 2009).

Although some sections of the older "professional" middle classes remain relatively active in challenging the social and political status quo, for example by building civil-society organisations, such activities remain strongly linked with foreign-aid flows. As a result, these efforts to pursue progressive social and political goals lie largely outside the realm of the established political parties and their activities. The new middle classes, although less educated, are also in part aligned with foreign aid, but through contracting and other local business interests. Such groups are also more closely involved with the politics of patronage that have characterised the state and the mainstream political parties (Alam 1995). It is the politics of this new middle class, and its frustration with the current unstable system of economic and political organisation, that is likely to hold a strong influence over Bangladesh's future. Some see the older elite as now in retreat, their secular Bengali values increasingly under challenge, and many recent generations preferring to opt for an international "exit" as global citizens living and working in the West and in other parts of Asia.

In geopolitical terms, Bangladesh's position is also problematic (see Map 1). Surrounded by India on all sides except for its coastline that faces the Bay of Bengal, relations with its giant neighbour are complicated by history, politics and ecology, in spite of India's role as "midwife" to the new country. There is a high level of ecological interdependence that has caused longstanding water-sharing conflicts, a long and porous border with high levels of labour migration and smuggling and allegations on both sides that each gives assistance to the other's rebel separatist groups. India is currently building a steel fence in an attempt to secure its borders, an act that perhaps signals less regional exchange and partnership. Yet Bangladesh's strategic position as a potential bridge between South Asia and Southeast Asia may be one important key to its own future development and to future regional growth. As Van Schendel (2005) reminds us, the "Bengal borderland" between India, Bangladesh and Burma is an area of political and historical contestation and an important site at which information, goods and ideas are exchanged. Such are the challenges and contradictions with which Bangladesh's people contend on a daily basis.

When the country does feature on the international stage it has tended to do so as a quintessential "developing country," with mass poverty and regular natural disasters. As such it has attracted considerable resources and attention from aid agencies, including a wide range of UN organisations, bilateral donors and NGOs. Within this outsider-led aid industry, however, perceptions of Bangladesh have oscillated wildly between pessimism and optimism. In its early days, the country was famously regarded as a "basket

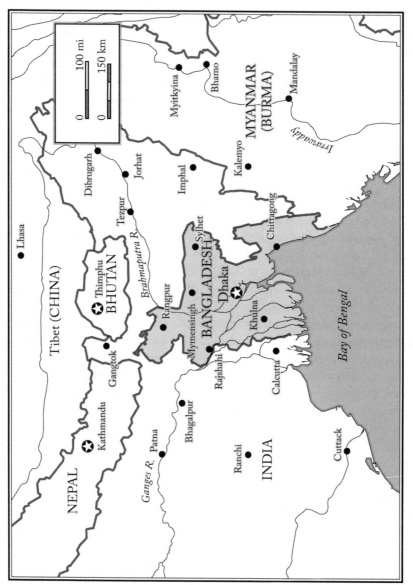

Map 1. Bangladesh in regional context

case" that was likely to remain substantially dependent on the international community for food aid long into the future. Negative views have persisted among many of the development donors, who despair over what are often seen as the country's fractured institutions and weak governance structures. But there are some voices in the aid world, including the World Bank in recent years, that have begun to speak of Bangladesh's progress in terms of a development "success story." They are enthused by the better than expected rate of economic growth in recent years, significant progress with key social indicators such as female primary education participation and a series of successes in the fields of health and family planning.

This shifting spectrum of different views, including more recently, the concerns about migration and terrorism, reflects two important facts about Bangladesh: the rapid scale of the economic, political and cultural changes that have occurred in the country since 1971 and the dispiriting regularity with which outsiders have been often been ready to attempt to encapsulate the country's complex and diverse experiences with simplistic banner headlines or sound bites around themes such as floods, overpopulation and poverty.

## Politics, Economy and Civil Society

Bangladesh's political history has been turbulent, and its institutions of government remain cumbersome, fragile and unresponsive to people's needs. Such problems have their roots in the colonial period and intensified further when the country became part of Pakistan. In the first years after 1971, Bangladesh was ruled by the country's founding father, Sheikh Mujibur Rahman, but his government lacked capacity, faced a crushing range of internal and external pressures and grew increasingly authoritarian. The government was brought down in 1975, when Mujib and most of his family were assassinated by army conspirators. The coup ushered in a period of military rule during which General Ziaur Rahman (known as Zia) took charge until his assassination in 1981, and then was followed in 1982 by a second military government led by General H. M. Ershad until the end of the decade.

In 1990, a combination of the longstanding "people power" opposition movement and, some have argued, pressure from international donors secured the end of Ershad's rule. Bangladesh then entered a period of parliamentary democracy up until 2006. National elections were held every four years, using a novel system of installing a neutral, temporary three-month caretaker government in order to ensure a fair vote. During this period, the two main political parties, the BNP, led by Zia's widow Begum

Khaleda Zia, and the AL, led by Mujib's daughter Sheikh Hasina Wazed, each formed governments under this system. However, the two parties' highly antagonistic relationship, embodied in the historic feud between their two leaders, soon paralysed the democratic process and periodically destabilised the economy.

It soon became clear to many people inside and outside the country that Bangladesh was falling far short of institutionalising a viable system of parliamentary government. For the first half of the 2000s, Bangladesh was annually rated by the TI anticorruption watchdog to be the most corrupt country in the world and, according to the World Bank, this was a major concern that put off potential international investors in the country. For many ordinary people, lack of security and deteriorating law and order had become intolerable. In 2007, the military intervened once again and set up what it called a transitional caretaker government that it claimed would restore law and order, address endemic corruption and oversee a fair election. In January 2009, a new AL government was duly elected with more than two-thirds of the vote. How far will this new government be able to challenge what many see as the prevailing norms of political dysfunction and deteriorating law and order, or will "business as usual" remain the order of the day? These questions are explored further in Chapter 3.

Despite these political and institutional problems, Bangladesh's economy began to fare better during the 1990s, its population growth rate was reduced and the country's overall poverty levels went into decline. By the end of the twentieth century, Bangladesh had achieved a consistent GDP growth rate of about 4.5 percent, while the population growth rate had declined from 2.7 percent in the late 1970s to about 1.7 percent by the late 1990s (Khan 2006). Development agencies such as the World Bank (2006a) began to identify Bangladesh as notable among other comparable developing countries in regard to the progress it has made in reducing poverty. For example, in relation to income poverty, data indicated that while 59 percent of the population was living in poverty in 1990, this had declined to 50 percent by 2000, with four-fifths of the decline taking place in rural areas. Recent government figures indicate that 41 percent of the population lives in poverty; two out of three of whom live in extreme poverty as measured by direct calorie intake (Rahman et al. 2009). At the same time, evidence for widening of inequalities remains a concern.

The government and some development agencies have also lately become more positive about the areas of social progress that have been made. They point to its relatively high level of progress towards the United Nations' MDGs, particularly in relation to eradicating extreme poverty and achieving universal primary education, compared with many other low-income countries around the world. For example, primary school enrollment has increased from 72 percent in 1980 to 98 percent in 2001, though dropout rates have remained high, and a longstanding gender disparity has been removed in relation to primary and secondary school enrollment. Between 1970 and 2003, infant mortality declined from 145 to 46 per 1,000 live births, and child mortality has been reduced from 239 to 69 per 1,000. This means that by 2015 the country will likely meet the MDG objective of reducing by two-thirds its 1990 child mortality levels. There has also been good progress with achieving food security (at least until the 2008 increase in global food prices), which has improved markedly, even for the very poor. The World Bank (2006a: 1) reports that fertility levels, infant and child mortality, contraceptive prevalence and crude birth and death rates are far more favourable than would be predicted for a comparable country in terms of income level, and suggests that these improvements have occurred "despite widely held perceptions of poor governance."

Bangladesh's economy is primarily agrarian, employing about 60 percent of the labour force and with close to one-quarter of the GDP coming from agriculture, forestry and fisheries. The main crop is rice, Bangladesh's staple food, and there has been considerable progress made with increasing the productivity of rice production during recent decades through the adoption of new technologies, including many new high-yielding hybrid rice varieties and an expansion of groundwater irrigation. In particular, the expansion of the winter *boro* rice crop has been dramatic, from 2 percent of land area in 1971 to close to 15 percent by the start of the new millennium. There has also been substantial diversification into wheat and vegetables. As a result, according to Robert Bradnock and Patricia Saunders (2002: 68), despite thirty years of low expectations, agricultural production has "more than kept pace with growing demand for food and agricultural products."

Three-quarters of the population live in rural areas, and Bangladesh, therefore, remains a predominantly rural society, with various village-level institutions continuing to play a central role in peoples' daily lives. At the heart of local rural society is the *paribar* or *gusti*, the local lineage group that may be composed of several related families within a village. The *gusti* has traditionally formed the basis for the organisation of agricultural labour and systems of reciprocity. Such rural institutions are often quite flexible, and it is common for poorer families to seek membership of a *gusti* in order to claim benefits and for better-off households to try to limit membership in order to safeguard resources (Jansen 1987). The local residential community in rural areas has long been understood, in the social science literature at least, to be the *samaj*, a word that also means "society" more generally. *Samaj* can be also seen as an associational realm animated primarily by the power of elite charismatic leaders and their supporters, framed by patron-client relationships located within neighbourhoods and based around village elders, known as *matbars*. These elders manage disputes over resources through the traditional dispute-resolution system of the informal *salish* village tribunal. The *samaj* helps to provide a framework for moral order, in which followers may have a means of redress if leaders are seen to behave in ways that offend norms of justice and morality. The *samaj* is also a somewhat flexible, negotiated local institution, relatively detached from local government structures and the religious bureaucracies (Bertocci 2001). Although the forms and roles of these traditional institutions are clearly subject to change, there are also signs that the pace of change in some rural areas has rendered them irrelevant. For example, when Kamal Siddiqui (2000) returned in 1997 to make a restudy of the village in southwest Bangladesh where he had undertaken detailed fieldwork twenty years earlier, he found that the *samaj* and *salish* had disappeared altogether.

The landscape of rural areas is therefore subject to increasingly rapid change, from the expansion of market forces, the penetration of formal administrative structures and the construction of rural infrastructure, leading some observers to question even more the validity of traditional rural and urban distinctions. A rural-urban continuum is increasingly visible around the country. Nonagricultural livelihoods in the form of rural services, construction and trade have expanded in relation to agricultural livelihoods (Toufique and Turton 2002). At the same time, local informal institutions increasingly rub up against formal ones, and such differences hybridise and blur. For example, although the *salish* has long been the main village-level dispute-resolution mechanism, traditionally controlled by the *matbars*, as with all local-level institutions it is undergoing evolution and change. In some areas, there is now increasing participation from other actors, such as representatives from the lowest rung of local government, the elected Union *parishad* (UP) (Lewis and Hossain 2008).

The "patron-client" relationship is defined in the Bangladesh context by B. K. Jahangir (1982: 88) as "a reciprocity of exchange based on unequal rank" with three important characteristics: economic structures of exploitation, political structures of domination and ideological structures of consensus and control. Although giving support to these local leaders does not necessarily guarantee followers any tangible benefits and resources, opposition may result in exclusion from any benefits that might arise (Bode 2002). These relationships are enacted within different arenas, from the local bazaar association to mosque and temple committees, where *samaj* leaders may build reputations through participation in public activities, such as the *jama'at* and its provision of *zakat* charitable redistribution.

Patron-client relationships are important at every level in Bangladesh. Within local village communities, patron-client relationships have long been the dominant mode of social organisation that structures relationships between rich and poor households. For landowners, these relationships may be used to "tie in" the poor into unfavourable or exploitative relationships around land tenure, sale of crops or moneylending. At the same time, patron-client relationships also provide a measure of social security in the form of an informal "safety net" for poorer households in times of hardship.

Like many other developing countries, Bangladesh is urbanising fast. In 1974, a total of 8.8 percent of people lived in urban areas, but this had risen to 23.4 percent by 2001. Currently, an estimated one-quarter of the population live in urban areas, and at a growth rate of 3.5 percent per year about 40 percent of the population will be urban by 2030 (Khan 2008). In rural and urban areas, the phenomenon of *mustaans*, a term that is used to refer to petty hoodlums engaged in extortion or to strongmen used by individual patrons or sometimes by political parties to enforce the payment of rents or other forms of exploitation, also forms part of this culture of patronage. From the point of view of a person without much power or influence, the negotiation of a patron-client relationship may provide a useful minimum access to resources and a measure of social security in the absence of formal rights or alternative livelihood options. A set of moral norms based on social and religious values and kinship obligations helps to balance these relations of exploitation.

In 1971, Bangladesh's industries were few, because it had predominantly been a source of raw materials for processing in West Pakistan. From the nineteenth century, Bengal had been the world's leading exporter of jute, a natural fibre used in rope and carpet making. Since the 1970s, its importance has declined and world demand for jute has steadily fallen because synthetic fibres became more widely used in the manufacture of these products. Instead, jute's contribution to Bangladesh's export earnings was superseded from the 1980s onward by what Stanley Kochanek (2001:154) described as "the most remarkable economic development in Bangladesh in the past two decades" – the emergence of an industrial sector manufacturing ready-made garments for mainly Western retailers. The sector was worth only $7 million in 1982, but by 1999 it was employing 1.5 million workers and contributing three-quarters of Bangladesh's $5 billion total exports. As we have seen, these garment workers have emerged as key actors in debates about Bangladesh's position in the global economy. How are we to understand this paradox of economic and social progress within a political and institutional system that appears to contain so many shortcomings, and what are the prospects for the future? These questions will be discussed in more detail in Chapter 5.

The positive gains made by Bangladesh in these areas need to be set alongside the continuing problems of governance and growing inequality. Bangladesh's GNP per capita of US$590 remains low even in comparison to other South Asian countries, with India's now standing at $1,770 (Sen 2011). A total of 53 percent of the rural and 37 percent of the urban populations remain poor (Ahmed and Mahmud 2006). Furthermore, the 1990s have seen rising levels of income inequality in the country as a whole and between rural and urban households (Khan 2006). There are many who take issue with claims coming from some of the development agencies. For instance, Joseph Devine (2008) writes of the "rotten core" at the heart of this apparent development success story, pointing to the extent not only of corruption and poor governance but also to the pervasive way in which violence, criminality and clientelism have come to characterise most levels of social interaction. As a result, many people face a high level of harassment (*hoirani*) as they go about their daily lives, including official obstruction, demands for informal payment for services and various forms of casual violence. This severely impacts upon peoples' quality of life but is an aspect of good governance that receives insufficient attention in generalised donor models that tend to focus on formal structures and institutions (Rahman 2009).

A distinctive aspect of Bangladesh is that it has become well-known for its extensive and high-profile "nongovernmental" sector – sometimes also termed *civil society*. Most visible are the country's development NGOs, emerging after 1971 as a result of a wide-ranging combination of factors: longstanding local traditions of voluntary action, the large-scale inflows of foreign aid and the weakly institutionalised state that could manage only limited levels of service provision and continued to exhibit a rigid and unresponsive bureaucracy. Today these NGOs are best known internationally for their microfinance work, but many are also active in the health education and agriculture sectors and in activities such as human rights and policy campaigning. BRAC, the country's largest NGO, is an organisation that has recently internationalised its work and now operates elsewhere in Asia and more recently in several African countries. Development NGOs have played an important part in the various gains made by the country outlined in the preceding text.

Civil society is more than just the development NGOs. Bangladesh's history encompasses a set of diverse civil-society experiences – from the older language movement (*bhasha andolon*) of organised resistance in the cultural sphere of the 1950s, to the nationalist groups, trade unions and cultural organisations that gradually became part of narrower, organised political interests under the AL. It also includes the movements that struggled against military rule, in support of improving the engagement between citizens and democratic political institutions and the wide range of religious civil-society groups (Lewis 2004). Today the country also has a number of think tanks, such as the Power and Participation Research Centre and the Centre for Policy Dialogue, that play prominent roles in the public policy debate. Yet the civil-society sector in Bangladesh remains poorly understood. It contains a wealth of contradictions, with organisations of wildly different competences and aims, and it remains an open question as to how far it represents, or even has the support of, many ordinary citizens. We examine these questions in more depth in Chapter 4.

### Religion and Identity

Along with class and ethnicity, religion constitutes a critical component of Bangladeshi identity. According to the 2001 Census, almost 90 percent of the population is Muslim, just more than 9 percent are Hindu, with the remainder made up of Buddhists (0.7 percent), Christians (0.3 percent) and Animists and others (0.1 percent). For the Muslim majority and the Hindu and other minorities, religion and family lie at the centre of social life, offering a framework for general social conduct and underpinning what remains a predominantly patriarchal social order. Religion gives meaning to people in the sense that "it offers a grounding to a moral universe that animates the everyday" (White and Devine 2009: 15). It contributes, for example, to the way in which some groups use ideas from reformist Islam to contest dominant developmental ideas such as microcredit interventions by NGOs.

Almost all Bangladesh's Muslims are Sunni. Islam in Bangladesh has been described in general terms as taking one of three main forms (Banu 1992). The first is what may be termed "modernist" Islam, which attempts to apply rational and scientific thought to the interpretation of the Koran and Hadith, envisages a personal role for religion in one's life and is generally found among a fairly narrow group of urban elites. The second is "orthodox" Islam, which insists on a literal and traditional interpretation of holy texts, which are found among better-off educated urban and rural households. Finally, there is the "popular" or folk Islam tradition, which is syncretic in character and combines traditional Islamic beliefs with many local beliefs, ideas and traditions (Haq 1975). This continues to have a strong influence among the rural and urban poor.

At the formal level, Islam opposes the social distinction of caste, which is an essential component of Hindu social organisation. Yet Muslim Bengalis have also traditionally recognised certain hierarchies of social status. For example, a longstanding distinction has been made between *ashraf* and *ajlaf* families, terms that refer to the idea of "noble" and "commoner" status. Many of the former group claim hereditary descent from high-status groups from North India that would have served with the government or army during earlier periods of Muslim rule (and from before that time), while others also claim descent from Arabs originally associated with the Prophet Muhammad. These families were therefore originally non-Bengali, and many would have preferred to use the Urdu language during the Mughal and British periods, sometimes in order to differentiate themselves from Hindu Bengalis. The latter *ajlaf*, who form the majority of Bengali Muslims, were believed to have converted much later to Islam, and may have originally been low-caste Hindus (Baxter 1998)

Such identities are complex, shifting and multidimensional. There were also divisions among the *ashrafs*, as well as a wide range of daily interactions between both categories of people. The same was true of relationships between Muslims and Hindus. M. Anisuzzman (2001: 48–9) points out that a broad range of exchanges between Hindus and Muslims took place during the Mughal and British periods, "even at the cost of displeasure of the orthodox sections of both communities." These may have included the veneration of common deities and *pirs* (holy men), the paying of tributes to common *dargas* (shrines) and *mazars* (tombs or mausoleums) and interest from sections of both religious communities in the cult of Tantra and in the ideas and practices of Yoga. The Sufi-influenced *baul* tradition of rural wandering devotional singers, still popular today in Bangladesh, is another example. In her influential account of the breakup of Pakistan, Jahan (1972) also goes on to distinguish between the rise of a "vernacular" elite, drawn from the less educated Bengali-speaking lower middle classes, and the "national" elites who dominated Pakistan at partition, drawn from traditional urban bilingual elites. This idea further develops the *ashraf* and *ajlaf* distinction, arguing that the former were largely drawn from the ranks of the politically active *ajlafs* and the latter from the Urdu-speaking *ashrafs*, many of whom had supported the integrity of Pakistan.

The role of religion in the construction of Bangladeshi identities has long been an important point of public debate. How do Bangladeshis balance their linguistic and cultural identity as Bengalis with their religious identities as Muslims, or as religious minorities? How do the small numbers of non-Bengali citizens fit into the whole? In 1971, as we have seen, some Islamists had opposed Bangladeshi nationalism on religious grounds and had sided with the West Pakistani army during the conflict, creating a legacy of bitterness and betrayal that, as we shall see, continues to haunt politics to this day. The fact that some of these Islamist political leaders have never been held to account for what was seen as their role in the genocide remains a key political pressure point. That some have also remerged since the 1970s as "mainstream" political leaders is also troubling for many Bangladeshis who still feel close to the country's independence struggle. For example, many people were horrified that Jama'at-i-Islami (JI), the main Islamist political party, was included as a key member of the centre-right coalition government headed by the BNP that was formed in October 2001.

Compared with the other nations of South Asia, the dominance of a relatively well-defined Bengali ethnic and linguistic group provides the country with a strong level of social cohesiveness. But it also conceals a number of longstanding issues of diversity and difference as B. H. Farmer (1983: 73) points out. Hindu minority communities are particularly located around India's borders, as well as the so-called Biharis, the term given in Bangladesh to those Urdu-speaking Muslims from all over India who had opted to reside in Pakistan, but who ended up stranded in Bangladesh. As non-Bengalis, they have remained marginalised, partly by language and partly because they have faced discrimination because they were thought to have had pro-Pakistan allegiances during the 1971 Liberation War.

In 1947, and for some time after, close to one million people from the present-day Indian states of Uttar Pradesh, Madhya Pradesh, Rajasthan and Bihar had migrated to East Pakistan. Before 1971, many Biharis, for example, had held scarce and desirable factory jobs because they had been seen by some within the Pakistani authorities as less militant than the Bengalis. Regarded as supporters of the West Pakistan government during the Liberation War, many of them suffered at the hands of Bengali nationalists. At the time of liberation, there were believed to be about six hundred thousand of these "Biharis." Many still remain in camps where, in theory, they await transfer to Pakistan (only a few have so far been officially moved), while others have managed to travel under their own efforts to Pakistan and elsewhere. Later generations have, in many cases, learned Bengali and integrated more fully into Bangladeshi society. There are also refugees in the south who have entered Bangladesh. Since the early 1990s, as many as three hundred thousand Rohingya Muslims (believed to be descendants from seventh-century Arab traders) have fled Burma's Arakan Province to Bangladesh in the wake of persecution and discrimination by the Burmese military junta. Many of these people now live in informal settlements and refugee camps located between the port city of Cox's bazaar and the Burmese border areas.

In addition to the Biharis and the Rohingyas, there are several other non-Bengali groups in society. The government estimates that there are close to two million classified as so-called tribal people, encompassing more than fifty different groups. These can be identified as being divided into three main clusters. The first, which includes the Garos and Khasis, found mainly in the Mymensingh area of Bangladesh, are part of larger ethnic groups that are concentrated mainly in the northeastern states of India. The second, which includes the Chakmas, Tripuras and Marmas are found in the Chittagong Hill Tracts (CHT) area of southeastern Bangladesh near the borders with Burma and the Indian state of Tripura, and many are Buddhists or follow Animist religions. A long-running armed conflict has taken place between the Bangladesh state and sections of these communities in the CHT, and this has only recently begun to move towards a resolution. Finally, there are the Santals, who are predominantly Hindu, and form part of a much-larger community in the Indian states of West Bengal, Orissa and Bihar. The numbers of all these tribal groups are believed to be consistently underrepresented within official data (Van Schendel 2001). The final non-Bengali minority group is the *bediya*, sometimes known as "river gypsies," another marginalised Muslim minority community that lives a seminomadic boat-dwelling existence selling spices and medicinal herbs, hunting and acting as travelling entertainers. The extent of this population is hard to judge, but an estimate during the 1980s put the numbers of *bediya* at 1.4 million, but recent suggestions are closer to half a million or lower (Maksud 2006).

Religion and politics were only weakly linked together in the public sphere during the years before and immediately after liberation, during which time a secular inclusive Bengali national identity was uppermost, but they have gradually become more closely linked. Throughout the years, political expediency has driven each of Bangladesh's postliberation national leaders to try to build bridges with the Islamists, with varying degrees of success. Bangladesh's military leaders needed to build political support in order to legitimise their undemocratic governments, while in the democratic era, minority Islamist parties became part of the negotiation to build governing coalitions. The result has been that new areas of political space have been created for Islamist forces. For example, during the 1990s, some conservative religious leaders and their supporters campaigned against some forms of rural development work, including attacks on NGOs such as BRAC and Proshika (Seabrook 2001). Government and NGO credit programmes have also sometimes been denounced as contravening religious rules that forbid moneylending, and some local religious leaders have viewed the mobility of women outreach workers and interventions aimed at women's empowerment work with suspicion.

Yet as Banu (1992: 148) has argued, there is a problem with a narration of Bangladesh's history that contrasts an earlier "secular" nationalist identity with a gradual increase in religiosity. The Bengali words *dharmanirapeksata*, used by Mujib and the nationalists in the early 1970s, did not refer to secularism in the sense of an absence of religion, but was more correctly translated as meaning secular in terms of "neutrality in religion." Mujib is quoted as saying,

The 75 million people of Bengal will have the right to religion. . . . Our only objection is that nobody will be allowed to use religion as a political weapon.

After the 9/11 attacks on the United States, and with JI installed as part of the ruling BNP government coalition led by Begum Khaleda Zia, the tensions quickly became far more pronounced. There were reports of increased cases of "communal" violence. Religious violence had taken place during and after the 2001 elections, and evidence soon began to emerge of the existence of militant Islamist groups operating in the country, some claiming international links. Since 1999, bombings of secular Bengali cultural festivals, open-air festivals and cinemas started happening in places such as Tangail, Mymensingh, Jessore and Dhaka. There had also been attacks on churches and on AL and leftist political party offices. In 2003, a militant organisation that called itself the Ja'amatul Mujaheedin Bangladesh (JMB) became visible to the authorities after a bomb factory exploded in the staff residence of a local *madrasa*. In 2004, members of the Ahmadiyya religious community (a minority group that considers itself a sect of Islam) were violently targeted by Islamist groups around the country. In the same year, grenades were thrown at Sheikh Hasina during a public rally in Dhaka, killing fourteen people and injuring three hundred. In August 2005, more than five hundred small bombs exploded in three hundred locations around the country, in all but one of the sixty-four districts, killing two people and further increasing the public profile of the JMB. Observers such as Ali Riaz (2004) began to ask whether Bangladesh was at risk of becoming a Taliban-style state.

*International Context: From Cold War to "War on Terror"*
When Prime Minister Mujib unveiled the new constitution in 1972, its basic principles were set out as nationalism, democracy, socialism and secularism. The constitution outlined a policy of peaceful coexistence with other countries and of nonalignment in foreign affairs, with Mujib even speaking at one point of the new country as "the Switzerland of the East." There were no issues of territorial claim on its neighbours, even though some initially saw a possible linkup with the Indian state of West Bengal (Bengal had originally been partitioned by the British in 1905, which is discussed in Chapter 2). Mujib was careful to put an end to any speculation that he hoped Bangladesh might one day be augmented by West Bengal, within a greater reunified Bengal, in a speech made during a visit to Kolkata in 1972. However, as Anisuzzaman (2001) recounts, when an amendment to the constitution was adopted in the Constituent Assembly that "the citizens of Bangladesh shall be known as Bengalis," Manabendranath Larma, the member from the CHT, strongly objected and later walked out in protest, predicting the destruction of the Chakma nation, on the grounds that although the hill peoples were Bangladeshi citizens, they were not Bengalis. The debate about whether the citizens of Bangladesh are Bengali or Bangladeshi remains ongoing between the political parties.

Despite the relative stability of the country's national borders, its internal and external environments were to prove highly turbulent. Within the context of the essentially bipolar world of the Cold War, the emergence of Bangladesh was seen by many Western powers as a strengthening of India's regional interests and, therefore, also as a likely addition to the Soviet Union's sphere of influence more generally. In this environment, the United States and China had aligned themselves with Pakistan. What followed almost immediately was a "tilt" by Bangladesh away from its original position of nonalignment and towards the Indo-Soviet bloc. Between 1972, when the Indo-Bangladesh Friendship Treaty was signed with Prime Minister Indira Gandhi, and 1974, there were trade agreements, cultural relations and commitments to solving boundary problems. Yet close links with India did not always play well with a domestic audience in Bangladesh, which was wary of India's unequal power and size, and little in the form of resources had actually materialised from the Soviet Union for economic reconstruction.

Although Mujib was relatively pragmatic about foreign policy and attempted to keep the door open for good relations with countries and regions such as the United States, China and parts of the Arab world that had, in 1971, opposed its independence, his flexible strategy did not prove particularly successful. Washington viewed Bangladesh as being within the Soviet bloc, and the United States was suspicious of Mujib's early commitment to socialism in the constitution. Beijing, which was relatively hostile to India at that time, decided to veto Bangladesh's application to join the United Nations in 1972. By 1974, Pakistan had recognised Bangladesh, and Mujib, eager to try to offset his earlier difficulties in seeking to build relationships with the United States and China, then began participating in the Organization of the Islamic Conference. This, in turn, brought an end to the early positive phase of Bangladesh's relationship with India (Huque 2002).

After 1975, Ziaur Rahman set about reordering Bangladesh's internal and external policies. As a result, Mujib's earlier, rather unsuccessful efforts to court the United States and China gradually began to turn into a reality. China recognised Bangladesh, and U.S. foreign assistance began to increase. General Zia also began to open up the private sector in Bangladesh and invested less heavily in publicly owned industries and in the public sector. With Mujib gone, the way was also opened up for Saudi Arabia to recognise Bangladesh. This fit in well with Zia's new emphasis on building a stronger Islamic identity in place of the earlier emphasis on an ethnolinguistic foundation. This shift also contributed to the creation of a more anti-Indian domestic political climate, which Zia was then able to draw upon in order to consolidate his power, and he began enlisting supporters from the political left and the right.

The new portrayal of Indian regional hegemony and its interfering role in Bangladesh's affairs proved to be a very powerful mobilising cry for building political support – and was a stance that was to continue and intensify during the regime of General Ershad, who came to power in 1982. Ziaur Rahman's reorientation of Bangladesh's foreign policy set the tone for future governments into and through the 1990s (Huque 2002). India's dominance was powerfully symbolised by the issue of water control, because Indian water-management interventions such as dams and barrages placed upstream were believed to have continuing negative implications for downstream water supplies in Bangladesh. Despite this, Zia managed to conclude a water-sharing agreement with India in 1977, in which the Ganges was recognised by India as an international resource, along with establishment of the principle of equitable distribution of its waters between both nations.

After seizing power in 1982, General H. M. Ershad's government continued to build on the positive relationship that Zia started building with the United States. In particular, the New Industrial Policy (NIP) set out in 1982 and the Revised Industrial Policy (RIP) of 1986 moved forward the United States' and other foreign donors' favoured policies of "structural adjustment" and liberalisation, which aimed at privatisation and the deregulation of public enterprises and institutions. Relations with China also continued to remain close, but unlike Zia, Ershad did not make any effort to maintain friendly relations with the Soviet Union, and he expelled a number of Soviet diplomats from Dhaka in 1982.

Two issues became recurring problems for foreign relations with India during the 1980s and the 1990s. The first was the continuing tension over water sharing. A new Memorandum of Understanding with New Delhi, signed in 1982, failed to build on the 1977 agreement, because it still did not provide a guarantee that there would be a minimum of downstream water available to Bangladesh during the dry season. India also continued to provide support to tribal rebels who were involved in a long-running conflict in the CHT, a continuing problem that would not receive serious attention until the 1996 AL government was elected. Relations with India were also worsened by Ershad's attempts to further Islamise Bangladeshi nationalism, as he tried to bolster popular support in the face of increasing domestic dissatisfaction with his autocratic rule. This effort culminated in the declaration of Islam as the state religion in 1988, by the Eighth Amendment of the constitution.

When Begum Khaleda Zia (Zia's widow, usually referred to as Khaleda) was elected in 1991, after Ershad's peaceful overthrow ushered in a new era of electoral democracy, the collapse of the Soviet Union removed the need to deal with the consequences of the deterioration of the relationship under the previous regime. The pattern of cordial relations with United States and China continued, as did the difficult relationship with India. This was complicated by a number of factors: the ongoing water-sharing problem, which Khaleda Zia unsuccessfully took to the United Nations in 1993, and the growth of a massive trade deficit with India. Another problem was the increasing level of Hindu nationalism in India, which sparked the destruction in 1992 of India's Babri Mosque and led to violence between Muslims and Hindus in India along with counterpart communal tension in Bangladesh with reports of increased attacks on minorities. Khaleda Zia attempted to reactivate the now-dormant South Asian Association for Regional Cooperation that had been established in 1985, but continuing regional tensions rendered such efforts fruitless.

The first democratically elected AL government headed by Sheikh Hasina Wazed (Mujib's daughter, usually referred to as Hasina) came to power in 1996 with a more sophisticated foreign policy agenda. The AL was faced with the problem that it was popularly regarded as "pro-Indian," a fact that did not sit well in the changed communal climate of the mid-1990s. Hasina cleverly defused this potential problem by refusing to renew the 1972 Indo-Bangladesh treaty that had come to be regarded as symbolising India's hegemony. This was an act that, according to Mahmudul Huque (2002: 213), helped the new government "to shed the burden of pro-Indianism from the beginning." A new water agreement with India was established, and this improved the longstanding tensions around water sharing, while a peace treaty was negotiated in the CHT that made it more difficult for insurgents to use the neighbouring Indian territory as a base for their operations. Requests by India for a special transit route in order to allow better communications with its territories on the other side of Bangladesh were not popular, and Hasina refused to grant India this concession.

During the second half of the 1990s, people inside and outside Bangladesh began to talk more frequently of the country in connection with the now-fashionable idea of "globalisation." International migration had increased substantially, and for the first time, remittances began to exceed income from international aid. Bangladeshi troops were now successfully placed within UN peacekeeping forces, generating much-needed foreign exchange and building the reputation of the country further as a responsible global citizen. The Hasina government elected in 1996 built on much of what had come before in the Ershad and Khaleda Zia era in order to continue to develop a foreign policy that further integrated Bangladesh into the world capitalist system. There was an increasing focus on the relationship with the United States as the key to foreign policy in the now unipolar post–Cold War world. There were three main dimensions: U.S. development assistance remained a crucial resource, it had become the largest importer of Bangladesh-made garments and U.S. companies started economic investment in exploring Bangladesh's extensive oil and gas sectors. Yet current globalisation, as discussed in Chapter 6, needs to be considered in the context of earlier histories of international restructuring of state in relation to capital.

What kinds of comparisons can be made between progress in Bangladesh and other states in India? From the 1950s onwards, the government in West Bengal embarked on a very different set of policies. Rural social relations were managed by the Left Front government through an agrarian reform process that reduced the power of ex-zamindar elites in favour of that of the rural middle classes, by the introduction of a land-reform process that began to restructure property rights. Yet as Ben Rogaly and colleagues (1999: 24) argue, the government's policies in West Bengal increasingly met with criticism, as the government's radicalism diminished in the face of electoral realities and problems of elite capture, patronage, and implicit gender bias became apparent. Each contributed to a reality that regularly failed to live up to the rhetoric of redistribution that has been peddled by politicians. Popular protests in recent years over the government's role in compulsory agricultural land acquisition on behalf of corporate capital have also highlighted growing inequalities within West Bengal.

The historical legacy of agrarian relations has played an important role. Blair (2008) explores the contrasting structural and cultural characteristics that may have influenced rural development pathways in the Indian states of Maharashtra and Bihar. In Maharashtra, outcomes have been relatively favourable, most notably with its innovative Employment Guarantee Scheme, which has subsequently replicated by many other Indian states. By contrast, Bihar remains characterised by many of the longstanding rural problems faced by neighbouring Bangladesh, such as high levels of poverty and vulnerability, the dominance and capture of development resources by elites and extensive corruption. Four sets of factors may help to explain the differences: land tenure, rural-urban linkages, level of outside control and political culture. First, Maharashtra's landholding system under the Bombay presidency allowed a relative level of freehold *ryotwari* tenure that encouraged productive investment by landlords in order to maximise income. By contrast, the *zamindari* system that was put in place by the British in Bengal and Bihar had an opposite effect because it rewarded exploitation and neglect by landlords. Second, with respect to the pattern of urbanisation, Bihar's capital Patna (like Kolkata) exploited its rural hinterlands by a heavy extraction of rural rents in order to maintain higher urban standards of living. By contrast, the cities of Mumbai, Nagpur and Pune in Maharashtra to some extent mitigated these impacts through a higher level of provision of state services, finance and trade that produced a measure of economic growth across the state. Third, there is a tradition of assertiveness in Maharashtra that contrasts with Bihar and Bengal's long history of being under the control of outside forces. Fourth, a political culture that has evolved in Maharashtra is characterised more by strategies for accommodation and negotiation than the "winner takes all" approach to politics found in Bangladesh and Bihar.

Since the 9/11 attacks on the United States, Bangladesh has increasingly come to be viewed by many Western governments through the lens of international "antiterror" activities. As a moderate democratic-majority Muslim country, what has been perceived as the growth of domestic Islamism and radical Islam in Bangladesh has now become more of a source of international concern. The rise of religious politics in Bangladesh has also been linked with the country's closer ties with the Middle East: the financial resources that have been received since the 1980s from Saudi Arabia and other wealthy Middle Eastern oil states in the form of aid and the large-scale labour migration and return of workers to and from the Middle East (Maneeza Hossain 2006). The international context has also changed with the idea of the BRIC (Brazil, Russia, India and China) countries. The term was developed in 2001 by Jim O'Neill, chief economist of Goldman Sachs, and became increasingly used during the first decade of the twenty-first century. It suggests that these four countries will overtake the economies of the six main Western countries within two to three decades and go on to form the mainstay of the twenty-first-century economy (Tett 2010). With China and India close by, the rise of the BRICs will have important implications for Bangladesh. Two years later, the same bank listed Bangladesh among the "next 11 countries" that were tipped to achieve similar status later in the century.

## Bangladesh and the International Aid System

Pakistan had already become a recipient of sizeable quantities of foreign aid from the 1950s onwards, particularly from the United States. During the Cold War era, Pakistan was a strategic U.S. ally and counterweight to India, which was seen as pro-Soviet. The first major investment of the newly emerged post–Second World War modern-aid system in Pakistan was the Village Agricultural Industrial Development (V-AID) initiative established in 1953. This was based on the philosophy of "community development," which had emerged at the end of the colonial era, and aimed to train community leaders to help organise their communities, discuss local problems and needs at newly formed village councils and provide a local framework for the transfer of technical and financial resources from government (Buiyan et al. 2005). Villages were organised into units of five to seven in what was called a development block, and new officials known as block officers were created to supervise the implementation of projects. The perception, however, that foreign aid was disproportionately benefiting West Pakistan at the expense of East Pakistan fuelled a sense of injustice that was to feed into the growing dissatisfaction with the Pakistan leadership that had eventually led to the Liberation War in 1971.

Nevertheless, in East Pakistan, three training institutes were set up in order to extend the V-AID programme, and under Pakistan's First Five Year Plan (FYP) (1955–1960) there were to be seventy-nine development areas brought under the programme. Yet by 1961, it had been declared a failure. A new two-tier village cooperative system developed by charismatic civil servant Dr. Akhtar Hameed Khan was seen as a much-improved solution to problems of agricultural modernisation. This became known as the Comilla cooperative model, as it was named after Comilla's rural development "academy" in the east of the country where the idea was pioneered by Khan. It was based on the idea of mobilising local effort and distributing government resources to local farmer organisations, based on principles of rural cooperation. The village was seen as an arena for social cohesion and mutualism, in which new cooperative structures could be built (Haq 1966). In its early years as a carefully managed local initiative, it was relatively successful (De Vylder 1982). But when it was later extended on a larger scale across the whole country, the results were extremely disappointing.

A pattern emerged within the developmentalist policy regime that followed, and which continues to this day, with the regular replacement of one type of development approach by another every few years. Sometimes different, often similar, a succession of approaches has each subsequently attempted to engage with longstanding development problems. For example, the mixed results derived in rural areas from Khan's Comilla cooperative model, particularly after it was replicated on a national level during the 1970s, later led to the use of integrated rural development projects (IRDPs) in the 1980s, and then to a new, stronger emphasis on NGOs as key rural development actors during the 1990s. The disappointments with the performance first of the IRDP approach, and later also with the various NGO approaches, in turn influenced the rise of new donor sectorwide approaches and budget support, and so on, in a cycle of endlessly changing approaches.

After the Liberation War, foreign aid quickly took on a new level of importance within the newly created country. Bangladesh rapidly came to symbolise the challenges posed by international aid as a form of poor-country support. This was a vision fuelled by the often-cited remark, mistakenly attributed to U.S. National Security Adviser Henry Kissinger, that Bangladesh was an "international basket case" country that would never be able to stand on its own two feet. (In fact, the comment was made by Ural Alexis Johnson, an under-secretary of state for political affairs at a meeting chaired by Kissinger in December 1971, to discuss the situation in South Asia, who was predicting that if the United States were to provide aid to Bangladesh, the country could turn out to have limitless needs.)

By the end of the 1980s, Bangladesh was receiving $1.7 billion in official annual aid flows. This amounted to about $15 per person and financed almost three-fifths of the country's total investment. Most of this aid was provided as grants or on soft-loan terms, which kept the country's debt-servicing ratio relatively low – at close to 12 percent of foreign exchange earnings or 20 percent if short-term liability on commercial loans is included (Mahabub Hossain 1990). Faaland and Parkinson (1976: 197), two economists who had worked with the World Bank in the early 1970s in Bangladesh, argued that the country was to be considered "a test case for development." Having made the argument for long-term and increased international aid, the authors concluded that if development can be made to work in Bangladesh, "there can be little doubt that it can be made to succeed anywhere else." By contrast, Sobhan (1982) instead suggested that foreign aid had created a "crisis of external dependence." Aid, he argued, had led to a range of undesirable outcomes that held Bangladesh back: it reduced government incentives to promote exports, sustained parasitic elites, contributed to a decline in savings and inhibited the emergence of domestic capitalism and disempowered the country's policy makers because they were made subservient to outside policy prescriptions.

Four decades later, many of the international donors are now relatively upbeat about what has been achieved. As we have seen, the expression "success story" – at least in relation to some economic and social indicators – has, perhaps for the first time, become part of some Bangladesh donor vocabularies. Two key drivers for this success were identified as long-term government commitment to an improved education policy and the NGO-led emphasis on microcredit programmes. This former policy began with primary schooling during the 1980s and then continued with a scheme providing stipends for female students during the 1990s. It has provided for the country, and for successive governments, a positive and coherent policy narrative that has found widespread support among both elites and masses. At the same time, the work of the Grameen Bank and other organisations in first developing and then implementing credit and savings programmes for the poor provided a material base for increasing women's status and well-being. It has also helped create a strong basis on which women were able to organise and access services such as health and family planning, skills training and opportunities for self-employment.

Donor political influence in Bangladesh has been substantial. Since the 1970s, foreign donors have been instrumental in promoting a programme of privatisation and economic liberalisation in Bangladesh. When General Ziaur Rahman had taken power in 1975, he had inherited an economy in which the government owned 90 percent of the fixed assets of the modern manufacturing sector and any foreign direct investment was only permitted if done so through the public sector. Western donors, led by the World Bank and the U.S. Agency for International Development (USAID), used their influence to advise the government to begin denationalising public industries and reducing the controls that Mujib's government had placed on private enterprises. This political role played by foreign aid has remained a central theme in Bangladesh, as Naomi Hossain (2005: 11) has argued:

The desperate need for aid undoubtedly steered the early shift to liberal economic reform, and continuing aid dependence has encouraged later governments to stay on the pro-market growth track. Aid donors apparently felt entitled to promote their policy preferences because of the evident need for aid. . . . Abandonment of "socialism" to comply with donor recommendations was followed by a considerable rise in aid flows.

This exercise of donor power continued under the regime of General Ershad, who made efforts to further intensify the slow progress with liberalisation reform. By the late 1980s, Western donors had also become enamoured with the development roles of NGOs – international and local – and were beginning to push for an expanded role for these agencies in Bangladesh.

Alongside these ideological arenas of donor influence, foreign aid has also provided resources that have remained important within Bangladesh's everyday political economy. In Blair's (2001: 192) analysis, the political economy of Bangladesh can be understood primarily in terms of an enduring alliance between three groups of elites: military officers, the upper echelons of the bureaucracy and the political leadership. He highlights a fourth "silent partner" in the form of a layer of dominant rural elites, made up of the landowning rural patrons who produced an agricultural surplus through labour hiring and through tenancy arrangements such as sharecropping. Like many other researchers, he draws attention to the way in which foreign aid has oiled the wheels of the machinery of these elites. The bureaucracy was given the job of turning the bulk of the foreign aid into development initiatives, and this provided large-scale opportunities for rent-seeking behaviour. At the same time, large amounts of aid flowed to the military and to political leaders (depending on who was in power). In the rural areas, when legitimate development activities such as credit, infrastructure or social services were initiated by the representatives of the various central government ministries, the resources tended to be "captured" and diverted by local rural elites.

Finally, as Wood (1997) suggests, foreign aid is about far more than simply financial resource flows – it is about the politics of power and the power of ideas to frame policy and action. By the 1990s, the aid relationship was not only one of the country's key defining features, but also it had come to represent the dominant cognitive framework through which much of Bangladesh had come to be known. At the international level, this meant that internationally commissioned donor studies often generated mountains of data about Bangladesh on a highly selective basis (reflecting shifting development fashions such as microfinance or flood control). At the local level, it meant that university-based academics were turned into consultants and villagers began to see the local landscape increasingly dotted with sign boards that advertised the names of internationally funded development projects or the acronyms of growing numbers of NGOs. The content and the representation of Bangladesh's economy and society had now become absorbed within the international project of developmentalism. Although aid is now undoubtedly less important to the country in terms of financial resources than it was during the 1970s and 1980s, it nevertheless remains a powerful influence at the level of ideas and policy.

Peoples' attitudes to foreign aid in Bangladesh are at best ambiguous – and at worst sometimes outright hostile. The reasons for this are a combination of a nationalist self-respect that resents foreign interference and influence and the widespread perception that international aid is a self-interested and inefficient business that achieves little of benefit for the country. For example, Huque (2002: 214) estimates that of the vast volume of Bangladesh's aid received during its first three decades (around US$26 billion), only 25 percent reached ordinary people and 75 percent was "looted" by bureaucrats, foreign consultants, politicians, contractors and other local urban and rural elites. He also argues that foreign aid has been received "at the cost of the country's self-respect." Externally, this has led Bangladesh to appease countries such as the United States and Saudi Arabia that had opposed the country's independence in 1971. Domestically, aid has been misused such that the country's politics and economy have become criminalised in an informal, shadowy corrupt nexus among politicians, financial professionals and donors and their consultants. Some economists have also pointed to the role of heavy inflows of foreign aid in making a significant contribution to high levels of capital flight that have long characterised Bangladesh (Quazi 2001).

## Conclusion: The Current Picture

Although its borders have remained constant since 1971, Bangladesh today is not the same country it was when it was established. It has experienced a wide-ranging set of economic, political and social changes during the four decades since the Liberation War. These changes have been felt in the expansion of infrastructure in the form of roads, bridges, schools and health facilities; in the efforts to decentralise power into new forms of

local government structure; and in the varied social and economic transformations associated with both in-country and international processes of
migration. There has been a long period of economic growth, and many
areas of social progress are visible. Despite these far-reaching changes and
indications of progress, Bangladesh remains a state in the making. The social
and political forces unleashed in the struggle for liberation from Pakistan
continue to animate events and still show no signs of settling. In 2007,
the JI Secretary General Mohammed Ali Ahasan Mojaheed controversially
described the Liberation War as a "civil war" and claimed that there were no
"war criminals" in Bangladesh, reigniting the AL's continued call for those
who had killed Mujib and collaborated with the Pakistan authorities during
conflict to be prosecuted (ICG 2008).

Tensions and synergies exist within the processes of modernisation, the
construction of religious identities and the externally and locally driven
impulses of development. However, progress towards a resolution of the
country's longstanding political crisis remains slow. Governing institutions
still betray their authoritarian origins in the British colonial period and
are only weakly institutionalised. Political parties continue to serve narrow
interest groups through a pyramid of patron-client relationships that stretch
from the centre down to the villages. In the formal structures of state
administration, there is widespread stagnation. The government and public
institutions of the state remain captured by a narrow national elite that still
tends to favour private gain over public interest. The result is government
that neither protects and fosters the rights of its citizens nor provides a
stable enough environment for business and investment. At the regional
level, Bangladesh remains locked into complex and long-running disputes
with India over issues such as water use, immigration and aid to separatists.
Finally, increased concern over the potential consequences of climate change
has in recent years begun to hover more ominously over Bangladesh's future,
adding a new urgency.

3

# Towards Bangladesh

## British and Pakistani Rule

Bangladesh's existence as a nation-state only dates from 1971, but the nation cannot be understood without reference to a much-longer historical backdrop. In this chapter we provide a selective historical overview leading up to the moment when Bangladesh emerged as a separate country, aiming to contextualise analysis of state and economy against the longer-term developments in the region. The chapter begins with a brief discussion of precolonial Bengal, a period with important implications for the shaping of the natural environment and of social and religious identities. It then moves to the period of British rule, first describing the role of the East India Company in securing the region as part of the British Empire, and then its gradual incorporation into the formal administrative structures of colonial rule, which brought lasting political and economic consequences, for example, in state formation. The weakness of the Bangladesh state today has important historical roots in the influence of more than three hundred years of economic globalisation during which the country moved from a position of relative economic strength and vitality to a position of structural weakness within the global economy (McGuire 2009).

The third section considers partition in 1947 and the period that followed when Bangladesh existed for more than two decades as East Pakistan. This was a time when the country experienced the disruption of internal economic colonisation, which led to growing resistance and Pakistan's civil war in 1971. Finally, the chapter summarises the years of Bangladesh's independence. Bangladesh's founder and first prime minister, Sheikh Mujibur Rahman, experimented with secular nationalist identities (1971–5) and built close ties with neighbouring India and the Soviet Union. The military regimes of General Ziaur Rahman (1975–81) and General H. M. Ershad (1982–90) gradually moved Bangladesh towards closer links with the United

States and other Muslim countries, particularly the Arab states, contributing to the strengthening of a Muslim Bengali cultural identity.

## Precolonial Bengal

Relatively little is known about the prehistory of Bengal. Some believe that the word *Bengal* may derive from a tribe known as the Vanga, one of several Stone Age Indo-Aryan and Mongol groups that may have migrated into the Indus and upper Ganges valley areas close to 1000 B.C., populating areas of what is now West Bengal, Bihar and Assam. Despite these communities, there were still relatively few human settlements around the lower Ganges and the Brahmaputra valleys, the areas that form much of today's Bangladesh. It was only with the advent of improved Iron Age tools five hundred years later that it became possible for people to make clearings in the dense forests and swamps and to develop the area for human habitation.

Early historical evidence relating to Bengal is found in records of the dynasty founded by Chandragupta Maurya in the early third-century B.C. The Mauryans controlled parts of Bengal along with northern and western areas of the Indian subcontinent, in a dynasty that encompassed a range of religious influences, including Hinduism and Jainism. The best-known ruler of this dynasty was Chandragupta's grandson Asoka, who famously converted to Buddhism. The Mauryan Empire was in decline by the end of the second-century B.C., and less is known about the states and rulers that followed. Bengal is mentioned in records from the Sunga (170–70 B.C.) and Gupta dynasties (320–510). Archaeological records and travellers' accounts indicate that there was already a measure of integration between north and west Bengal within a wider region of "networks and centres of mobility running from Iran to Bengal and from the Oxus to the Narmada" (Ludden 1999: 45). Bengal was mainly ruled by local chieftains, who would have paid tribute to imperial authorities in the Indian heartlands. However, movements of northern peoples had not reached very far into Bengal, discouraged by its hostile ecology and unfamiliar tribal communities (Bhattacharya 1969). Much of the river-delta area that makes up present-day Bangladesh therefore remained a backwater, relatively isolated from its nominal rulers in the north.

In middle of the seventh century, Bengal came under the control of a Kshatriya tribal chief named Gopala, who founded what became known as the Pala dynasty (c. 750–1159). The Palas were Buddhist Bengalis who controlled large areas of the Ganges valley, competing for influence at its borders with other dynasties such as the Gujara-Pratiharas based in western India (Gujarat), the Rashtrakutas based in the Deccan and the Cholas from South India. A total of eighteen successive Pala rulers controlled the territories of what is now Bengal and Bihar until the middle of the twelfth century, ruling the area from their capital at Pataliputra (Patna in modern-day Bihar). The city of Vikrampur near Dhaka is believed to have been a regional capital. The Palas were strong opponents of Brahminism and were known for their art, literature and universities. The Palas influenced the direction of Tibetan Buddhism during the reign of Pala king Nyapala. The Palas were in decline by the middle of the twelfth century, when they gave way to the Sena dynasty, founded by Lakshman Sen, a powerful non-Bengali Hindu patriarch from Karnataka in South India. The Senas ruled Bengal from close to 1095 to 1245. Grandson Vijayasena became the king of Gaur, an important city located in present-day West Bengal, which had previously been the capital of the kingdom of Sasanka during the seventh century. Gaur later became the Sena dynasty capital during the eleventh and twelfth centuries. Some historians have argued that the Sena dynasty's lack of tolerance for Buddhism and its efforts to reassert the values of the Hindu caste system contributed to the readiness of sections of the population to begin to convert to Islam at this time (Baxter 1998).

The earliest documented Muslim influences in the Indian subcontinent are usually recorded as the arrival of Arab traders on the Malabar Coast of South India during the seventh century and a series of eighth-century Arab military incursions into Sindh. By the early eleventh century, Muslim influences started to be felt in Bengal, when the Afghan Mahmud of Ghazni began extending his power base into northwestern India. By the twelfth century, Ghaznavid power had been displaced by that of the Ghurids, rulers who brought Afghan, Persian and Turkish influences and who captured Delhi in 1193. This was the beginning of the period of what became known as the Delhi Sultanate, established in 1206 by the Ghurid general Qutb-ud-din Aybak. Most of present-day Bihar and Bengal gradually came under the control of the Delhi Sultanate, the centre of Muslim power in the region, as it extended its power eastwards. By 1245, Bengal had been brought under Muslim rule and was controlled by a succession of largely independent sultans, exercising varying levels of control over Bengal from Delhi. These Muslim kingdoms began with the Slave (or Mamluk) dynasty founded by the Turks, was followed by the Khaliji (1290–1320), the Tughluq (1320–1413) and Sayyid (1414–51) and ended with the Lodhi dynasty (1451–1526), who were Afghans. Yet Bengal remained an area with a high degree of independence and was only very loosely incorporated into the institutions of rule from Delhi. Local Bengali chieftains, such as Shamsuddin, regularly challenged the authority of the Delhi rulers. At this time, as Sufia Uddin (2006: 19) describes, Bengal was only "nominally" under the rule of the Delhi Sultanate and achieved a de facto political independence, owing to its geographical distance from the capital.

In 1346, after a successful rebellion against the Tughluq rulers in Delhi by the Bengali Fakhruddin Mubarrak Shah, what became known as the Bengal Sultanate began and continued for almost two centuries. This era is often identified as the start of Bengal's proper independence, as the Tughluq Sultanate in Delhi failed, despite several attempts, to recover control of Bengal (Uddin 2006). Founded by Shamsuddin Ilyas Shah (1342–57), the Ilyas Shahi dynasty ruled Bengal until 1490. During this period, much of the agricultural land in Bengal had come to be controlled by Hindu landowners, which created occasional tensions with Muslims. For example, the Ilyas Shahi dynasty's rule was resisted by Raja Ganesh, a powerful Hindu landowner who briefly managed to place his son on the throne of Bengal in 1415, although the Ilyas Shahis were again restored upon his death in 1432 (Uddin 2006). The late 1480s saw the rise of an Abyssinian slave dynasty in Bengal. People from Abyssinia had originally been brought by the Ilyas Shahis as slaves (*Habshi*) to serve as soldiers in their armies. Four Abyssinian kings briefly gained the throne in succession. However, the periodic tensions between Hindus and Muslims at this time were less significant than the numerous lines of cleavage and conflict that regularly arose between different Muslim religious and cultural identities. For example, Anisuzzaman (2001: 47) describes the way that different areas of conflict and tension existed: between Sunni and Shia contributing to schisms in administration, a Mughal distrust of Afghans and the consequent reluctance to appoint them to high office and the persecution of the Abyssinians (*Habshis*) by Sultan Husain Shah that ultimately led to their expulsion from Bengal.

After a period of instability, Ala al-Din Husayn Shah gained control of Bengal in 1494, after serving as chief minister under the last of the Abyssinian sultans, and went on to rule until 1519. Ala al-Din Husayn Shah was originally a Meccan Arab but had lived in Bengal for many years. He founded the Bengali Husayn Shahi dynasty, which ruled from 1493 to 1538, and was known to be tolerant to Hindus, employing many of them in his service and promoting a form of religious pluralism (Uddin 2006). Despite the inequalities of landholding that existed, Muslims and Hindus were both active in governing Bengal during the succession of independent regimes that held sway in the Bengal Sultanate period. This era is often regarded as a golden age in which the territory of Bengal extended to the edge of

West Bengal and as far as the west of the present state of Assam, and included areas of Burma, Orissa and Tripura.

### The Mughals and the East India Company
The Delhi Sultanate period came to an end when the Mughals established control in Delhi. Babar, the founder of the Mughal Empire, had defeated the last Lodhi ruler at Panipat in 1526. The period of independent Bengal was ended first by the rule of the Afghan Sher Shah Suri, who gained control when he challenged the authority of the second Mughal emperor, Humayun. He was followed by the Karranis, another Afghan dynasty, who went on to rule Bengal until Humayan's successor, Emperor Akbar (and Babar's grandson) defeated Sultan Daud Karrani at Tukaroi in 1576. This made Bengal a province of the Mughal Empire, at least in name, because there were many Bengali attempts to resist Mughal rule. One of the best known was the Bara Buiyan group (the twelve landlords) that was led by Isa Khan, a wealthy farmer who owned large landholdings in Comilla and Mymensingh, and who operated from his base at Sonargaon near Dhaka. Joining with other landlords, including many Hindus, the group inflicted notable defeats on the Mughal navy in 1584 and 1597. Isa Khan, who had effectively acted to try to defend Bengal against Urdu-speaking outsiders, was a name later invoked as an early Bengali hero during the 1971 Liberation War.

Bengal developed and prospered under Mughal rule. The capital of Bengal was moved from Gaur to Dhaka in 1610, a city that had by now become economically successful and politically important, in part due to the emergence of its distinctive and renowned handloom textile industry. During the Mughal period, Dhaka saw the construction of many new buildings such as the Lalbagh fort and impressive mosques and gardens. A wide range of cultural influences were also at work in the city, including those from Samarkand and Persia, and the latter brought Sufi ideas and philosophy to the region. At this time Bengal was also opened up further to traders from both the east and west operating across overland and maritime routes. However, when the Bengal provincial capital was relocated from Dhaka to Murshidabad in 1715, this contributed to the decline of Dhaka as a city of political importance and reduced its prosperity.

The Portuguese were the first Europeans to reach Bengal, establishing settlements during the fifteenth century. But it was the British East India Company, founded in 1600 and given a trading monopoly over India by Elizabeth I, that was to impact more forcefully on the fortunes of the province. Crucial to its expansion was the Company's organisation as a joint-stock enterprise. This made it possible for its traders to operate more easily within an uncertain business environment far from home because they could now pool resources and share risks. Because traders could raise substantial resources through this new type of company structure, they were more than a match for local Indian merchant families (Metcalf and Metcalf 2002). The Company had originally traded spices profitably in the islands of the East Indies, but competition from the Dutch had led to a new strategy to centre its activities on India. Faced with the strength of the Mughal Empire, the British negotiated entry to Indian markets, and this was welcomed by Mughal authorities because they were seeking to counterbalance the growing power of the Portuguese. The Company began to develop trade in indigo dye, saltpetre (used for gunpowder), and Indian textiles, which were handmade and of high quality, all of which found ready markets in Europe. Britain's economy boomed after the 1660s, and the demand for Indian textiles began to grow very rapidly, with fabrics such as muslin and calico now forming the mainstay of Britain's trade with India. The Company had initially been a trading company that had set up its first warehouse in Surat in western India in 1612, but it slowly grew into a vast military and administrative organisation that served to develop and secure British colonial interests. In Bengal, a warehouse was established in Kolkata in 1690 and trading stations were soon installed at other locations such as Dhaka and Chittagong. There was particularly strong demand for the high-quality *jamdani* muslin cloth produced in Dhaka, which was also known at this time as an opulent centre of fine embroidery and lacework.

Bengal became a mainstay of the Company, accounting for 75 percent of its traded Indian goods by 1750. Seeing Bengal as an almost inexhaustible source of wealth, the Company became determined to secure ever-greater profits, and the British had "begun systematically abusing the right to free trade awarded them by the emperor," with the selective sale of free trade rights to "Indian favourites" and the extension of such permits into illegal activities such as trade in restricted internal grain markets (Metcalf and Metcalf 2002: 50). From the 1660s onwards, the power of the Mughal Empire started to wane. A deterioration in regional security led the Company to begin fortifying its facilities around India, including Chennai (then known as Madras), Mumbai (then Bombay) and Kolkata, after some were raided. Both locally, and back in Britain, there were critics of the Company who saw it was out of control. When the last Mughal emperor, Aurangzeb, died in 1707, Mughal decline had created political space for Indian provincial governors to begin to assert their autonomy. In 1756, the young *nawab*

Suraj-ud-Daula assumed the throne of the independent dynasty that governed Bengal, with an agenda to challenge what he saw as the excessive power of British trade interests that were operating in his province. He attacked and briefly captured Kolkata, and survivors from the fort were held in what became known in British school history books as the "black hole of Calcutta," in which a hundred British subjects reportedly perished. In order to restore British power, Colonel Robert Clive (1725–74), who started his career as a clerk in the Company, launched an expeditionary force from Madras and recaptured Kolkata in 1757.

In the same year, at the battle of Polashi ("Plassey" in the British history books), Robert Clive defeated Suraj-ud-Daula. From this point on, Bengal was ruled by the Company by using a series of "puppet" *nawabs*. Suraj-ud-Daula had recognised that the European merchants now posed a threat to the sovereignty of Bengal. He wished to see all foreign merchants made to trade under a more evenhanded set of rules and had taken steps to curb this power, revoking the right of the Company to trade without taxation. He also ordered the removal of a recently built British fort in Kolkata, seeing military power as having no place in a trading relationship. When Drake, the British Governor of Calcutta, offered a noncommittal response to this demand to demilitarise the Company's trading practices, the *nawab* marched on Kolkata and secured Fort William after three days. Compelled to withdraw, the Company's forces regrouped at Fulta and began to devise a new strategy that would exploit rivalries and tensions in the Bengali leadership.

After an unsuccessful attempt to support two pretenders to the *nawab's* throne, a force led by Clive was then sent from Madras, where he had defeated the French five years before, and arrived in late 1756. Clive managed to make a deal with Mir Jafar, the *nawab's* commander in chief, in which he would restore the privileges of the Company and pay compensation in return for British backing to overthrow Nawab Suraj-ud-Daula. This deal was achieved by conspiring with a group of bankers led by Jagat Seth, who had become disaffected with Suraj-ud-Daula's tax regime and who, in turn, conspired with Mir Jafar, who agreed to make substantial payments to the merchant bankers and the Company in return for being helped to gain the throne. At the "battle" of Polashi on June 23, Mir Jafar simply gave way to the Company's forces. Five days later, Mir Jafar had replaced Suraj-ud-Daula, who was executed soon after by Mir Jafar's son. But Mir Jafar was merely a puppet *nawab*, and from this point on the East India Company, supported by its army, became a powerful vehicle for its members to build their personal fortunes. British bullion was no longer needed to finance the purchase of the Company's goods, and instead it became possible to use internal tax revenue from Bengal to fund the purchase of the goods it shipped to England each year (Metcalf and Metcalf 2002: 51).

Polashi had been little more than a skirmish, in which the outcome had already been negotiated. An army of fifty thousand Bengali soldiers were ostensibly defeated by an irregular group of eight hundred Europeans, who had faced superior numbers and firepower. For Laurence Lifschultz (1979: i) Polashi set the tone not only for British rule in India but also for many of the subsequent twentieth-century "covert operations" or coup d'états that have been carried by both Western and other interests' powers against unwanted regimes because the opposing commander had simply been bought off beforehand. By now the governance of Bengal had become effectively destabilised by the Company. Mir Jafar was replaced in 1760 by another puppet ruler, Mir Kasim, who nevertheless also attempted to challenge the authority of the British and built up support in northern Bengal and Bihar. A final confrontation took place at the battle of Buxar on October 23, 1764, where the British defeated the Mughal emperor Shah Alam II, the Nawab of Awadh and Mir Kasim. The incident at Polashi therefore ushered in, as Lifschultz (1979: v) puts it, "the longest and deepest colonial experience in modern history."

In 1765, the Company signed a treaty that secured from the Mughal emperor, also by now a British puppet, the right to collect land revenue (*diwani*) of Bengal, Bihar and Orissa. This provided the Company with the right to raise taxes in Bengal and, therefore, its de facto rule over the province, although the administration of justice remained nominally under the control of the *nawab*. As governor of Bengal, Clive was unwilling to risk the Company's successful trading relationship by taking on formal rule. Over the coming years, driven by simple greed and expediency, the success of its policy of "military fiscalism" nevertheless meant that the Company gradually moved fully into the project of the conquest of Bengal, even though the Mughal emperor remained nominally in charge. In 1772, the Company appointed Warren Hastings as governor general of all the Company's Indian possessions, and Kolkata became its capital. The East India Company pursued an "indirect rule" policy based on local patronage and the playing off of local princely rulers against each other. The Company prospered in its commercial activities, bolstered by the new opium trade, which allowed it to build a regulated system in which opium growers in India were advanced credit, the crop was purchased and then taken to China in order to finance the purchase of tea and other goods. Yet by this time other British traders, who saw the potential for exploiting Indian resources and markets, started to campaign against the Company's trading monopoly in India, which was consequently ended by Parliament in 1813.

The growth of Britain's own industrial textile industry altered the nature of its trading relationship with India, with the new availability of cheap textiles dramatically reducing the value of Indian handmade cloth. The relationship with India began to shift to one of colonial dependency, in which agricultural raw materials (such as cotton, tea, wheat and oil seeds) were grown by Indian peasant cultivators and then bought at below-market prices. Indian farmers became primary producers, often heavily indebted by production loans provided by intermediaries and merchants who, in turn, were financed by the colonial capitalists in Britain. There was a move back to subsistence agriculture as artisan producers in Bengal (and elsewhere) now found that their markets had been undermined. Local demand also fell as increasingly resource-strapped princely courts could no longer afford locally made luxury items. Commodities such as cotton were exported to Britain for manufacture and then reexported at considerable profit. The decline in domestic cotton production in Bengal was gradually replaced by the production of jute, a crop that was well suited to the fertile deltaic soil. Jute was a high-value natural fibre that was in high demand on the international market and was used to make rope and carpet backings. The jute industry remained the exclusive project of British capital, and jute boomed in the period up until the First World War. Yet the jute cultivators of East Bengal were subordinated to a peripheral status within the wider organisation of production. They remained producers of raw jute that was then transported to Kolkata for processing or shipment overseas. In 1947, when Bengal was again divided, not a single jute mill existed in East Pakistan (Boyce 1987).

Economic uncertainty contributed to demands for land revenue reform as a way of stabilising the Company's finances. At the same time, early Indian nationalist critics were increasingly arguing that, because India's export surplus had become crucial for Britain's balance of payments, there was an exploitative drain of wealth from India that could have made an important contribution to India's development if it had been invested in the country. According to Sugata Bose and Ayesha Jalal (2004: 81), such criticism led the colonial state to begin "tempering the rules of governance in India." Believing private property to be central to economic prosperity, in line with current British liberal thinking of the time, governor-general Lord Cornwallis tried to stimulate agricultural productivity in Bengal through the creation of a new class of Indian "gentleman farmers." This idea was

formalised by the Permanent Settlement Act of 1793, which vested zamindars (intermediaries who collected revenue from the farmers) with full
landownership rights over new "*zaminadari*" estates. However, this was a
complete transformation of the traditional *zamindari* role that had dated
back to Mughal times, where it had simply designated "the lowest layer of
sovereignty" (Ludden 2002: 167). Zamindars had previously been middle-
men who took a percentage and then passed the rest on to the government.
They were not full landowners, but merely one party within a dispersed
set of cultivation rights distributed among themselves, the peasant farmers
and the government. After the reform, the cultivators were transformed
into peasants without rights, and although the zamindar could now assume
control of the estate, he could also be forced to sell it if he defaulted on
the required taxes. In Bengal, the transformation of the *zamindari* undermined agrarian relations. The hoped-for agricultural modernisation leading to higher production never materialised, with much of the countryside
instead degenerating into a stagnant system of landlord rentiers and per-
petually poor tenant farmers.

Furthermore, as many as one-third of the *zamindari* estates changed
hands during the two decades that followed the Permanent Settlement.
Many of the new purchasers were high-caste Hindus who had worked for
the Company, and this group understood to their advantage the workings
of the new tenancy system. By the 1820s, the zamindar landowning class
in Bengal had become predominantly Hindu, which began to contribute to
increased social tensions and would have far-reaching consequences. Indian
Civil Service (ICS) officer and historian W. W. Hunter observed in 1871 in
*The Indian Musalmans* (quoted in Ahmed 2004: 109)

We usurped the functions of those higher Mussalman officers who had formerly
subsisted between the actual collector and the government. . . . It elevated the Hindu
collectors, who up to that time had held but unimportant posts, to the position
of land-holders, gave them a proprietary right to the soil, and allowed them to
accumulate wealth which would have gone to the Mussalmans under their own
rule.

This change in agrarian relations would have long-lasting consequences.
Much later, when a significant element of the zamindar elite left East Bengal
for India at partition, the Muslim majority remained in a disadvantaged
position that was to leave them vulnerable to exploitation by the industrial
bourgeoisie of West Pakistan (Wood 1981). At the same time, as Bengal
became integrated into the global economy under British colonial rule, and
as part of a strategy to counterbalance the power of Hindu elites, a mainly

Muslim class of *jotedar* rich tenant farmers were given tenure rights through a patronage relationship with the colonial state. They emerged as producers of jute and other cash crops, though they paid rents to the zamindars. After the departure of Hindu zamindars in 1947, these rich peasant classes gained power in East Pakistan as property rights became established and *jotedars* began to move into politics, creating a period of social transformation that would eventually lead to the demand for separation from West Pakistan.

A key political outcome of the Permanent Settlement was also the creation of the culture of the *bhadralok* or "respectable people," the term that became associated with this mainly high-caste Bengali Hindu rentier class: "the *bhadralok* gentleman was the antithesis of the horny-handed son of the soil" (Chatterji 1994: 5). As incomes from agriculture began to decline towards the end of the nineteenth century, the *bhadralok* had become increasingly associated with a Western education, modernising views and an enlightened view of itself as a progressive class carrying forward a "Bengali renaissance." It played an important role in shaping the continuing nationalist resistance to British colonial rule, drawing on various forms of Hindu tradition, but ultimately also became associated with the view that Hindus should dominate Bengal and therefore with an anti-Muslim position at the time of partition in 1947 (Chatterji 1994).

As the condition of the Muslim Bengali peasantry worsened, various types of resistance to British rule began to form. Some of these drew on religious forms, such as the *fakir* movement that was active during the second half of the eighteenth century. These *fakirs* (religious mendicants) were used to raising alms from villagers, which was frowned upon by the colonial authorities. Farmers organised by the *fakirs* refused to pay rents, and there were several violent clashes, such as the 1793 attack and subsequent occupation of the Company's Dhaka warehouse. More influential in the long term was the Faraizi movement, led by Haji Shariatullah (1781–1840). Shariatullah, while studying for many years in Mecca, had become inspired by Wahabi ideas and on his return led a religious reformist movement that aimed to free Bengali Muslims from Hindu influence through what he saw as the renewal and purification of their religious practice. This call to promote the *farad*, the set of basic obligatory religious duties set out in the Koran, gave its name to the movement. The movement continued its opposition to the unequal system of landholding and rights that had been created by the Permanent Settlement under the leadership of Titu Mir (1782–1831), another Wahabi-influenced leader, whose movement declared independence from British rule. Titu Mir was killed, along with 250 of his followers, in November 1831.

The legacy of the Faraizis was important for the future country of Bangladesh. As Laurence Ziring (1992: 9) recounts, Shariatullah's son Dadu Miyan continued to build the movement, which became an attractive option to a peasantry that found itself increasingly exploited by landed interests:

Dadu Miyan divided the eastern section of Bengal, where Muslims were the majority population, into a number of administrative circles, each comprising between 300 to 500 families. Each circle was made the responsibility of a Siyasi Khalifa, a political-spiritual leader. This was born the rural-based organization which later inspired Bengali nationalism and produced leaders like Fazlul Huq of Barisal and Maulana Bhashani in Mymensingh. Sheikh Mujibur Rahman, a disciple but contemporary of these older personalities, was also a product of the later Faraizi movement.

Relations between Muslims and the British authorities began to improve again after 1870, when a *fatwa* was declared by religious educator and reformist Karamat Ali (1800–73) that stated that Muslims who resisted British rule were being un-Islamic. Karamat Ali's view was that India under British rule was *darus salam* (a land of peace), and this fatwa therefore helped revive and further Islamic tradition and reunited Faraizis into the mainstream Bengali Muslim community (Ahmed 2004). By the 1880s, there was now what Salahuddin Ahmed (2004: 87) describes as "an Islamic renaissance movement in East Bengal." A key aim within this movement was to spread the use of English as a strategy to empower Bengali Muslims, a move associated with the Dhaka Mohammedan Friends Association, which was established by Maulana al-Obaidi in 1883.

### British Rule

The Rebellion of 1857 persuaded the British government to take control of India from the Company, which had by now become a source of concern in London, by passing the Government of India Act in Parliament on August 2, 1858. At the same time, the British government was slowly beginning to give more credence to the growing recognition that Indians should have more of a role in their own governance. This shift was an outcome of two main sets of factors: (1) the gradual whittling away of British resistance by increasing demands from grassroots movements and Indian political leaders and (2) the changing character of British domestic politics in which conservatism and evangelicalism started to give way to the influence of Liberal party politics, which was, in general, more sympathetic to the idea of "home rule." The government's first major change was the 1861 Indian Councils Act, part of which established a new executive council for the state of Bengal, which by now included Orissa and Bihar. Although the governor-general remained in power overall, the council was given administrative and legislative powers, and for the first time, Indians were not excluded from membership. In 1882, elected district and municipal boards were established in which two-thirds of the seats would be held by Indians because it was still extremely difficult for Indians to enter the civil service, for example. This was first put into effect in the state of Bengal. Many local administrative officers opposed these changes, which they saw as being imposed from London. Nevertheless, the reform meant that the area that is now Bangladesh experienced an early system of local government, despite its frequent lack of effectiveness (Baxter 1998: 36).

Municipal government structures were also slowly being put in place in the presidency cities. In 1872, Kolkata was provided with a municipal corporation that was run by an official, but with two-thirds of its members elected by local taxpayers. In 1923, there was the creation of an elected mayor and fully elected council, but this was still under only a limited electoral franchise. Those Indians who entered the system and gained electoral and administrative experience within these limited political reforms tended to be predominantly Hindu. A few Muslims did reach influential positions through opportunities presented by the 1882 India Councils Act, which moved away from direct election to appointments on the basis of suggestions from local bodies such as business associations and universities.

Some Muslims began to define a need for separate forms of political action to pursue their interests in order to avoid what they saw as the threat of domination by Hindus. Although Bengal was a centre of Indian political resistance to British rule, much of it could be portrayed as having been Hindu-led. For example, one of the main leaders at the close of the nineteenth century was Suredranath Banerjea, a Bengali who, for a while, had successfully entered the ICS and been active around India in the consolidation of various political associations. In 1885, he formed the Indian National Congress Party, with another Bengali, Woomesh Chandra Bonnerjee, as its president. The Congress, as it became known, was initially supported by Muslims and Hindus, but at the same time there were also separate Muslim-led efforts in process that aimed to increase Muslim political participation in more specific ways.

For the colonial authorities, an alliance with Muslim landowning classes was an obvious and logical counterweight to the increased assertiveness of Hindu elites in Bengal. Among the national elite in Bengal, Muslims, such as the Kolkata Suhrawardy family, and Syed Amir Ali, who in 1876 had founded the Central National Mohammadan Association after earlier being part of the Bengal Legislative Council and the Viceroy's Legislative Council, were playing important political roles. There were some Muslim leaders who argued that they were better off under British rule than they would be under the rule of the Hindu majority and distrusted the Congress Party for this reason. Sir Syed Ahmad Khan (1817–98), who had been an official within both the Mughal and the British authorities, urged Muslims against joining Congress. From an aristocratic Delhi family, Sir Syed had been loyal to the British during the 1857 Rebellion, but had been disappointed by the way that the Muslim community had been blamed and subsequently excluded from government positions and the professions. He consequently feared for the long-term well-being of the Indian Muslim community, as Daniel Thorner (1980: 28) writes,

Sir Syed set himself very early the task of reconciling the Muslims and the British.... In arguing with the British for a reversal of their policy, he contended that the revolt was far more than a Muslim rising, that many Muslims had remained loyal, and that wise policy could reconcile even those who had been hostile. To his Muslim brethren, bitter over the discrimination practised against them, he pleaded for the ending of anti-British sentiment. As British rule was here to stay, the sensible thing, he argued, was to appreciate its power and enjoy its benefits.

Khan was also one of those arguing the case that there were two distinct religiously based entities in India. This influential idea would later become known as the "two nation theory," which gained currency from the 1930s, that rejected the principle that Hindus and Muslims could be successfully contained within a single united India.

By the turn of the century, the province of Bengal had grown as British influence had expanded northwards and now included Bengal, Bihar and Orissa. Viceroy Lord Curzon now considered that the territory had grown too large to be properly administered from Kolkata. This was a problem that could perhaps have been addressed less contentiously simply by separating Bengal from the non-Bengali-speaking areas such as Bihar, but in 1905, Bengal was partitioned into two new administrative units: East Bengal and Assam, on the one hand, and West Bengal, Bihar and Orissa on the other, with Dhaka as the capital of the first unit. With a Muslim majority of approximately three to two, this act of partition was primarily motivated by the strategy of divide and rule, intended to curb growing resistance to British rule by the Hindu-educated elites and to give more power to loyalist members of Muslim elites such as Sir Syed Ahmad Khan. Partition was, therefore, firmly opposed by Hindus, and for the next six years there were regular demonstrations, parades and boycotts that grew into the strongest opposition to British rule since 1857, mobilised around the central demand for *swaraj* (self-rule) and reaching as far beyond Bengal as Punjab.

There were nonviolent protests such as those organised by members of the Kolkata elites such as Rabindranath Tagore and Surendranath Banerjea as well as violent underground revolutionary activists such as Sri Aurobindo and the Jugunda Party. In 1911, the partition of Bengal was abandoned under this pressure. In the reshuffle, Assam became restored to a chief commissionership, Bihar and Orissa were separated from Bengal, and the province had its eastern and western halves joined back together again. Yet by this time, Muslims now felt increasingly threatened by Hindu social and economic dominance, and Bengal's reunification led many Muslims to begin pressing for autonomy. The capital of the British Raj was moved from Kolkata to Delhi in 1912. Kolkata remained economically dynamic, but East Bengal suffered neglect and grew more underdeveloped. Many Muslims by now were supporting calls for repartition and the creation of a separate state.

When Lord Minto took over as viceroy after the departure of Lord Curzon in 1905, he began to further the agenda of increasing the role of elected representatives within decentralised councils. This, in turn, fed the concerns of Muslims who feared that they would suffer during elections in most areas of India where they were outnumbered. At a key meeting in 1906 at Simla, a Muslim delegation led by the Aga Khan presented Minto with the idea of creating separate electorates for Muslims. By constructing a separate electoral roll, the idea was to allow for Muslim electoral representation on councils and local bodies. This later bore fruit in the form of the 1909 Government of India Act, which provided just this, along with a corresponding arrangement for Hindus in the Muslim-majority areas of Bengal and Punjab. These legislative councils had only limited decision-making powers, and almost half the members were appointed rather than elected, but this move did further the Muslim political agenda and as a consequence was not supported by Congress.

In December 1906, the All-India Muslim League, a new political party in support of Muslim interests, was formed in Dhaka by a group of Muslim leaders drawn from across India. The aim was to follow Sir Syed's view that the British offered the best protection against Hindu domination, and the new party pledged its loyalty to the Crown. It stated the aim of advancing Muslim political interests without promoting hostility or prejudice towards other religious communities. The Aga Khan presided over the League until a system of electing presidents was put in place in 1913. The League contained many individuals drawn from Sir Syed's Alighar Muslim University, which had replaced the Central National Mohammadan Association that he had established in 1876. Yet the Muslim League, while it was to become a key player under the leadership of Muhammad Ali Jinnah (1876–1948) during the period that led up to the formation of Pakistan, represented only a transient moment in relation to East Bengal between the agricultural tenancy reformist politics of the Krishak Proja Party (KPP) and the Bengali nationalism of the AL.

The Bengal Legislative Council that was formed in 1909 contained Muslim representatives from both the national elites (including members of the Dhaka *nawab's* family and from the Ghaznavis) and from the vernacular elite such as Abul Kasem Fazlul Haq, a member from 1913 to 1947. Fazlul Haq had joined the Muslim League but was more closely aligned with Bengali nationalist interests. He argued that the ordinary rural Bengali Muslim was oppressed by both Hindu and Muslim landlords and did not share the broader India-wide goals of the League. Another Government of India Act (1919) inched forward Indian participation but failed to satisfy either the Congress or the League, both of which had expected that the end of the First World War would usher in more far-reaching change. Elections to the Bengal Council in 1920 were boycotted by Congress, and there was a turnout of only 20 percent. By this time, Gandhi's noncooperation movement was also underway.

In the 1936–7 elections for the first premier of Bengal, there was a struggle for the support of the Bengali Muslims, structured strongly along class lines. A. K. Fazlul Huq's (1873–1962) KPP, originally established in 1929 to campaign for tenant rights, took on the Muslim League in the competition for Muslim votes. Another party, the United Muslim Party (UMP), had been set up in 1935 by the *nawab* of Dhaka Nawab Salimullah, with Huseyn Shaheed Suhrawardy (1892–1963), who was soon to become a key politician in Pakistan (and later Bangladesh), as its general secretary. The UMP was, however, seen by Fazlul Huq as an elite Bengali Muslim Party, and he branded it the "zamindar party," leading to a dispute between the two parties that required the intervention of Jinnah in order to reconcile in the interests of maintaining Muslim unity. The result was that the UMP merged with the Muslim League, but Fazlul Huq, at first agreeing to do the same, then changed his mind. He preferred to keep control of what he saw as the Muslim politics of Bengal, rather than lose ground to wider Muslim leadership under Jinnah. In particular, he advocated the abolition of the *zamindari* system, but this was a radical demand that Jinnah would not countenance because he wished to keep the UMP in the alliance (Ahmed 2004).

Underpinning issues of religion and ethnicity within the society of East Bengal was the importance of class politics. For Taj ul-Islam Hashmi (1992: 2),

Peasants' political activities, motivated by conscious efforts to improve their socio-economic conditions, led to the creation of a separate homeland for the Muslims in the region, East Pakistan, and in the long run the state of Bangladesh.

Yet Hashmi (1992) shows that this was not simply a bottom-up peasant movement of unmediated subalterns, but rather that it was also a class politics of factions and patron-client relationships mediated by elites. Fostered by the British authorities as a counterweight to the Hindu nationalism promoted by the high-caste professional elites and zamindars of Bengal, an alliance arose based on a false "consciousness" of common interests among a Muslim aristocracy, rich peasants and the rural poor in support of a Muslim homeland, and this weakened class alliances. This tradition of vertical patronage and factional ties continues to this day and helps to explain why there are relatively few cases of peasant movements in rural Bangladesh based on "horizontal" solidarity, despite the efforts of some of the more empowerment-minded NGOs, particularly efforts during the 1980s to build such grassroots movements. As the idea of Pakistan continued to take shape, in 1940, Fazlul Huq, the Bengal premier, set out the Lahore Resolution at the session of the Muslim League, which asserted that Muslim majority states should be grouped into independent, autonomous, self-governing states. This was intended as a clear statement to the Congress Party, which was now increasingly being seen by Muslims as having betrayed its initial founding principles of inclusivity. Instead, it had become, for many a tool of the Hindu revivalists who aimed to establish "Hindu Raj," and for Jinnah, the influence of Gandhi was seen as one of the key drivers of this shift.

The 1940s were a traumatic decade for Bengal. A devastating cyclone hit the coastal areas in 1942, which killed thousands of people and damaged the autumn *amon* rice crop. The Allied forces were defeated by the Japanese in Singapore, and that year the British colonial authorities began to stockpile food in Bengal in preparation against an expected Japanese invasion of Bengal. This, combined with administrative incompetence, led to a breakdown in local food distribution and marketing, particularly because additional food imports from Burma were now impossible due to Japanese occupation. Both factors contributed to the terrible Bengal famine of 1943–4 that led to the deaths of between 1.5 and 3.5 million people. Amatrya Sen's influential book, *Poverty and Famines* (1981), famously argued that far from being due to the decline of food availability as conventionally argued, the famine was the result of a lack of "exchange entitlements" among certain rural classes, such as landless agricultural labourers who faced decreasing demand for their services and were ignored by the colonial government's public food-distribution system. As Van Schendel (2009: 76) observes, the famine was the first of three "enormous shocks" to a generation of Bengalis, to be followed by partition in 1947 and the War of Liberation in 1971.

### The Pakistan Period

The name *Pakistan* had been coined in 1933 by Choudhary Rahmat Ali (1897–1951) in the pamphlet *Now or Never: Are We to Live or Perish Forever?*, which was written while he studied law at Emmanuel College in Cambridge (Rahmat Ali 1933). The pamphlet advocated a national homeland for India's Muslims, and the word *Pakistan* was derived from the names of the main Muslim majority provinces including Punjab, the North West Frontier or "Afghan" Province, Kashmir, Sind and Baluchistan. In this document, Ali had set out an early argument that these provinces should become part of a separate federation, so that Indian Muslims would avoid political domination within a future Hindu-majority state. Interestingly, the province of Bengal was not mentioned at all (perhaps because it seemed so far away from the other areas) and therefore did not form part of this initial rationale for "Pakistan" (Ahmed 2004). In hindsight, this was an ominous foretaste of what Jahan (1972) later termed Pakistan's "failure of national integration."

After the Second World War, it had become clear to Indian leaders that European power had waned further. The logic of Indian independence was becoming stronger, causing additional anxiety among Bengali and other Muslims that they would be repressed in an independent India. In 1946, Jinnah laid out details of the new country of Pakistan in which he stated that it would take the form of a democracy, with autonomy for each of its constituent parts. Yet there were still Muslim political leaders who did not accept the premise of the "two nation theory," and who preferred to continue to support Congress. For example, in the North-West Frontier Province (NWFP), Khan Abdul Ghaffar Khan, the practitioner of nonviolence and an associate of Gandhi, led Congress to win a majority of Muslim seats in the 1947 election. The factors that ultimately led to the creation of Pakistan remain a longstanding area of debate among historians. The combination of Jinnah's lack of flexibility and the inability of Congress to remain open to the idea of Indian Muslim rights undoubtedly served to reinforce each other. But underlying the logic of partition were far deeper structural factors that resulted from longstanding political struggles around land and property rights. In the eastern part of Bengal, the fact that most zamindars were Hindu while most tenants were Muslim generated what David Ludden (1999: 216) terms "a symbolic repertoire for popular mobilization." The wider struggles between landlords and tenants took on distinct cultural identities as Hindu landlord and Muslim tenant leaders "projected" these identities into wider political discourse. The result was that, by the 1920s, there were few opportunities for alliances across a political divide that had increasing become publicly identified as one between Hindus and Muslims.

The period leading up to partition raised many complex questions around national, religious and territorial identities for Bengalis. Riots in Kolkata in 1946 hastened the rush to draw up plans to partition British India. Within the existing Indian Union, Bengali-speaking peoples were located in East Bengal and West Bengal, Assam, Meghalaya and Tripura, and there were initially various ideas that this bloc might form a politically recognised territorial unit within an independent India. For example, the 1946 Cabinet Mission Plan envisaged three Indian substates with devolved power in northwest, central and eastern India but was rejected by Congress in favour of the idea of partition into two separate states of India and Pakistan, which took place on August 14, 1947. A vote in the Bengal Legislative Assembly in June had decided that Bengal would be divided, with Hindu members voting for partition by a large majority, while Muslim-majority area members voted against – but under the British plan accepted by both the Muslim League and Congress, if one side were to vote for partition, then it would be accepted.

Pakistan was, in Van Schendel's (2009: 107) words, "a unique experiment in state-making," with three distinct sets of characteristics. First, it was a state established on the new hybrid principle of religious nationalism. Second, it was at the same time located within two separate geographically dispersed sections, finding its population split 45 percent/55 percent between the two wings. Third, the new state was forced to establish itself without any of the central institutions of the former colonial authorities – such as the bureaucracy, military or police, all of which were inherited by the new Indian state. Furthermore, the new east wing of Pakistan was, at the same time, a severely fractured version of the old state of Bengal because it was now without its capital, Kolkata, which had contained its industrial base and main port. It was composed only of a large and backward agricultural hinterland, along with the tea-growing district of Sylhet that had previously been part of Assam (Sobhan 1993:79). Nevertheless, given its sizeable population, East Bengal became Pakistan's largest province, with forty-four representatives as against twenty-eight from the west. The new country was to be governed by a new Constituent Assembly of Pakistan in Karachi, with Jinnah as its president, and elections duly took place in July.

During these elections, Bengal was the only Muslim-majority province that returned a Muslim League majority, winning all twenty-nine Muslim seats, while Punjab, Sind and NWFP failed to form Muslim League governments. This fact would later rankle with many Bengalis who felt that Jinnah and the other Muslim League leaders had failed to acknowledge their contribution and support. Bengali Muslims saw themselves as having made a considerable contribution to the establishment, evolution and eventual success of the Muslim League over the years. For example, Nawab Salimullah had helped establish the Muslim League in Dhaka in 1906, and Fazlul Huq had attended and played key roles in many of its subsequent meetings. H. S. Suhrawardy, a key influence on the young Sheikh Mujibur Rahman at the time of partition, had attended the first Central Parliamentary Party of the League in Lahore in 1936. But tensions between national Muslim politics and Bengali Muslim politics had proved persistent. Suhrawardy had fallen from favour with Jinnah by supporting the idea of a united Bengal, and Khawaja Nazim-ud-Din – from the Dhaka *nawab* family – became chief minister of East Bengal. The new cabinet was mainly composed of Urdu speakers. This meant that it was now the "national elite" who were in dominant positions in the new province. Bengali interest and involvement in the Muslim League began to fade as rapidly as it had arisen. The League had never been a mass-based party that had connected with ordinary people and had instead relied on gaining control of the remnants of colonial bureaucratic institutions to secure power. At the same time, the League's political critique of the colonial status quo, such as it was, had essentially evolved in opposition to the rise of Congress and had little content of its own apart from the vision of a new separate Muslim state.

Two important priority areas that required political action immediately came into play in the aftermath of Pakistan's formation. The first was the agrarian reform agenda. In 1948 the East Bengal State Acquisition and Tenancy Act was passed, dismantling the *zamindari* system, and this prompted many Hindu landlords and professionals to leave for West Bengal. The reform limited individual landholdings, whether owned by Hindus or Muslims, to one hundred *bighas* or close to thirty-three acres, and compensation was issued to those from whom land was seized in a process that continued until 1956. The second was the difficult task of framing the new constitution, to which little thought had been given in the immediate prepartition period. In 1949, the assembly had set up a Basic Principles Committee to begin the task, but its interim recommendations published in 1950 were immediately seen by many East Bengalis as strongly biased towards the interests of Pakistan's Western wing because they proposed giving central government a set of draconian emergency powers that would override provincial autonomy and recommended that the official language of the state be Urdu. There were meetings, protests and demonstrations across East Bengal.

When Jinnah died in 1948, he left a power vacuum. He was succeeded by Khwaja Nazim-ud-Din as governor general of Pakistan, though it was clear that the real power was held by Prime Minister Liaquat Ali Khan, who had been Jinnah's principal lieutenant as general secretary of the Muslim League since 1936. It was on Liaquat's advice that Nazim-ud-Din appointed Nurul Amin as chief minister of East Bengal, even though this was against the wishes of the Parliamentary Party of the Muslim League. In 1951, Liaquat was assassinated in Rawalpindi and Nazim-ud-Din resigned from his post to become prime minister, only to be dismissed two years later in 1953 by Ghulam Mohammad the former finance minister of Punjab, who had taken over as governor general. According to Ahmed (2004: 135), this was the start of the intrigue and tensions that would lead to military rule and to the unravelling of Pakistan in 1971. Despite Nazim-ud-Din having the support of the Constituent Assembly, Ghulam Mohammad was apparently backed by Punjabi assembly members and by the army, and this can be seen as "one of the first signals of planned domination by the west Pakistani civil-army coterie over East Pakistan" (Ahmed 2004: 135). Ghulam Mohammad was not a Muslim League member and had no interest in democratic politics. The Constituent Assembly and the majority Muslim League Party were too weak to challenge his decision to invite another outsider, Mohammed Ali (not a member of the assembly but ambassador to the United States at the time), to form a new government.

The issues that motivated Muslim Bengalis to support the movement for the creation of Pakistan and later motivated the movement separation from Pakistan were not, as Sobhan (1993: 83) points out, separate historical events but part of "a continuum within the consciousness of the Bengalis of eastern Bengal." This centred on the struggle for political power and economic control over resources, whether against successive domination by the Mughal rulers from northern India, from the British *raj*, or from the Bengali Hindu zamindar class. As Sobhan (1993: 82) has argued, the

Muslim Bengalis remained the most marginalised of the Indian Muslim communities:

Of all the divergent social forces which constituted Pakistan, the Bengalis had the most ambitious expectations because they remained perhaps the most deprived of the Muslims of India. Even in the minority provinces of India Muslims were well represented in commerce, professions and artisan skills in the South and West of India. In the Northern regions of the Hindi speaking belt, Muslims were part of the dominant class of landowners and professionals whose mother tongue, Urdu, was indeed the shared language of the upper classes of the region.

There was absolute deprivation in East Pakistan in terms of a lack of resources and infrastructure, but there was also a new element of relative deprivation within the new country as power began to be exercised over the East by the West.

Pakistan, with its two separate land blocs separated by a thousand miles of Indian territory, faced a series of important contradictions and tensions. Although the economy of East Pakistan grew, it had no facilities of its own to process its jute crop for export. It was, therefore, transferred to industrial facilities in West Pakistan for processing. This led to an exploitative system of internal transfer within Pakistan that disadvantaged East Pakistanis in two ways. First, raw jute was purchased from East Pakistani growers at a disadvantageous rate of exchange, and then second, little of the value added from subsequent jute processing and exportation was returned by the government to East Pakistan. Pakistan found itself at partition with few highly trained civil servants because the majority of those working on the British administrative system had been Hindus, few had been senior and most had opted to remain in India. This was a particularly acute problem for East Bengal because most of the Hindus in the Bengali administrative service had left at partition, and it was therefore mainly trained West Pakistanis, usually Punjabis, who took up civil service posts in the East, not Bengalis. Many were not culturally attuned to Bengali life and were therefore seen as "outside masters" (Baxter 1998: 64). It was not until 1954 with the appointment of Fazlul Haq that a Bengali would hold the highest administrative office.

Attempts were made to remedy the lack of Bengali representation in the civil service, a priority that was mandated in the constitution drawn up in 1956, though only in relation to "nondefence" areas of federal administration. Pressure from Bengalis led to the creation of a quota system in the new Civil Service of Pakistan (CSP), which was to ensure that 40 percent from the east and the west would be represented, along with 20 percent of positions to be filled only on merit, based on results in the annual civil-service examination. However, the reality was that few Bengalis reached the top, and among those that did most were from the Urdu-speaking national elite. The West Pakistan elite had monopolised most of the key positions in the new state of Pakistan, from banking and administration to business and banking, and also dominated the armed forces. As Ziring (1992: 14) puts it: "Bengali demands for a proper distribution of the country's resources and opportunities went unheeded."

The critical focus of Bengali dissatisfaction and nationalist aspiration rapidly "crystallized" around the issue of language (Ziring 1992: 15). In East Pakistan, what was regarded as Pakistan's declaration of Urdu as the national language led to protests in Dhaka in 1952 and the birth of the language movement. Urdu had been widely looked upon as the language of India's Muslims because it had evolved during the Delhi Sultanate and Mughal periods with Persian, Arabic and Turkish influences. It was written using Arabic script rather than the Devanagari script used in Sanskrit and Hindi and from which written Bengali evolved. For this reason, Bengali was viewed in some quarters in Pakistan as an "un-Islamic" language (Afzal 2001).

Bengalis recalled that during Jinnah's only visit to East Bengal in 1948, he had told those assembled to hear his public address: "Let me make it very clear to you that the state language of Pakistan is going to be Urdu and no other language." For Ian Stephens (1964: 61), Bengali was a regional language, while Urdu had no local roots but was a kind of *lingua franca* with "a loose wide web of intelligibility" among the diverse communities of West Pakistan, giving logic to the assumption that it would eventually become Pakistan's national language. In 1952 Prime Minister Nazim-ud-Din, a Bengali, visited Dhaka and declared that Urdu should be the state language. Yet the strength of Bengali Muslim cultural attachments had been severely underestimated by the authorities in West Pakistan. In the demonstrations that ensued, students and other groups marched to demand equal status for Bengali, and twelve people were killed when the army fired upon the protesters. These grievances were not simply cultural but also were underpinned by the growing sense of economic and political discrimination felt by Bengalis in relation to the central authorities. For example, the imposition of Urdu would mean that Bengalis would be at a disadvantage when applying for government employment (Bano 2008). A decision from Pakistan's constituent assembly in 1954 that Urdu and Bengali and other languages could each be official languages of Pakistan, and the equal billing of languages in the 1956 Constitution, was seen as representing "too little too late," and serious political damage had already been done.

Despite their shared Muslim Pakistani identity, there were other cultural tensions between the West and East that went deeper than language. Although there were many West Pakistanis who did not view Bengalis as inferior or second-class citizens, some sections of Pakistani officialdom, particularly Punjabis in authority, despised Bengalis, reflecting an attitude sometimes observed more widely in West Pakistan. As Richard Sisson and Leo Rose (1990: 8–9) observed:

politically influential groups in the West perceived the Bengalis as latter-day Muslim converts still corrupted by Hindu practices, unlike descendents of the founders of Islam or conquerors like themselves, and as secessionists in league with their "co-culturalists" in India.

In June 1949, the Awami Muslim League (the "Muslim" part was soon dropped) was founded as a new Bengali nationalist opposition party and an alternative to the Muslim League. Prominent Bengali Muslim League leaders such as the leftist propeasant leader Maulana Abdul Hamid Khan Bhashani (1880–1976) and H. S. Suhrawardy had become dismayed by the new politics of Pakistan. The Muslim League had lost respect in the eyes of many East Bengalis during the period after 1947 and was now viewed as largely indifferent to the needs and concerns of the Bengalis. Furthermore, the Muslim League had prohibited non-Muslim membership, and there were many Bengali Hindus who were also dissatisfied with the turn of events in the new country. New organisations such as the East Pakistan Muslim Students League, with Dhaka university student Sheikh Mujibur Rahman as its secretary, also began to give voice to the opposition among Bengalis to the central government.

In 1953, the AL joined with Fazlul Huq's revived Krishak Sramik Party (KSP) (formerly the Krishak Proja Party [KPP]) to form the Jukto (United) Front. The Jukto Front aimed to unite and mobilise Bengalis to pursue a range of demands set out in its historic *Ekush Dapha* (21 Points) document. This document formed the basis for contesting the 1954 elections, the first to be held on the basis of universal suffrage. The two key demands were for full autonomy for Bengal (though stopping short at a separate military or currency) and for formal recognition of Bengali as a state language. Also demanded was the establishment of a Bengali Academy and a public holiday to commemorate the Bengalis who had died during the protests on February 21, 1952. Although Prime Minister Mohammad Ali Bogra (a Bengali, but seen as serving West Pakistani interests) campaigned in East

Bengal for the Muslim League, he encountered little or no support. The elections resulted in a massive defeat for the Muslim League, and the Jukto Front gained 228 out of 237 Muslim seats in the East Bengal Assembly. The victory made little impact on the Pakistan central leadership, which refused to make changes in the central administration or the Muslim League–dominated legislature. Yet as Jahan (1972: 39) points out, the election "marked the loss of power of the old ruling elite."

A new government was briefly formed in East Bengal under the leadership of Fazlul Huq in 1954. However, this government was soon dismissed by the central government after criticisms that Fazlul Huq had made statements during a visit to Kolkata that could have been construed as secessionist because he had made reference to a larger Bengali identity and to the historical and cultural ties that existed between East Bengal and West Bengal. He was put under house arrest, along with two hundred students, and forced to retire from politics. In a precursor to events later in 1971, ten thousand troops were sent to East Pakistan to maintain public order, and Iskandar Mirza was appointed as the new governor of East Bengal. He immediately began arresting activists of the United Front, including the young Mujib. Ghulam Muhammad declared a state of emergency and dissolved the constituent assembly, and a new "controlled democracy" was created at the centre of which was the so-called cabinet of experts, a government that included General Muhammad Ayub Khan and General Iskandar Mirza. This military presence was to signal the end of Pakistan's initial system of parliamentary democracy.

When new elections to the Constituent Assembly were held in 1955, the result was a Muslim League majority in West Pakistan, but one that needed support from the AL or KSP to form a viable government, and it began to split into factions. Both Ali Bogra and Ghulam Muhammad became ill and were replaced by Chaudhury Muhammad Ali and General Iskandar Mirza, respectively. The former was succeeded by Suhrawardy as prime minister in September 1956, but there was an increasingly fragmented politics in East Pakistan. By the end of the 1950s, while the AL had constituted the spearhead of the language movement, it had nevertheless struggled to contain two main but different tendencies. One was an elitist faction led by Suhrawardy, who had supported the imperial powers, speaking out, for example, in favour of the United Kingdom, the United States and France during the 1956 Suez intervention. The other was a more rural-based populist faction under Maulana Bhashani, which split away in 1957 to become the National Awami Party (NAP). This then left Mujib, who was politically committed to the elitist tendency, but whose personal political style appealed to the populist supporters, "to bridge the gap between the elitist leadership of the AL and its popular mass base" (Alavi 1972: 168).

The political instability in West Pakistan led, in October 1958, to a military coup and the imposition of martial law across the whole country. This brought the abrogation of the constitution that had finally been passed in 1956, the dismissal of the prime minister and chief ministers, and the installation of General Ayub Khan as chief MLA. The national election which was to have taken place in 1959 was thwarted by the imposition of martial law, further convincing the Bengalis that they would never be able to gain a fair share of political power at the national level. When H. S. Suhrawardy died in 1963, the Bengalis lost their only major public figure with a national constituency and an aspiration towards national power. Ayub ruled as chief MLA until 1962, when he deposed President Iskandar Mirza in order to become president. As Ayesha Jalal (1995: 56) argues, although he promised to restore integrity to government and public life, Ayub was primarily motivated by the knowledge that his own position rested on the need to maintain the support of the Punjabi federal bureaucracy and its army. This reliance also fed into perceptions that elements within West Pakistan's governing elites were prone to assert values of cultural superiority over the Bengalis. Ayub Khan famously observed that Bengalis "have all the inhabitants of downtrodden races and have not yet found it possible to adjust . . . to freedom." Baxter (1998: 11) has suggested that Ayub's attitude was "almost racist."

The new constitution set in place by General Ayub Khan in 1962 was a "fait accompli" that "allowed certain political parties to function within the restricted domain of his new political order" (Jalal 1995: 56). It centralised power at the expense of the East, denied Bengalis a direct franchise and vested absolute power in the hands of the chief executive. Ayub's efforts to strengthen local democracy and improve Pakistan's public administration did, however, bring some important changes and set in place some of the infrastructure of local government in Bangladesh that exists today. The so-called basic democracy programme that was proclaimed in 1959 attempted to build on existing local government structures in order to create a system of local "union" *parishads* or councils. A total of seven to fifteen individuals were to be elected by direct franchise and given some limited local powers of revenue collection, administration, adjudication and management of development activities. The unions were positioned under another new tier of subdistrict government, known as the *thana* in East Pakistan (and the *tehsil* in the west), and these, in turn, were accountable to a set of district councils. These new officials were designed to act as "basic democrats," who would also elect the president and the national and provincial assemblies, and were carefully matched at forty thousand in each of Pakistan's wings.

However, the new "basic democracies" strategy also implied a return to old colonial policies of divide and rule, combined with selective co-option and collaboration. In practice, this was a means for patronage to be extended to selected local groups in exchange for support for quasimilitary rule (Jalal 1995: 56). Although this strategy did produce a measure of economic growth for certain sections of society, it also maintained a centralised political structure that ran counter to Pakistan's federalism. It stifled, for example, the provincial demands of East Pakistan and perpetuated social inequalities that quickly gave rise to a renewed sense of grievance:

During the 1960s the Ayub regime orchestrated a process of social class formation by linking policies of differential economic patronage with its overall goal of depoliticization. Encouraged by its international patrons and their main vehicles of economic control, the World Bank and the International Monetary Fund, the regime unabashedly accepted the logical consequences of "functional inequality" in an attempt to achieve rapid growth. Betting on the strong to expand its economic base in the shortest possible time, the regime unfurled a spate of policies that assisted the transformation of landlords into capitalists and merchants into industrialists... [and] presided over an economic boom that contained all the explosive ingredients for a massive political bust. (p. 57)

In 1965, Ayub embarked upon an ill-advised war with India in an attempt to secure Kashmir, but the conflict ended without a change to the status quo when the Soviet Union convened the Tashkent peace conference. This war turned out to be "the swansong of a regime slouching under the combined weight of Pakistan's multiple political and economic woes" (Jalal 1995: 59). Ayub was eventually forced by the army to resign in 1969 and the presidency passed to General Agha Muhammad Yahya Khan. Ayub's period of rule in Pakistan had seen substantial economic growth, but the disproportionate weighting towards West Pakistan continued to create a striking disparity between the two wings of the country, and this added to the grievances felt by the Bengalis. This increasing sense of grievance among the East Pakistan Bengalis underpinned the further rise of Mujib's AL. It was now the main political party in Pakistan, and when elections finally took place in December 1970, the AL secured an absolute majority when it won 160 out of the 162 seats from East Pakistan, while Bhutto's Pakistan People's Party gained 81 of the 138 seats allocated to West Pakistan.

The union with Pakistan had negative economic consequences for the east, with resources diverted from the east to the west through a set of "subtle and powerful" transfer devices. These included an overvalued rupee that disadvantaged the jute producers, a balance-of-payments system that meant that the east's external trade surplus went straight into servicing West Pakistan's foreign account deficit and the Western wing's monopolisation of foreign aid (Faaland and Parkinson 1976: 7). By the end of the 1960s, the transfer of resources from the east to the west had become far less acute, but by then the political logic for separation had become the dominant force. Nevertheless, the disparity in incomes that had been around 20 percent at the start of the 1950s had by the end of the 1960s become 50 percent higher in West Pakistan (Faaland and Parkinson 1976: 9). Muslim Bengalis in the east, along with most Hindus, had voted for the AL. Within East Pakistan, as Ziring (1992: 15) argues, what subsequently came to be termed "communal" divisions were not at this time a binding force, and a nationalist identity based on ethnicity and heritage rather than on religion had instead become preeminent. With the east controlling 167 of the 313 seats in the new National Assembly of Pakistan, General Yahya Khan was unable to accept a Bengali-dominated Pakistan government and suspended the assembly, leading to waves of further student unrest and political violence. Yahya decided to delay the transfer of power in order to try to find a negotiated settlement that would allow the maintenance of the status quo against the demands of East Pakistan and West Pakistan for concessions. However, by this time, such a settlement had become impossible, not because the differences between the two wings and the centre were irreconcilable, but because, as Jalal (1995: 62) argues, "a decade of military and quasi-military dictatorship" had severely restricted the emergence of an open, national-level political culture in which such differences could be negotiated within an atmosphere of trust.

In the midst of this disorder, an act of nature then further added to the human misery. On November 12, 1970, a severe cyclone struck the coast and claimed a reported five hundred thousand lives in East Pakistan. What was seen by most Bengalis as an inadequate relief response to the disaster further worsened the distrust of central government felt by people in East Pakistan. The negotiations broke down, and on March 25, 1971, the Pakistan government began its military crackdown, and the Bengalis declared their sovereign state of Bangladesh. In the violence that followed, hundreds of thousands of people died and millions fled to India as refugees, leading India to send forces to Bangladesh in December 1971 in support of the new country. Yahya's loss of East Pakistan in the war of 1971 led to his resignation and to a government formed by Zulfiqur Ali Bhutto.

### Formation of Bangladesh

The creation of Bangladesh was the end point of a longer-term politics of dissatisfaction among leaders in Bengal. In 1966, Sheikh Mujibur Rahman published *Six Points: Our Demand for Survival* and presented what became known as his "six point programme" at a conference of opposition leaders in Lahore, as part of efforts to launch a national opposition movement against the Ayub regime. The roots of the Six Point Programme went back a long way. The 1954 Jukta Front's electoral declaration in Lahore had demanded complete autonomy for East Pakistan except for defence, foreign affairs and currency, which would be left under the jurisdiction of a central Pakistan government. But this time the demand was revived in a sharper form, seeking to bring currency under local control in order to redress the problem of unequal transfers of capital within Pakistan. There was also a point relating to the control over the allocation of foreign-aid resources, which had previously been disproportionately claimed for use by the West Pakistan elite. Yet, as Sobhan (1993) shows, between 1966 and 1971 there had been little or no interest from West Pakistani leaders in discussing the six points, which might easily have formed the basis for the settlement of Bengali grievances. As we have seen, when negotiations on the transfer of power finally took take place in March 1971, "by that time the Pakistan army had decided that the issue of Bengali nationalism would be settled by blood and fire and not by political negotiations" (147). The Six Point Programme was significant not simply as a statement of democratic resistance, but also because it showed that the Bengali leadership was focused on securing self-government for Bengalis rather than simply trying to capture national power by the removal of Ayub.

In the two years between March 1969 and December 1971, a political mobilisation that started with the AL campaign to win the 1970 national elections had crystallised years of Bengali Muslim nationalist struggle into the tangible gain of statehood. What had changed, according to Sobhan (1993), was the movement's transformation from a middle-class urban movement into a mass struggle, after Mujib's AL had enlisted the mass of rural households in the struggle for self-rule, motivated by the desire to address the problems of absolute and relative deprivation among ordinary Bengalis. This effectively offset the efforts being made within the Pakistani state to accommodate the demands of the Bengali middle classes in the form of better civil-service positions and public investment in rural productive enterprises. As Jalal (1995: 61) has put it:

The Awami League's six-point programme for maximum provincial autonomy with its confederal overtones was anathema to the West Pakistani dominated establishment, but it won the enthusiastic support of Bengali middle class professionals, students, small and medium scale businessmen and industrial labourers. A poverty-stricken peasantry also responded to the Awami League's clarion call, having been the main victims of inter-regional economic disparity and neglect during a catastrophic cyclone in the fall of 1970.

When General Tikka Khan was sent in early 1971 from West Pakistan to eliminate Mujib's supporters, some of the small numbers of Bengali units in the Pakistan army rebelled and joined the resistance. Yet still Ayub Khan viewed the source of the problem merely as one of a "few intellectuals," and he believed that a brief violent response would silence the movement, explaining that "a few thousand dead in Dhaka and East Pakistan will be quiet soon." He failed to see that the demand for separation had now become a mass movement. The failure of the West Pakistan elite to recognise the changed nature of the Bengali nationalist movement was the crucial factor in what turned out to be a disastrous decision to try to suppress Bengali nationalists by force – disastrous because it ultimately caused the destruction of the Pakistani state and was, in Sobhan's words, "the ultimate measure of the failure of governance in Pakistan" (149).

Mujib was arrested at the start of Pakistan's military crackdown, which was termed Operation Searchlight, immediately after he had made his patriotic address at the Race Course Rally in Dhaka on March 25, 1971. He remained in prison in Dhaka Cantonment until April 1, and was then flown to West Pakistan where he remained in captivity until December 22, 1971. On March 27, Major Ziaur Rahman, then a young army officer who had been decorated for bravery during the 1965 war, announced Bangladesh's independence through the Swadhin Bangla Betar Kendra radio station in Chittagong. The radio station had been captured by the new group of *mukti bahini* fighters who had responded to the call for independence and, ignited by Mujib's arrest, started resisting the Pakistani army. The Liberation forces were commanded by Colonel Osmani, appointed as army chief of staff by the new Bangladesh government in exile established by senior AL leaders in West Bengal. Shiekh Mujibur Rahman was declared president of the new country on April 17.

The result of General Tikka Khan's crackdown was massive loss of life among the Bengali population. Along with the *mukti bahini* rebels, Hindus and intellectuals were specifically targeted by Tikka's troops. In the violence that followed, tanks shelled the Dhaka University campus and residences because it had been identified as the location for many of the "Hindu intellectuals" whom Pakistani authorities were claiming had helped foster the rebellion. Hindu neighbourhoods in Dhaka were also shelled by tanks. As the army ran amok, Bengali intellectuals, business people and other "subversives" were systematically hunted down and shot. By June, there was a large-scale guerrilla war taking place, leading to even more brutal army tactics. During this period there were documented reports of the killing of civilians, use of napalm against villages and systematic use of rape by soldiers as a tactic to weaken the Bengali "race." The Pakistan army recruited a special force of volunteers from among the minority of Bengalis who remained loyal to Pakistan and from some of the non-Bengali Urdu-speaking population known as *razakars*, a term that has become closely associated in Bangladesh with the worst of the violence committed against the pro-Liberation Bengalis.

The scale of the carnage has never been authoritatively established but has been internationally recognised as one of the twentieth century's genocides. There is a broad consensus in the literature that at least a million Bengalis lost their lives at this time. Some sources, such as Ahmed (2004), put the figure as high as three million people, and this is widely accepted by many in Bangladesh who lived through this traumatic period. The Pakistani administration reported at the time that the Bengali "insurgents" had killed one hundred thousand "non-Bengalis" and that only about thirty thousand Bengalis had died (Afzal 2001). There was, at the time, a comprehensive attempt by Pakistan and its supporters to produce propaganda that played down the scale of the carnage, such as L. F. Rushbrook Williams's book *The East Pakistan Tragedy* (1972). This provided a highly partial account of the events of 1970 and 1971 from the perspective of Yahya Khan's government, in which it was the AL supported by India that perpetrated the "true genocide," and was a book described by one reviewer as a "one-sided an account of one of the most harrowing episodes of our time" (Roselli 1972: 527).

More recently, the Indian journalist Sarmila Bose (2005) has begun constructing a revisionist history of the war, accusing Bangladeshis of "unsubstantiated sensationalism" and "the cultivation of an unhealthy 'victim culture.'" Needless to say, such work has met with outrage in Bangladesh and elsewhere. For example, Nananika Mookherjee (2007: 121) countered Bose's work with a eviscerating methodological critique of the bias she argues is inherent in the work because Bose "talked to Pakistani military authorities and accepts everything they say to be true but considers all Bangladeshi accounts as predominantly fabricated." Nevertheless, it is clear that women were brutalised by both sides, as oral history research with Bihari women still resident in Camp Geneva in Dhaka testifies (Saikia 2004). The consensus figure given in most accounts is that close to a million people died during the conflict, although, later, General Tikka Khan would admit to having killed "only" thirty-five thousand Bengali intellectuals. He was never brought to account for these war crimes and, on the contrary, became seen by many in Pakistan as a hero. In 1989, he became governor general of Punjab Province. For Jalal (1995: 187), the fact that East Pakistan ultimately slipped out of the control of the central "military-bureaucratic state" was unsurprising in view of the political tensions and economic inequalities that had emerged during the past two decades, but the sheer scale of the atrocities committed by the Pakistan army "will continue to astound the voices of sanity in South Asia for many generations to come." In a recent analysis of Pakistan, Lieven (2011: 10) observes that although the failure of the original conception of Pakistan was clearly unsustainable, the tragedy is that "a situation made for a civilised divorce should instead have ended in horrible bloodshed."

By November, Dhaka was under Pakistani control and the country was "occupied," with more than ten million people having fled to camps in India. Border clashes between the armies of India and Pakistan grew as the *mukhti bahini* moved back and forth across the Indian border. When Pakistan's air force preemptively attacked Indian forces on December 3, India responded by invading the new country and took Jessore on December 7, creating a new front from the west in addition to the ongoing *mukhti bahini* and civilian resistance. On December 16, General Niazi of Pakistan signed the surrender documents. Some argue that the U.S. Navy's 7th Fleet was on its way to aid Pakistan but was too late to make a difference to the outcome of the conflict.

The movement embodying the aspirations of Bengalis in East Pakistan became organised around the secular issue of language because it helped to jointly mobilise the impoverished rural masses excluded from economic opportunities and the movement's small group of elite leaders (Alavi 1972: 167). The latter had been excluded from, and now sought entry into, the bureaucratic establishment and the government jobs that this would provide:

There were, therefore, two traditions in the Bengali movement: (1) a petty-bourgeois elitist tradition for those who hoped to rise to senior positions in the bureaucracy or to become members of the newly-created business community in Bengal on the strength of governmental financial support and subsidy; and (2) a rural populist tradition that articulated the frustrations and aspirations of the long-suffering sections of the extremely poor Bengal peasantry. The two traditions were intertwined but remained distinct. The educated sons of rich peasants had other aspirations than those of the peasantry in general.

A key problem after Liberation was that the government that had come to power on the promise of emancipation from Pakistan's economic exploitation and political domination had no specific policy programme. It faced the immediate problems of restoration of law and order, creation of a constitution and establishment of diplomatic relationships. But there was no consensus among the leadership about building a new economic system. As Nurul Islam (1977) has described, the government was now answerable to a quite disparate set of interest groups, including surplus farmers, a mercantile class of traders and market intermediaries, small-scale entrepreneurs, industrial trade unions, organised students with a wide spectrum of ideologies, public servants, the army, professionals and intelligentsia.

As the new country began to move forward, each group saw the job of government as opening up the economic opportunities – in terms of trade, industry and administration – that had been denied to them by West Pakistan. The government attempted, unsuccessfully, to balance these interest groups – a strategy that resulted in indecision and, within a relatively short space of time, to a widespread disillusionment that led to intervention by the military.

## Conclusion: Past and Present

This historical overview has briefly contextualised the analysis of state, economy and civil society that will follow. It has provided a glimpse into the range of different cultural and religious influences in the region, and into the economic and political forces to which Bengal became subject during its history. This history began with a discussion of precolonial Bengal, the role of the East India Company in bringing the region within the British Empire, the anticolonial struggles that led first to the formation of Pakistan in 1947 and later to the creation of Bangladesh from East Pakistan. During the prepartition period, Muslim and Hindu politics were shaped not by the rigid ideas of religious affiliation suggested by the "two nation theory" but by a variety of local and regional factors that played out across different parts of India. In the eastern part of Bengal, there was a more complex and diverse set of nationalist narratives that included Muslim and Hindu voices, each seeking inclusion within an emerging set of political, religious and cultural ideas about the nature of a post-Independence India.

After partition, the continuation of earlier processes of colonisation and resistance were to lead eventually to the 1971 Liberation War and to the birth of Bangladesh as an independent nation. This substate nationalist movement led to "the only case of secession from a post-colonial state" until the disintegration of the USSR two decades later (Bertrand and Laliberté 2010). The motivation for Muslim Bengalis to lend support to the creation of Pakistan, and later to the movement for separation from it, hinged on long-standing struggles for political power and control of economic resources, against successive domination by the Mughal rulers from northern India, from the British *raj*, and from the zamindar class. In the Pakistan period, the language movement became the dominant cultural expression of the struggle for Bangladesh, but it was firmly underpinned by this earlier history. Each of these periods and processes has helped to shape the landscape of contemporary Bangladesh. At the same time, although this past remains an influence on the present, it does not determine its precise shape, nor does it fully circumscribe the room for a manoeuvre of key actors within state, economy and civil society.

4

# State, Politics and Institutions

This chapter analyses the development of Bangladesh's political institutions and considers the tensions and transformations that have taken place in relation to the main political actors and processes. A period of nation building followed the 1971 Liberation victory under the leadership of Mujib, which was based on the secular nationalist principles that had labelled Islamic political parties as collaborators with the Pakistani army. However, disillusionment ensued as it became clear that Mujib's increasingly rigid and repressive regime had failed to capitalise on the momentum of Liberation. After the 1975 coup, the government of General Ziaur Rahman (Zia) ushered in a new period of military politics. This brought a series of efforts at limited administrative decentralisation, partly as a mechanism designed to build political support and legitimacy for unelected government. After Zia was assassinated in 1981, General H. M. Ershad continued military rule until the restoration of democracy in 1991 after a long mass-opposition movement was eventually translated into a peaceful "people power" removal of Ershad from power.

Four elected governments have now served since that time (two led by the BNP and two by the AL), as well as a two-year period of an extended military-backed caretaker government that took power in 2007–8. The main activities and achievements of these governments are discussed in key areas such as the ongoing government decentralisation, the partial peace settlement achieved in the CHT and the progress with regional negotiations over water sharing with India. The chapter also explores the emergence of the confrontational politics that have characterised government-opposition relationships during this period and considers the main roots of these problems. Understanding the limitations of the political system requires an historical perspective on state formation and recognition of the ways social institutions such as patronage still tend to dominate political institutions. Evidence of a revival of Islamist politics is also considered, notably in the election of the 2001–6 BNP government that, for the first time, included JI coalition members in the cabinet. It concludes by considering the dominant perception among citizens and outside observers of an increasing inability of the state to govern within a political system that has been described as an "illiberal democracy." A lack of confidence in the capacity of the state to provide basic law and order for citizens or a sound investment climate for national and international capital reached a crisis point at this time when a combination of pressure from the international donor community and a faction within the army led to the imposition of an extended military-backed caretaker government on January 11, 2007. Dr. Fakhruddin Ahmed, a former civil servant, World Bank economist and governor of the Bangladesh Bank, was appointed as the chief adviser. This intervention initially met with considerable public support, and the new government attempted a set of wide-ranging reforms that were aimed at tackling corruption, building political leadership and strengthening the independence of the judiciary. When elections eventually followed, almost two years later in December 2008, the AL achieved a massive majority and formed its second elected government, bringing some new expectations but also continuing many of the old discredited characteristics of dysfunctional politics.

### Governing Bangladesh (1): From Nation-building to the Military Era

*Sheikh Mujibur Rahman (1971–1975)*

In 1971, Bangladesh's state institutions were, quite understandably, fragmented and weak. The key problem for the new country was the lack of a viable foundation on which to build a resilient and responsive state, because the colonial state and the Pakistan state had been similarly distant and top-down in character and had excluded all but a tiny minority of East Pakistan elite from participation. A small, educated elite that had previously been present in East Pakistan was now depleted. The senior ranks of the military and the bureaucracy had previously been predominantly occupied by West Pakistanis, who had now left for Pakistan. Significant numbers of the Bengali elite had been killed. The human-resource base for the new government, in terms of skills and experience, was weak. In this new context, state power now rested in very different hands than it had under Pakistan. A new set of class-based political relationships began to shape a struggle to determine the form and character of the new state. Van Schendel (2009: 178) writes,

Gone were Pakistan's "twenty-two families" and their allies, the landlords and the armed forces. Instead, economic power was now in the hands of the delta's surplus farmers, small-scale entrepreneurs and industrial trade unions. Each expected that its support for the Awami League would translate into greatly expanded economic opportunities.

There was a political and administrative vacuum created into which two main groups moved and started to compete for power. The first was made up of the returning politicians and activists who had supported the Liberation War from neighbouring West Bengal, while the second was made up of members of the nationalist resistance who had remained within Bangladesh during the conflict. Further tension between these groups was created by the return of an additional group of bureaucrats and military personnel who had been stranded in Pakistan, known as *Pakistani ferat* (returnees), some of whom also faced distrust.

In addition to the challenges the country had inherited from the British colonial era and then from the Pakistan period, there was now a raft of new problems to engage the national leadership. The challenges that faced the new government were daunting ones: they needed to establish law and order, convert still-armed groups of freedom fighters into peaceful citizens and rebuild the country's already limited infrastructure that had been battered by the conflict and the November 1970 cyclone. Perhaps the most urgent of all was the need to put in place a set of policies that would help steer Bangladesh on a course towards economic development and begin to move the country forward from decades of poverty and economic stagnation. Although Mujib's approach to politics had been very well suited to agitation and resistance, it soon became clear that he possessed few of the political skills needed to equip him for providing effective leadership nor the capacities required for the difficult task of building national unity. The AL in government rapidly began to place its own leadership and party interests before those of the new state, setting a strong precedent for Bangladesh's future pattern of the "politics of patronage" (Van Schendel 2009: 178). It managed growing factionalism within its ranks by appointing party loyalists to key positions in the bureaucracy regardless of competence, which crippled the state's capacity for effective policy formulation and implementation and put in place a system of competing patronage networks that perpetuated rival claims on securing a share of state resources. Party loyalists were rewarded with positions running nationalised industries that they often had no knowledge or experience of and with import licenses that opened up opportunities for personal profit through illegal trade in rice and jute, often across the border with India.

The first phase of Bangladesh's political system lasted four years. When Mujib resigned as interim president and became prime minister in January 1972, he did so with the objective of building a parliamentary political system with a constitution that aimed to guarantee civil liberties and remove the repressive tendencies of earlier British and West Pakistani rule. Mujib began to take steps to bring the military and the bureaucracy under political control. Although the basic principles of a liberal democratic state existed in theory, the reality of the system was "highly personalized, centralized, and increasingly repressive" Kochanek (1993: 52). There were some elements of a socialist vision at the core of Mujib's new Bangladesh. The size of the public sector increased from 34 percent of industrial assets in 1969–70 to 92 percent by 1975, then falling to 40 percent by 1986. The AL began as a party representing the vernacular elite of East Pakistan, and as it gradually acquired a mass base it also built an ideology of economic nationalism that was based on opposition to West Pakistani control of economic assets and the idea of nationalisation of private industry. In this way, a radical platform was constructed that initially linked political and economic nationalism. This was also a response to earlier forms of Western "development" thinking:

It came as a reaction to the uneven pattern of growth that had resulted from the development model of the 1950s and 1960s, which had stressed the vigorous pursuit of macro-level economic growth as a solution to the poverty of the region. In the late 1960s, this development model came under attack by those who demanded greater economic equality and distributive justice. (p. 74)

When the AL had taken power, it did so having rejected calls for a coalition government based on the broad consensus of the Liberation Movement. It did not have a clear ideology of how to govern, but was quickly carried along by events. One immediate issue was to dispose of property and assets formerly owned by West Pakistanis, and in January 1972, the government seized more than seven hundred firms and placed them under the control of the Ministry of Industries, though many of these were effectively plundered by these party supporters.

The Planning Commission was established, headed by four key academic economists sympathetic to the AL, which devised the country's First FYP (Nurul Islam 1977). Many of the abandoned, non-Bengali–owned busi-nesses had been nationalised. In March 1972, the commission adapted a radical policy to transform the economy by also nationalising Bengali-owned businesses including the industrial sector, banks and insurance sector and limit the emergence of a capitalist class. Mujib began speaking of a move towards socialism as part of the heart of the new FYP. Small-scale private-sector businesses were permitted, but government was allowed to nationalise those it judged were being mismanaged. Foreign investment was to be permitted, but only as joint ventures with the public sector with a maximum of 49 percent equity, and, as Kochanek (1993: 81) points out, "few foreign firms rushed to take advantage of these new opportunities to invest in Bangladesh." Under these rules most private business people quickly transferred their economic activities away from production towards the more lucrative trade and construction enterprises. The small community of Bengali Muslim business elites quickly became disillusioned with Mujib's leadership.

Meanwhile, the FYP was adopted by Mujib without adequate consultation with other wings of the government or population, which meant that it had little in the way of wider government "ownership" (in the current parlance of donors) across the rest of the bureaucracy. When the economy went into decline, the result was that the commission was blamed. Many senior bureaucrats were more sympathetic to the state-regulated capitalism of the previous regime and resented the new power being given to what they saw as inexperienced, overly academic economists. On top of these problems, the new economic policy was also opposed by the international donor community led by the World Bank, whose power quickly increased in Bangladesh once it became clear that Soviet and Indian assistance had failed to materialise in any quantity. Within the policy process, a precedent was set of weak accountability and low levels of responsibility, which according to Kochanek (1993), arose from the fact that nondominant groups were unable to gain public representation, due to the weak press, courts and opposition parties. Decisions were made in private and, therefore, did not need to be explained or defended to anyone. Even within government, ministries tended to compete and, once excluded from a decision, felt no obligation to implement it, as in the case of the Planning Commission's First FYP. This culture of government has dominated the polity up to the present period. Domestic political conditions created incentives for a high level of individual accumulation, through the plunder of the country's already meagre resource base. There was a lack of experience among those controlling power at the state level, where rapidly promoted politicians and bureaucrats quickly found themselves out of their depth. Another problem was the basic lack of attention that was given to economic matters. This was partly the result of a widely held belief that once the exploitative layer of West Pakistani control had been removed, an unblocking of the economy would occur and logic of economic growth would quickly and simply follow.

The macrolevel power structure that emerged after Liberation, and which continued in varying configurations until the fall of General Ershad in 1990, was one in which three urban groups – the senior bureaucracy, military and political leaders – jostled for control within a central alliance. This alliance sustained its power through a relationship of "mutual convenience" with the rural landowning elites who maintained the rural social order, within a process in which foreign aid served as an overall "lubricant" (Blair 2001: 190). Two further shocks also affected the state and the economy in the form of the 1973 oil crisis that suddenly increased international prices and the reappearance of famine during 1973–4. Both events severely afflicted the new country that was still reeling from the aftereffects of war and natural disaster. This was still an economy that already "suffered from low productivity, an excessive money supply, deficit financing and galloping inflation" ( Jalal 1995: 88). The new nation's economic performance, and therefore the standard of living of the majority of the population, rapidly went into decline. By 1973, agricultural production was 84 percent lower than it had been just before the war, and industrial production had fallen by 66 percent. Although the cost of living for an agricultural labourer increased by 150 percent, real incomes fell to 87 percent of their 1970s levels (Van Schendel 2009).

By 1973, the terrible overall state of the economy, combined with Mujib's increasingly inept and unpopular approach to politics, had eroded much of the support he had counted on across a range of social groups for the first few years of the country's independence. The Bangladesh economy collapsed in July 1974, from a combination of internal political and administrative failings and external pressures. A devastating famine that year caused the deaths of an estimated 1.5 million people. Mujib was forced to give way to pressure from both the old business elites and the newer AL supporters, who had benefitted from the early years of nationalisation and now wished to invest their gains, and to the international donors. The result was the lifting of many of the restrictions on local and international private investment. Although Bangladesh started turning itself more fully towards the West, at the same time, Mujib was trying to restore his failing political powerbase. However, the country's continuing economic deterioration had created a formidable "anti-Mujib alliance" between an army that had become frustrated by the growing level of resources commanded by the paramilitaries, and a new capitalist class interested in accessing state power for private capital accumulation ( Jalal 1995: 88). Mujib's response to his waning popularity was increasingly authoritarian. In 1974, he declared a state of emergency, making himself president of Bangladesh. As he began to lose support from most sections of society, including the army, he set about trying to establish a socialist state and disbanded political parties to be replaced by a new national political party – the Bangladesh Peasants and Workers Awami League or BAKSAL. By January 1975, the system had been transformed into an authoritarian one-party state. Mujib set up his own force of loyal paramilitaries, known as the *rakkhi bahini* ( *jatiya raksi bahini*, or National Security Force), which intimidated the population and tortured political opponents. This was an attempt, as Jalal (1995) argues, to build a new populist alliance between the AL and small peasants and workers, in the face of failing support from the "intermediate classes," bureaucrats, military and political groups who occupy the space between capital and labour, upon which he and the AL had previously depended. But it was only a matter of time before opposition to Mujib was translated into decisive action. In August 1975, a violent military coup took place by disaffected army officers and resulted in the assassination of Mujib and the murder of his family, aside from his two daughters who were away in Europe at the time.

Indian journalist Anthony Mascarenhas (1986: v) writes that Mujib had become "the most hated man in Bangladesh within three short years of its founding," who was seen by many as having betrayed the sacrifices made by the country during the Liberation War. Van Schendel (2009: 177) suggests that the first half-decade of Bangladesh's independence was a period in which "the government squandered its popularity chiefly because it was seen to contribute to the deep malaise in the economy." Furthermore, Mujib had been unable to translate his considerable attributes and skills into a convincing, institutionalised form of political leadership, there were high levels of corruption and cronyism within the administration and widespread concerns that he was allowing India to interfere in Bangladesh's domestic affairs existed. In short, Mujib's efforts to occupy the political middle ground had failed, as he was first rejected by disillusioned colleagues on the left and then later discarded and swept away by the right in a coup that, in retrospect, was to provide the transition to the globally integrated Western-aid influenced regime that Bangladesh was soon to become.

### General Ziaur Rahman (1976–1981)

After Mujib's assassination, there was a period of political chaos, with both a coup and countercoup. Khandakar Mushtaq Ahmed became president and declared martial law, banning all political activity. Four months later, a coup took place that gave Brigadier Khalid Musheraf power for four days. He was then killed in another coup, which led to a military government led by Abusadet Mohammed Sayem, chief justice of the Supreme Court, who ruled for two years as president and martial law administrator (MLA), with the army chiefs as deputies. In 1976, General Ziaur Rahman took over as MLA, and then also became president upon Sayem's resignation in 1977. The key to Zia's political rise to power had been his ability to mobilise a broad-based alliance of diverse and disaffected AL opponents, which included his own anti-Indian faction within the army and the bureaucracy, right-wing pro-Pakistan elements of the old Muslim League and Islamic political parties and significant parts of the left-wing pro-Chinese NAP (Kochanek 1993: 90).

Like Mujib, Zia inherited a country facing a major economic crisis, but he lacked the room for manoeuvre that, in theory at least, had been open to the AL at the start of 1972. Instead, Zia was under pressure from several directions. Leftist factions within the army, such as Major Abu Taher and the Jatiya Samajtantrik Dal Party (JSD), were pushing for a return to a radical programme of social transformation and self-reliance. The JSD had been set up by younger radicals within the AL who had lost confidence in Mujib and now favoured the introduction of "scientific socialism" with the aim of building a more egalitarian socialist revolution. The emerging Bangladeshi business elites were looking for greater access to opportunities for strengthening private sector. By 1977, such a shift was now openly being encouraged by the World Bank and other international donors, who saw the chance to engage with Bangladesh and move it more firmly onto the path of capitalist development through modernisation within a liberalised economy.

Under the guidance of the World Bank, the government began to reha-bilitate the private sector. The NIP had ushered in a set of policies designed to stimulate private-sector investment. One new provision, which was to have huge significance, permitted producers to import fabric duty-free on the condition that it was for making garments for export (Kabeer 2000). The Dhaka Stock Market was also reactivated, and many of the restric-tions on foreign investment were lifted. Some public assets, such as a few of the smaller government-owned enterprises that recovered from de-parted West Pakistani owners in 1972, were sold off to the private sector. Zia's administration relied heavily on senior former CSP officers who had been involved with the implementation of Ayub Khan's growth-oriented modernisation policies during the 1960s. Although such policies had not worked to the advantage of East Pakistan because of the dominance of West Pakistani interests, many believed that the approach of state-regulated capitalist economic development was still sound, and that it would now serve Bangladesh's national interests more effectively. With its pragmatic approach to leadership, Zia's government moved to create a mixed economy in line with the demands of business elites and donors, leaving behind the socialist vision of his supporters on the left. The result was that economic growth began to get underway, and along with the arrival of high levels of foreign aid, the economy began to strengthen.

Zia also began consolidating his political power. Taher was sentenced to death in 1976 for treason and the JSD was systematically intimidated and dismantled. The ideology of "Mujibism" had depended on the four principles of democracy, nationalism, socialism and secularism. Mujib's regime had been – at least in part – an experiment in the creation of a secular identity. But the secular nationalist identity that had formed during the liberation struggle could not easily be sustained within a society in which religion, predominantly forms of Islam but also Hinduism and other minority religions, played a major role in everyday life. In seeking to consolidate his power, Zia began to reconfigure the four principles. In 1977, with the Constitutional Amendment Order, Zia removed secularism and replaced it with a commitment to the values of Islam. A national presidential poll in 1978 gave Ziaur Rahman an overwhelming victory. Zia created a new political party to embody this new order, the BNP, which won two-thirds of the national assembly seats in a 1979 election.

Martial law was lifted and a measure of stability returned to Bangladesh. Zia attempted to build support in rural areas through the introduction of the *gram sarkar*, or "village government" system. This was to be based on a system of elected local leaders, though this was not operationalised, and attempted to establish a youth programme to recruit local support for government development programmes. In the foreign policy sphere, the country moved away from its earlier ties with the Soviet Union and the nonaligned India towards building a stronger relationship with the West and with the oil-rich Arab countries. Yet Zia also met with criticism from business interests. Although he had successfully dealt with his critics on the left, his modernising policy shift towards a mixed economy did not go far enough for many within the business community. Zia's Second FYP (1980–5) was still listing the public sector as the central driver of development. Such voices now argued that large-scale nationalised industries such as the jute mills should be returned to private ownership, as a precondition for genuine private-sector growth and development. But by the end of the 1970s, the economic recovery had stalled, with only 8 percent of the GDP coming from an industrial sector that compared poorly with an average of

19 percent in similar low-income countries. Zia's efforts at liberalisation were thwarted by persistent high levels of restriction, regulation and uncertainty that continued to push local investors into nonproductive economic activities such as trade and construction. Although there had been an average of 6 percent annual economic growth between 1976 and 1981, this now fell to 1.1 percent in 1982. Foreign aid and international trade had declined, and there had been a series of poor harvests for which the government appeared unprepared, and all of this contributed to an atmosphere of uncertainty and stagnation.

Mascarenhas (1986) describes how, just like Mujib, General Zia had squandered his earlier popularity "and became the target of 20 mutinies and coup attempts in five years." These coup attempts had been ruthlessly put down, which, according to Kochanek (1993: 94), "had decimated the ranks of both the officer corps and the *jawans* (enlisted men)" and had reduced the number of leftist opponents among the army officers. In May 1981, the twenty-first coup attempt killed General Zia. Without a clear successor, Justice Abdul Sattar became acting president of Bangladesh. In the general election that followed, he won 66 percent of the vote as a BNP candidate, and for a while the country's stability seemed to improve, though it was by now clear that the government lacked the coherent policies required to deal with the economic crisis. The political system that Zia had put in place struggled on for some months under its newly elected president, but in March 1982, a bloodless coup brought General H. M. Ershad, the army chief of staff since 1978, to power. A second new military government was formed under the control of General Ershad, who had led a coup against Abdus Sattar's civilian government in March 1982. He dismissed the president, suspended the constitution and restored martial law.

General Zia's regime had ushered in the second phase of the Bangladeshi political system, which was, according to Kochanek (1993: 52), essentially a restoration of the bureaucratic military state that had been constructed by Pakistan between 1958 and 1969:

Zia restored the bureaucracy to its former position of dominance, rehabilitated and expanded the size and rule of the military, and after several years of martial law, civilianized his rule by creating the Bangladesh Nationalist Party (BNP) out of an amalgam of prominent anti-Awami League forces. General Zia also amended the 1972 constitution to strengthen the presidential system, altered the religious and economic objectives of the state, and became supreme leader of party and government.

The BNP was to become the main political party alongside the AL, taking a more promarket policy and espousing a reframed view of Bangladeshi identity that brought a renewed emphasis on Islamic religion alongside Bengali language and culture (Bhardwaj 2011).

### General H. M. Ershad (1982–1990)

General Ershad's new cabinet was composed from a mixture of army and political leaders, and a return to democracy was pledged within two years. Ershad immediately began to set about consolidating his power through the opening up of new lines of patronage that would build support across key areas of the military and the bureaucracy. For example, he provided land in the up-and-coming north Dhaka residential area of Baridhara to senior military officers. At the same time, he faced a less factionalised army because Ziaur Rahman had purged many of its radical leftist elements after a succession of failed coups.

Ershad then proceeded to develop three new areas of policy. The first was in relation to economic affairs. The NIP had finally made a conclusive break with the economic nationalism favoured by the AL. It liberalised control of the private sector and set in place measures to protect new industries and give incentives to improve investment. A high-profile decision was made to return the jute and textile mills to private ownership, but this was strongly resisted by trade unions, students and opposition parties. The NIP was the brainchild of Shafiul Azam, a senior member of the CSP elite from the Pakistan period, who had earlier contributed to Ziaur Rahman's industrial policy and was now heading the ministries of commerce and industries. In General Ershad, Azam found an even more pragmatic listener looking for ideas to fill the vacuum created by his own lack of an economic model or a political ideology with which to establish legitimacy and consolidate power. Hearing of the success of the East Asian "tiger" economies, facing foreign pressure for more private-sector investment and facing domestic demands from the business community for the return of assets, Ershad was receptive to the NIP (Kochanek 1993: 96).

The process of denationalisation of twenty-seven of the country's cotton textile mills and thirty-three of its jute mills, representing about half the country's overall capacity in both sectors, was fraught with difficulty. The former owners were forced during the hand-over negotiations to accept responsibility for prenationalisation liabilities relating to the enterprises and for absorbing large numbers of employees on terms that led to resentment on both sides and did less than expected to improve economic performance. Two years after the launch of the NIP, trade union opposition to what was seen as Ershad's assault on the public sector had become increasingly militant, and the emphasis of the policy shifted to slightly less contentious reforms such as the creation of privatised "public private partnerships."

Nevertheless, the World Bank claimed that the NIP had been a success, and industrial growth boomed between 1983 and 1985. Critics complained that the public sector still remained too dominant to allow the private sector to develop, and that the growth was the result of the ready-made garment industry and the shrimp export markets, both of which predated and had little to do with the NIP.

By 1985, the country's economy was again in a downturn. According to a World Bank study of Bangladesh's trade and investment policies, a key structural problem was that the industrial sector possessed a dual character. There was one highly inefficient subsector composed of import substitution industries and another more efficient subsector that focused on the high-value exports of garment and shrimp. The study recommended further deregulation of the more dynamic export sector. Eager to restore life to the faltering economy, Ershad decided to build reform of the export sector into his 1986 RIP plan, which promised to deepen the process of liberalisation and deregulation of the private sector. Yet the RIP served only to mobilise the AL and the political opposition around the defence of the public sector, and domestic privatisation was again largely stalled. Despite the veneer of liberalisation implied by Ershad's economic reform policies, the reality was that centralised decision making, resistance to implementation, bureaucratic red tape and pervasive corruption remained in place. Combined with two consecutive years of destructive floods, there was little chance to find out whether these reforms would have contributed to improving Bangladesh's economic performance.

Ershad's second major policy contribution was his reorganisation of local government. He set up a new administrative structure for decentralised local government in 1982. Ershad set up the *upazila* subdistrict system of local government, in which elected councils formed the local distribution point for centrally dispensed resources, in an attempt to plant roots and build support at the local level. The government put together a committee to consider administrative reform, which recommended that each *upazila* was to have a representative body called an *upazila parishad* (subdistrict council) under a directly elected chairman. The *upazila* subdistrict system was primarily an attempt by the military regime to build political allies in the rural areas in create legitimacy (Crook and Manor 1998). *Upazilas* were provided with an elected council and were given revenue-raising powers, but the key principle was the dispensation of central resources to appointees in the subdistricts. Two sets of elections were held to newly formed *upazila parishads* in 1985 and in 1990, but after Ershad's removal from power, the principle of the elected *upazila* council was abandoned once military rule ended and the first democratic BNP government was elected. Despite its shortcomings, the *upazila* system was an important first step in the decentralisation process. For example, in their study of the 1990 *upazila* chairman elections, Richard Crook and James Manor (1998) found evidence to suggest that voters were, to a degree, able to discipline unpopular local leaders. More recently, there are signs that progress with local government reform, combined with bottom-up civil-society pressure, is giving grounds for cautious optimism. There may be a loosening up of a local power structure previously characterised as one in which most external resources were captured and diverted by local elites (Lewis and Hossain 2008). New *upazila* elections were held in January 2009.

The third area of major policy intervention was the innovative adoption by Ershad's government of an essential drugs policy. As in the case of the progress made for *khas* land reform (see Chapter 6), this was a process that was strongly driven by the NGOs. Under Ershad's regime the country's growing NGO sector had come of age, despite a somewhat uneasy coexistence (see Chapter 5). Gonoshasthya Kendra (GK) (which means "people's health centre") was an NGO established in 1972 by left-wing health activist Dr. Zafrullah Chowdhury and his colleagues initially to provide postconflict relief, but which soon evolved into a programme to provide people-centred rural health services across the country. One of GK's objectives was to persuade the government to put in place an "essential drugs policy" that would address the basic health needs of the population by using low-cost locally produced medicines. This was controversial because it challenged the dominance of the international pharmaceutical companies and the medical establishment in Bangladesh, both of whom profited from high-value specialised treatments to elite groups.

The UN World Health Organization (WHO) had set out the blueprint for its essential drugs scheme in 1977, after some progress with placing basic generic drugs at the centre of public-health policy had been made in countries such as Sri Lanka, Cuba and Mozambique (Mamdani 1992). The basic idea was to challenge the dominance of the profit-driven multinational pharmaceutical firms, which sold a wide range of costly and often-inappropriate products in poor countries such as Bangladesh. The aim was to focus instead on the provision of primary health care based on a narrow range of the most useful and cost-effective medicines available. However, the policy had not been adopted anywhere and had been strongly resisted by drug companies, importers and medical practitioners, as well as by some Western donors with strong pharmaceutical lobbies. Chowdhury had worked with Ershad's chief health adviser, Major General M. Shamsul Huq, during the Liberation War and national professor, Dr. Nurul Islam, and so the connections opened the way to building government support for the idea. But the government's lack of democratic credentials also made it a hazardous venture given the prodemocracy stance taken by most organisations within civil society.

For Ershad, the essential drugs policy offered a highly visible populist tool with which to legitimise his regime. The policy was adopted by Ershad in June 1982 under martial law conditions and without public consultation. It was a triumph of opportunistic political advocacy by a coalition of nongovernmental individuals and organisations, the consequences of which had been underestimated by the new and inexperienced government. Ershad's government was quickly brought into bitter and protracted conflict with the drug companies, doctors and more conservative donors such as the World Bank. Ershad was forced to set up an expert review committee made up of six military doctors, and despite strong lobbying pressure from private interests, stood firm on the policy, bolstered by carefully organised international civil-society pressure. The policy succeeded in increasing the market share of local drug companies from 20 to 25 percent in 1982 to 50 percent by 1988, but its critics pointed to the increase in poor-quality local drugs and smuggling. In 1987, Zafrullah Chowdhury, believing the policy to have been sabotaged, persuaded Ershad to carry out a review and the secretary of health was removed. A new drug policy tightened up on the products that were allowed in Bangladesh and revised drug prices, prompting a more organised reaction than in 1982 from the better established and networked Bangladeshi pharmaceutical industry and its drug industry association. The second policy was eventually adopted in 1989 but was later blocked by court action.

General Ershad's efforts to build political legitimacy were, however, doomed to failure. As part of the plan to "civilianise" his administration, he founded the Jatiya Party, just as Ziaur Rahman had earlier established the BNP. National elections were promised for 1985, but these never materialised. A concessionary "referendum" was held instead but was roundly dismissed by the opposition parties. A series of subsequent announcements promising a measure of political reforms did not amount to anything of substance. In October 1986, after a presidential election that had been boycotted by the AL and the BNP, and widely denounced as fraudulent, General Ershad was sworn in as president, martial law was lifted the following month and the constitution restored.

Although Ershad had tried to follow Ziaur Rahman's approach to building legitimacy through a gradual process of "civilianisation," he was less successful in doing so, partly because he lacked the former's popularity as a hero of the Liberation War, and partly because the Jatiya political party he established remained without much grassroots support (Kochanek 1993). The result was that Ershad's regime was forced to rely on a power base of largely opportunistic supporters from the military and business communities maintained through the heavy use of patronage. Instead, Ershad's regime became "one of the most centralized and corrupt in the history of Bangladesh" (53). It was clear that people without the key resources of money, status and connections were largely excluded from the political system. Direct action and protest became the only option, but this also further stifled public debate and negotiation. The grievances of social groups such as trade unions or doctors quickly escalated into political, regime-threatening demands. For example, when the anti-Ershad Movement eventually coalesced, it included doctors fighting the health policy, students, political parties and lawyers (Kochanek 1993).

A series of natural disasters had devastated Bangladesh during Ershad's rule. There were severe floods in 1984 that caused widespread damage and loss of life. In May 1985, a cyclone struck the coast and killed eleven thousand people and left almost one-third of a million without shelter. In 1988, the worst monsoon floods for forty years claimed three thousand lives and caused massive damage to crops and infrastructure, wiping out 10 percent of Bangladesh's agricultural production. Ershad's government gained some hard-won credibility in some quarters from the relatively efficient way it handled the 1988 relief effort, which mobilised large-scale international resources. Ershad also received a UN award in recognition of his implementation of family-planning policies (Ahmed 2004).

Although the economy had grown from the mid-1980s, it had again stagnated by early 1990. Popular discontent, which started to take shape in a broad-based mass movement that first took to the streets in 1987, increased to a crescendo of *hartals* and opposition rallies during the summer in Dhaka and across other main cities. By now, General Ziaur Rahman's widow, Mrs. Khaleda Zia, had emerged as a popular opposition leader at the head of the BNP, and this had helped to create a rallying call for Ershad's resignation. Mujib's daughter, Sheikh Hasina Wazed, was now also leading the AL, and both parties increasingly offered democratic political alternatives to military rule. At the same time, much of the military's support for Ershad had also started to wane. The students were active with the opposition parties in calling for Ershad's resignation and were joined by public-sector employees and middle-class professionals in an increasingly inclusive *gono andolon* (peoples' movement). In many ways, this relatively peaceful movement was reminiscent of the "people power" protests that had successfully brought down the military regime of General Ferdinand Marcos in the Philippines, three years earlier.

In November 1990, the so-called siege of Dhaka protest was organised by the main political opposition and resulted in thousands of arrests. In December 1990, the broad-based mass movement, which had first started three years earlier, successfully forced Ershad from office. The last in a series of mass protests had finally persuaded the military to withdraw its support to Ershad's beleaguered and now almost entirely unloved regime. Representatives from the international donor community were also believed to have played a key role in these final stages, threatening to withdraw the support on which the military government depended. The country's development NGOs, which had also kept a distance from the movement until the last moment, also lent their support to Ershad's removal and the introduction of parliamentary democracy.

### Governing Bangladesh (2): From Democratic Renewal to "Illiberal Democracy"

#### The First Khaleda Zia BNP Government (1991–1996)

Bangladesh now entered what many hoped would be a period of renewed democratic politics. It began well. In order to guarantee free and fair elections, it was decided that a three-month neutral "caretaker government" system should be put in place to oversee the national elections due to happen in early 1991. This was convened under the acting presidency of Chief Justice Shahabuddin Ahmed, a neutral choice that was acceptable to the opposition movement representatives. The 1991 election was reasonably free and fair and resulted in the return of a BNP government, surprising many who had assumed the AL to be the natural party of government for the new era. But it seemed that an overcomplacent AL had conducted a campaign that had been out of touch with many of the country's younger generation, who were more interested in economic issues than in political rhetoric that seemed preoccupied with unfinished business relating back to the Liberation War.

In the election, of the 300 directly contested seats, the BNP gained 140 and the AL trailed with 88, Jatiya with 35, and JI with 18, leaving the BNP without an outright majority but able to form a cabinet. Begum Khaleda Zia was sworn in as prime minister. However, this had been a narrow victory, and the percentage of the popular vote won by the BNP was only 31 percent as compared with the AL's 30.6 percent. This margin was believed to have dissuaded Khaleda from proceeding with the BNP's policy of maintaining the presidential system because it might not have been possible for her to have won such a tight popular vote as a presidential candidate. The government's position was further strengthened when it won twenty-eight of the thirty additional indirectly elected women's seats (with the other two given to JI in exchange for its support for the government).

The first major policy step taken by the BNP government was the abolition of the *upazila* councils. These councils had been set up by Ershad as a means of delivering resources to local areas, mainly as a means to consolidate his power and build legitimacy for his planned shift from military to civilian government. The incentive for abolition was that in 1990 *upazila* elections had returned a Jatiya Party majority, followed by the AL. The BNP, with its urban power base, came in a poor third, although both parties had, to varying degrees, boycotted the election. The new regime did not wish to try to work with a tier of local government that it did not control. The economy got off to a reasonably strong start under the new government. Finance Minister Saifur Rahman removed certain foreign-exchange restrictions and new export-tax exemptions were provided in support of the garment industry. New rules on foreign investment made it possible for outsiders to wholly own industrial companies, and the U.S. government wrote off almost one-third of a billion U.S. dollars of Bangladesh's debt (Baxter 1998). The economy began to grow from 1991 onwards, and the establishment of a new Dhaka stock market started to attract some investment from outside the country.

At the time, there was a measure of optimism about the new democracy. For Kochanek (1993: 346), the fall of Ershad "marked a new beginning for Bangladesh." It had ushered in a BNP government that had moderate policies, secured the support of the major elite groups and maintained good links with the army. But he also pointed out the vulnerability of the government and the system:

Although the new government enjoys a cushion of safety, it must demonstrate effective performance in order to establish its legitimacy. If it fails, the opposition will take to the streets, and the military will once again intervene. The cycle of military coup, martial law, civilian-military rule, mass movement, and systemic collapse has not yet come to an end. If civilian government fails again, a new generation of military leaders will intervene, believing that it can do a more effective job.

Events were soon to provide this analysis correct. Subsequent democratic governments have only rarely managed to maintain popular support by demonstrating their effectiveness because the power of interest groups and the politics of patronage have persisted and the law-and-order situation has gradually deteriorated.

A number of setbacks soon befell the new government. A major cyclone struck southern Bangladesh in April 1991, with a force exceeding even that of 1970. It resulted in the deaths of close to 150,000 people, though the existence of improved early warning systems and of large numbers of new purpose-built cyclone shelters meant that the numbers of fatalities were half those of the earlier tragedy. In the political sphere, a key unresolved political issue was reopened when Golam Azam returned from Pakistan in 1992 to head a renewed JI political party. In 1971, Azam and the JI had opposed the Liberation War, and he was now regarded by many Bangladeshis as a war criminal who had lost his citizenship rights by opting to live in Pakistan after the Liberation War. The AL and other opposition parties began boycotting Parliament and organised public demonstrations, but by mid-1993 the Supreme Court had backed a decision that he could retain his citizenship and the protests died down.

In the changed climate of the post–Cold War world, religious identities were also beginning to reassert themselves during the 1990s, with some unexpected ramifications for the Indian subcontinent. Cases of violence committed against Bangladeshi Hindus after extremists in India had destroyed the Babri Mosque in Ayodhya in December 1992 were played down by the authorities in Bangladesh, but they shocked many citizens who had assumed higher levels of religious tolerance in the country. The writer Taslima Nasrin (1994: ix) wrote,

[I]t is disgraceful that the Hindus in my country were hunted by the Muslims after the destructions of the Babri Masjid. All of us who love Bangladesh should feel ashamed that such a thing could happen.

Nasrin's controversial novel, *Lajja* (shame), fictionalised these events in order to draw them to public attention. The writer's proto-feminist poetry had already offended some religious groups in Bangladesh, who saw it as blasphemous, and she was forced to leave the country and go into exile in Europe.

The AL was also keen to make up for its earlier defeat and began preparing to recover power. The Dhaka and Chittagong municipal elections took place in 1994, and they were conclusively won by the AL. However, a few months later, the BNP won a by-election in Magura, a traditional AL stronghold, leading to accusations of vote rigging. This quickly escalated into confrontation, both in Parliament, which was boycotted by the opposition, and in the streets, where the AL organised a series of *hartals* (stoppages) and protests.

It was at this time that the fault lines in the new democratic system first became apparent. There were low levels of trust in the capacity of public institutions to ensure a fair political process and a declining confidence in the legitimacy of the main political parties. The AL began calling for regular *hartals* in the run up to the 1996 general election, demanding that that the BNP step down before elections were due to hand power over to a ninety-day transitional caretaker government. Khaleda nevertheless went ahead and attempted to hold national elections in February 1996, but these were boycotted by the major opposition parties. All this contributed to a deepening political crisis in the country, with violent street protests instigated by the AL creating an atmosphere of political deadlock. The stalemate was eventually broken by the action of a civil-society group, the Federation of Bangladesh Chambers of Commerce and Industry (FBCCI). After a meeting of almost five hundred of its businessmen members, the FBCCI issued the BNP government with a forty-eight-hour ultimatum to annul the February elections and set a new date for elections under a caretaker government.

The FBCCI was joined by a coalition of trade unions, NGOs, journalists and lawyers demanding the government's resignation at public rallies. In March 1996, there was an indefinite strike declared by civil servants. Eventually, Khaleda Zia gave way to these mass demands for the proper institutionalisation of the caretaker government system. The Thirteenth Constitutional Amendment was enacted in March 1996, and it called for a nonparty caretaker government – headed by a chief adviser in a position equivalent to that of prime minister – to be installed within fifteen days of the dissolution of Parliament, which would then assist the Election Commission in ensuring that elections would be held within ninety days. The amendment also specified that the chief adviser and the caretaker government's council of advisers would have to be drawn from nonparty political sources. In 1996, this new formalised caretaker government system was introduced and headed by retired Supreme Court judge Justice Habibur Rahman.

### Sheikh Hasina's Awami League Government (1996–2001)
When the national elections were held in June 1996, the AL now emerged as the largest party in Parliament, polling 146 seats to the BNP's 116, and duly went on to form a national government. During this period, there was also an attempted military coup, when President Biswas accused the Chief of Army Staff General Abu Saleh Mohammad Nasim of refusing an order to remove two of his generals who had become involved in party

politics against military rules. The general ordered his soldiers to march on Dhaka, but they were prevented from taking any action by loyal troops that surrounded the president's palace (Islam 2002).

In order to secure a majority, Sheikh Hasina formed her new government with support from the Jatiya Party, a deal that was reportedly premised on an agreement for the early release from prison of Ershad, who was granted bail in January 1997. Another early political act was the lifting of immunity from prosecution of those involved in the 1975 coup. In 1998, fifteen former army officers were convicted of the killings. Yet there were still serious problems at the heart of the political process. Parliament continued to be boycotted by the opposition, which paradoxically argued that the government was abusing its majority to prevent discussion of important national issues. A new Public Safety Act was passed in January 2000, which provided for detention of terrorists and "enemies of the state" for up to ninety days without trial, and this further alienated the opposition, some of whom saw it as a new means of harassing political opponents.

The Hasina government did, however, manage some significant achievements. Within the domestic economic sphere, this period saw significant increases in Bangladesh's food-grain production, though this may have been more due to favourable weather than specific policies. The water-sharing treaty with India in November 2006 and the CHT Peace Accord of December 1997 were both partially successful attempts to resolve long-running problems. Finally, the government managed to complete the large-scale Jamuna Bridge project, which was a significant and much-needed piece of infrastructure that improved communications between the two halves of the country. Less positively, the government seemed unduly concerned with the historical legacy of Mujib, naming public buildings – including the new bridge – after him, instructing his photo to be hung in every public servant's office and even passing a law to allow Hasina to live in his former residence in perpetuity. All this gave the impression of a government that was more adept at looking back and proclaiming past glories than one that had the vision to steer Bangladesh towards a more prosperous future. Perhaps more significantly, by the end of its term the AL government had become highly unpopular, seen by many as having become inefficient and highly corrupt.

### Khaleda Zia's Second Bangladesh Nationalist Party Government (2001–2006)

In 2001, Latifur Rahman, another retired chief justice of the Supreme Court was placed in charge of the second caretaker government under the new institutionalised system. In October, the BNP was returned to power with

193 seats within a prearranged electoral alliance with JI (which won 17 seats), Ershad's Jatiya Party (4 seats) and Islami Oikya Jote (2 seats). This manoeuvre included a surprising rapprochement with its former enemy, the Jatiya Party, allowing the BNP to form and then lead a coalition government with a two-thirds majority. Even though the AL had only won sixty-two seats, it had received the largest single share of the votes with 40 percent, and this was more than it had gained in 1996.

Khaleda was returned for a second term of government. The first session of Parliament was immediately boycotted by the AL, and the opening session was for the first time started without an opposition in attendance. The gridlock between the two main political leaders had, by this time, reached unprecedented heights. One of the first acts of the new government was to charge Hasina and some of her former ministers with corruption, just as the former government had filed similar charges against the leaders of the BNP. Ironically, Bangladesh was to be, for the five successive years between 2001 and 2005, placed by the international organisation TI at the bottom of its influential and widely cited *Corruption Perceptions Index.*

The inclusion of religious political parties in the ruling alliance angered many and emboldened militant religious groups in the country. Increased attacks began to be documented against minority groups, and an attempt was made to single out the Ahmadiyya Muslim sect in particular for persecution, as part of a quid pro quo with extremist religious interests that had now become included within the government. A new law was passed in January 2004 that banned the sect's religious publications. The deterioration of law and order in the country had become a key issue for politicians and citizens alike. There was a major recruitment of new police officers, and a new paramilitary initiative known as "Operation Clean Heart" was initiated in October 2002, drawing on army and Bangladesh Rifles (BDR) personnel, the country's paramilitary border guards, in a violent anticrime drive. It met with widespread criticism from local and international human-rights groups, and more than forty people had reportedly died in police custody or had been shot while being arrested by the time the operation ended in 2003.

The human-rights situation has continued to deteriorate. In 2004, an elite paramilitary unit known as the Rapid Action Battalion (RAB) was set up within the police force with the involvement of military service personnel. RAB had the stated aim of fighting crime and terrorism. The unit quickly became the subject of condemnation from human-rights groups, and by the end of the decade even RAB had admitted that 622 people had been killed in "crossfire," a phrase that was usually used as a euphemism for extrajudicial killing. In December 2010, Wikileaks published evidence that suggested that the British government had been involved with aspects of RAB's training (Karim and Cobain 2010).

### The Military-backed Caretaker Government (2007–2008)

On January 11, 2007, after the intervention of the army, a state of emergency was imposed on a country that had reached what Joseph Devine (2008) described as "the brink of social and political collapse." The confrontational and dysfunctional party politics, which had characterised Bangladesh since the Ershad period, finally ground to a halt. As with many such events, there was considerable speculation about motivations and of possible outside donor involvement in what became known as Bangladesh's "1/11." Yet the intervention was to the evident satisfaction of many ordinary people whose everyday needs as citizens had long been ignored, or worse still, actively blighted, by the realities of power and politics at national and local levels.

The provisional military-backed caretaker government that was put in place brought growing levels of street violence to an end, raised hopes that corruption and instability would be tackled and attracted support – or at least a quiet compliance – from diplomats and donors. The situation was initially greeted with a cautious measure of enthusiasm across the national and international communities. The new government activated the Anti-Corruption Commission (ACC) that had been established in 2004 but had remained dormant, and the ACC began to prosecute a number of high-profile politicians and civil servants. By May, the press was reporting immediate economic benefits to the country, such as a study that found that Chittagong Port had increased its traffic by 30 percent since the imposition of the state of emergency earlier in January, and that the cost of doing business in Chittagong had fallen by 40 percent.

But soon concerns about human rights and democracy began to take hold. The provisional government banned political-party activities and restricted freedom of association under its Emergency Power Rules. Economic hardship was also growing. There was extensive damage caused by two floods, a major cyclone and a crisis prompted by a massive increase in food prices, all of which contributed to widespread unease. In April 2008, there were riots in Dhaka as urban households reacted to a one-third increase in the retail price of rice. Yet with the caretaker government in place, some local areas reported that there was a marked reduction of political and criminal interference in issues of local governance, such as the allocation of relief resources such as food-for-work and test relief, and in the tendering process for market licenses and local construction projects (Lewis and Hossain 2008).

## The Second Hasina Awami League Government (2009)

The election originally scheduled for January 2007 was eventually held on December 29, 2008. The result was a landslide election victory for the AL, which gained 230 out of the 300 seats. This majority meant that it was able to govern without the support of the fourteen-part alliance that it led into the election campaign, and the BNP held only thirty seats. Some observers argued that the AL's victory in part reflected its strategy of seeking to engage the large proportion of younger voters. Its campaign manifesto included the slogan of creating a "digital Bangladesh" by 2021, as a mechanism for improving the country's governance and institutions.

The government has moved forward on several fronts. In the domestic arena, it has begun prosecuting several senior figures in the JI accused of war crimes in 1971 and pursued corruption cases against Khaleda Zia and her son Arafat Rahman. It also began to discuss the idea of reviving the secular constitution of 1972, which would negate Zia's later amendment that allowed religion-based political parties to participate in domestic politics. At the same time, the government has been more open with the public than the previous BNP government about the existence and activities of several small terrorist groups in the country, and it has utilised the army and police more proactively in order to maintain control of the internal security situation. Increasing inflation, rising food prices and shortages in the country's creaking power supply remain pressing domestic challenges. Although the first few years of the second AL government were relatively stable and free of the confrontational *hartal* politics that characterised previous regimes, the BNP soon responded to what it saw as an attack on its political leadership with a renewal of street-based protest and capitalised strongly on the widespread hardship and subsequent protests by garment workers that occurred during the second half of 2010.

## Understanding the State, Politics and "Illiberal Democracy"

### Nation Building and the State

For Jahan (1972: 3), Pakistan's central problem was its failure of "national integration," defined as the "creation of a national political system which supersedes or incorporates all the regional subsystems." She argued this posed a twofold challenge to a postcolonial developing country in which a national ideology and accompanying institutions had to be created, and different groups needed to be integrated into a new national system. Contrasting the process of "nation-building" with that of "state-building," Jahan argued that, unlike in many developed countries where nation has followed state, countries such as Bangladesh have been faced with the complex challenge of undertaking both these tasks simultaneously. The ruling elite in this situation tend to concentrate only on ensuring the state, which then leads to a fundamental neglect of nation-building activities such as maintaining law and order, creating efficient administrative capacity and guiding the economy in favour of the predominant need to concentrate authority. In Pakistan and in the new state of Bangladesh, these two tasks started to contradict each other quickly.

In common with many postcolonial contexts, the key role of "gatekeeper" that had been a central characteristic of the colonial state had been preserved after partition and was once more quickly reproduced under the new conditions of Bangladesh's liberation. As Cooper (2002) has argued in relation to Africa, the experiences of many leaders of anticolonial liberation struggles had made many of them very aware of the vulnerability of state power once achieved, and they came to the conclusion that a continuation of a state gatekeeping strategy was the best way to maintain a grip on power. Lacking the coercive power necessary to underpin and back up this authority, many instead resorted to the use of patronage as the means to hold onto power, creating new and fundamentally weak states that had inherited and reproduced aspects of the problems of late colonial states. In postliberation Bangladesh, a comparable pattern emerged, with the emergence of a strong patronage politics as the dominant form of political practice.

Hamza Alavi (1972) also identified the emergence of a "military-bureaucratic oligarchy" as a defining characteristic of the postcolonial state. The state mediates through patronage between the interests of three competing classes: the landed classes, indigenous bourgeoisie and metropolitan neocolonialist bourgeoisie. In this way, the state's role is relatively autonomous and does not represent the interest of any one of these classes, making it possible for the military and bureaucracy to control the state through its position at the top of the hierarchy. The realignment of these interests in Bangladesh, which had been disrupted by the rupture with West Pakistan, had by the mid-1970s created a military-bureaucratic state that now moved to the centre of the country's politics.

The military has remained an important political actor, though its role has evolved and changed in recent decades. It remains largely organised along the lines introduced by the British into army, air force and navy. Although some equipment was inherited from the Pakistan army after 1971, much of the equipment now in use has been supplied by China, with some aircraft acquired from the United States during the 1990s and eight fighter jets ordered from Russia in 2002. There are now more than one hundred thousand army personnel organised into seven divisions. The army provided 2,300 troops to take part in the first Gulf War in 1991, and since then has become a leading participant in UN peacekeeping activities in places such as East Timor, Kosovo and Sudan. By 2005, a total of 9,529 troops, military observers and police were deployed within peacekeeping operations in eleven countries, and its missions had generated more than $450 million in foreign exchange (GoB 2006).

This has proved a wise political strategy because it has provided the country with a useful source of foreign currency. In particular, it has given the army a prestigious international profile that has perhaps made it less interested in domestic political involvement. This is one reason why successive governments have been able to retain the support of the army during nearly two decades of democratic rule. However, this relative stability was disturbed by two recent events. The first was the military-backed caretaker government that took power in January 2007, suggesting that there was still a military threat to civilian domestic politics. The other was the violent mutiny by sections of the BDR in February 2009, which led to the deaths of more than seventy army officers and civilians. The BDR has its origins in the Eastern Frontier Rifles established in the late nineteenth century by the British and is administered by, but not part of, the army. Although the origins of this tragedy remain unclear, it is believed that some BDR were reacting against their exclusion by their army officer superiors from the proceeds from smuggling in Bangladesh's border areas.

### Patronage Politics

As outlined in Chapter 2, patron-client relations have long played a central role in political and economic life, with rural social structure characterised by subtle distinctions of status and rank based on wealth, land, education and power. Patron-client relations are a cornerstone of society in Bengal, combining political, economic and religious elements of social organisation. By the 1970s, the older nineteenth-century descent-based distinctions between *ashraf* and *ajlaf* were perhaps now less important than other forms of social status. Instead, households of all types as basic social units needed to negotiate reciprocal exchanges and dependencies inside and outside the family "in which people of higher rank are accorded the right to extract labour, services, and respect from people of lower rank" in return for support from patrons (Kochanek 1993: 44). This creates a hierarchical web of dyadic relationships and mutual obligations, as Eirik Jansen (1987) has outlined, with households and individuals competitively seeking to elaborate a set of constantly shifting networks. The concept of *daya* (grace or blessing) underpins social relationships within the family and outside it, creating among people a sense of moral entitlement to subsistence and respect from other better-placed individuals.

Society is, therefore, structured around a complex network of interpersonal patron-client relationships, which are reinforced by economic components, such as credit and employment opportunities, and political components such as protection. This makes it more difficult for people to develop horizontal relationships or build corporate units based on politics, kinship or locality, which has implications for the operation and stability of public institutions and for the opportunities for collective action. Instead, it is argued that such conditions favour "a system of individual traditional patrimonial leadership based on charisma, patronage and corruption," and that as a consequence there is a relatively low level of trust in society (Kochanek 1993: 44).

Two sets of factors have combined in order to ensure a chronic and persistent problem of instability at the heart of Bangladesh's political institutions: class interests and patron-client networks (Khan 2000). These are intertwined in the competing efforts of dominant groups to claim and control resources, forming a network of linkages and relationships in the shape of a pyramidal structure. Political parties form the top of this "pyramid," and their efforts to lead and organise a range of other groups and classes through a complex series of patron-client networks forms the base, with its roots stretching out to penetrate all levels and sectors of society. In this system, coalitions are built around a broad factional base of clients, but once mobilised these inevitably disintegrate when it becomes clear that not all groups can be adequately rewarded. For example, although Mujib's election victory in 1969 had been a significant achievement, his AL Party quickly began to fall apart once it had been installed in government after the Independence War, as factions struggled over limited rewards.

Bangladesh's political parties are, therefore, highly factional and regularly split into groups led by dominant charismatic individuals. Each group is made up of other smaller factional coalitions, cutting across classes and social groups, as Mushtaq Khan (2000: 17) outlines,

These basic patron-client factions are ubiquitous and range from neighbourhood groups led by petty mafia bosses known in Bangladesh as *mastans* to village factions led by somewhat more respectable *matabbars, dalals* and *upazila* chairmen.... Bargaining power depends on the number of people who can be occasionally mobilized by the faction for elections but more generally for maintaining local level enforcement networks, organizing civil protests, demonstrations, enforcing general strikes, and other forms of activity which aim to inflict costs on those who refused to make deals or offer payoffs to that faction.

Much political activity is organised and led by members of the "intermediate classes," such as rich farmers, educated middle classes, urban petty-bourgeoisie and urban professionals, who play the role of political entrepreneurs. These are groups whose political roles are highly factionalised and so never achieve the momentum of the class-based action of landlords or industrial capitalists in other areas of the subcontinent. It is the pragmatic nature of these alliances, which are often based on changing loyalties rather than longstanding allegiances, particularly lower down the "pyramid," which had made the emergence of long-term solidaristic grassroots organisations or interest groups, such as poor people's rural social movements, relatively rare in contemporary Bangladesh, despite the rhetoric of some NGOs. Although forms of collective action do take place, these are usually centred on narrower factional aims. As Sobhan (2004) argues, the dominant forms of collective action are those used by members of the bureaucracy against attempts by the authorities to curb their rent-seeking behaviour.

As a result, the historical transition to capitalism in Bangladesh remains a partial one. Unlike in other parts of the subcontinent, there was no real development of industrial capitalism in East Bengal during the colonial period. Later as East Pakistan, a process of internal exploitation by using exchange-rate manipulation in which West Pakistan benefitted from the East's raw jute ensured that this low level of industrialisation continued. At the same time, there was the evolution of a small class of commercial peasant farmers from the early twentieth century onwards, and this took place alongside the growth of the administrative sector and the professions in Bengal. The outcome was a form of politics in which a key aim was for this group and its political leaders to gain control over government jobs and resources (Khan 2000). For upwardly mobile rural households, investment in state patronage of this kind was usually a more attractive prospect than that of consolidating agricultural landholdings, particularly in view of the high levels of land fragmentation created by Muslim inheritance laws and rapid population growth. The processes of primitive accumulation that have taken place in Bangladesh during the second half of the twentieth century have not, therefore, led to the growth of a strong capitalist sector, but have instead generated resources that are transferred by the state to these competing political factions. For example, money received from international donors was regularly loaned to businesses by the state-owned bank sector, with little expectation of either repayment or investment in productive business activities.

The people at the bottom of the pyramid have little interest in the symbols of political ideology deployed by the competing parties, such as nationalism and religion, and instead are engaged in a battle of survival in which they make rational calculations about material outcomes. Part of this calculation, Mushtaq Khan (2000: 37) argues, is the recognition that the meagre gains to be made from factional allegiance and patron loyalty (such as a retainer payment or physical protection) are still likely to outweigh those that might arise from class-based political action. At the same time, the logic of factionalism helps to explain why political alliances tend to fall apart once they achieve power. A "paradox of success" is created in which an opposition faction that manages to secure power then finds that it has insufficient resources to distribute to each of its faction leader supporters to keep them "on board."

Aid resources aimed at promoting a liberal pluralist model of development therefore tend to achieve very little in cases in which the state is dominated by patron-client institutional systems, as E. A. Brett (2009: 216) argues with his concept of "blocked development." Such states, almost by definition, lack preconditions in the form of working systems of rules that can allow the successful promotion of individual freedoms and rights through the introduction of democratic and civil-service reforms, the strengthening of private property rights and regulatory regimes or the construction of a viable propoor civil society. Instead, where such reforms are attempted, they will be likely to fall foul of endemic corruption, bureaucratic clientelism, exploitative business practices, mismanagement of elections and sectarianism, all of which serve to generate perverse incentives that perpetuate governance problems. Such incentives make it more likely that the reforms are unsuccessful, or even that they make things worse. They may produce elections that fuel violence and political breakdown, market liberalisation that contributes to more unemployment and exclusion, privatisation that transfers assets to cronies and fails poor people in need of proper services and participation processes that simply increase levels of inequality and inefficiency.

### State and Identity

As in the case of any country, people hold multiple identities in Bangladesh that are based on issues such as nation, culture, language, religion, gender and class. However, it has become necessary in the case of Bangladesh to pay close attention to distinctive areas of complexity among citizens within a state that is historically defined by a mix of Bengali culture and Muslim religion. In this sense, despite the relatively high level of homogeneity within Bangladeshi society in terms of culture and language, the legitimacy of the state forty years after independence is still bound up with the continuing search for a Bengali identity that is distinct from India and a Muslim identity separate from that of Pakistan. As a result, political identities in Bangladesh can appear ambiguous and unclear. For example, a distinction is conventionally made between two dominant rival nationalist identities in Bangladesh. For the Bengali nationalism associated with the AL, an emphasis is conventionally placed on the idea of Bengali-ness, with its signifiers of language, literature and landscape, yet there is no suggestion that it would be a good idea for Bangladesh to reunite with West Bengal. For the Bangladeshi nationalism associated with the BNP, the emphasis is on the distinctiveness of East Bengali Muslim culture.

Although there are many people for whom such ideologies are deeply held and strongly felt, and there are regular debates in public space about identity issues and emphases, Mushtaq Khan (2000: 16) argues convincingly that in contemporary Bangladesh such questions should be primarily understood as matters of expediency rather than as straightforward identity or ideology issues. Contemporary political debates around the politics of nationalism rarely carry real implications for national sovereignty or policy but are instead driven by the logic of trying to define one particular version of "nationalist camp" in opposition to another that is currently in power. Tensions around secularism or nationalism are essentially superficial and instead conceal a deeper political process in which coalition of interests compete for resources in the process of what Marx termed "primitive accumulation." This is the transfer of resources from precapitalist sources into new capitalist forms that make possible capitalist enterprises, a transfer that occurs through a variety of processes including taxation, unequal exchange, colonial plunder or land enclosure.

Nor are the distinctions very clear-cut. Even during the 1970s, Bengali nationalists intervened in support of Muslim sensibilities, such as Mujib's release in 1973 of 33,000 alleged war criminals who had associations or sympathies with Islamist politics, and they have continued to do so. Rather than being based on fundamental questions of religion, culture or sovereignty, such identities seem to be deployed on a flexible basis and are loose at best. Although subsequent attempts by Ziaur Rahman and H. M. Ershad to use Islam as a means of stabilising their governments had limited political success, it can be argued that these efforts did nevertheless better reflect Bangladesh's wider society and culture than Mujib's relatively half-hearted attempt to build elements of a secular identity in the years that followed 1971.

### Weak State, Strong Society?

Following the work of Joel Migdal (1988), Sarah White (1999) identified Bangladesh as a "weak state" within a "strong society," in which the state is simply unable to resist the continual claims made upon it by a wide range of social groups. For example, successive governments' repeated efforts at decentralisation and reorganisation of local administrative units, or their relatively ineffective attempts to prohibit dowry or redistribute *khas* land to the poor, have made little impact on a society that is organised around powerful interests. These interest groups tend to "capture" any attempts to influence or challenge the prevailing power structure, however tentative such efforts may be. These interests that act effectively upon the state reflect a dynamic and strong society, which can become organised into acts of political mobilisation (such as *hartal* or *gherao*), corruption or perhaps more benignly in forms of social entrepreneurship that are sometimes apparent within the extensive NGO community (Lewis 2004). At the same time, the state remains a source of "considerable bureaucratic power, underpinned by a latent military threat" (Davis and McGregor 2000: 56). McGregor's notion of the "patron state" is based on the idea that the state serves as the main delivery agent for development resources and acts as "the patron of last resort" at the microlevel.

In seeking to build patronage relationships, the result is that there are only weak systems of citizen accountability, low-quality social-welfare services, a lack of an independent judiciary and a failure to mobilise local resources in the form of taxation. Today, the government's collection rate for direct taxes remains one of the lowest in the world. The Bangladesh state can therefore be characterised variously as both "strong" and "weak" depending on whether this is assessed according to its formal presence and power, or according to the quality of the services it provides to its citizens. Since 1971, the state has also become more embedded within the dominant global ideologies of neoliberalism. As a result of its patronage relationships and the outside ideology of structural adjustment that has been propagated by the aid industry, the state has tended to shed elements of its responsibility for service provision and citizen accountability by the "franchising out" of service-delivery roles to NGOs and the private sector. These now work within a model that caters to citizens as "consumers" with the result that privatisation in Bangladesh may be leading further towards a "state without citizens" (Wood 1997).

## The "Everyday State"

The formal structures of the state conceal a less formal reality that is experienced by most ordinary people. Barbara Harriss-White (2003) emphasises the existence in India of a "shadow state" of informal actors – advisers, brokers, criminals, contractors and political activists – who operate informally in order to ensure that the activities of the state as far as possible serves the interests of key sections of its employees. In this environment, the bulk of the poor are left vulnerable within an informal world of governmentality in which they must depend on brokers to reduce their vulnerability and try to survive. For example, patients visiting a government clinic in Bangladesh, although nominally free, must pay intermediaries to help them access medical professionals, and a whole range of informal costs are incurred at every stage of the process of accessing a service (Sida 2010).

Yet the state helps to structure the lives of ordinary people in ways that are both positive and negative. As Stuart Corbridge and colleagues (2005: 8) highlight in their work in relation to India, the idea of the state remains important even when it is seen to regularly "fail" to meet the needs of many of its poorest and not so poor citizens. For example, government jobs remain valuable assets, and it is desirable to get someone from a poor family into public service because it will provide job security, welfare benefits and perhaps inside access to economic opportunities through licenses or ration cards. Such engagements also form the ways in which citizenship rights are enacted, very often revealing the inequalities and discrimination that exist among difference groups and the legitimacy with which the state is viewed:

A low-caste man who is treated with respect by a teacher or a Block Development Officer might come to see the state in a very different way than an *adivasi* woman who is kept waiting for hours to see *sarkar*, who sees gangs of males push in front of her in what passes for a queue, and who is made to touch the feet of the official she finally meets (perhaps with the help of a *dalaal*, or local broker) at the end of rough or uncivil language.

One important issue that is often underplayed in the donor accounts of Bangladesh is the everyday insecurity that ordinary people experience as they try to go about their daily lives, characterised by Hossain Rahman (2009) by the term *hoirani*, which refers to small-scale harassment and the more serious forms of abuse by those with power. Nevertheless, the author argues that such new forms of governmentality still open up potentially important new "spaces of citizenship" (5), partly by using the "good governance" agenda that is imposed by government and donors from above and partly by using popular mobilisations that may take place from below. These issues are explored in more detail in Chapter 5.

### The Politics of State Governance

The important role played by patron-client relations contributes to a highly particularistic form of policy making, in which policy goals easily become captured by individuals. The result is that broad policies often become subject to special exemptions or restrictions, or are selectively enforced, for example, when public-sector loans are treated as grants. As a result, policy making is characterised by uncertainty and lack of transparency and is a situation in which goals are rarely turned into action. Although the government publicly outlines its policies as aiming to benefit everyone, the reality is that projects tend to be deliberately chosen to advance the interests of influential individuals with the result that priorities become distorted and resources are wasted (Kochanek 1993: 342).

This means that both sides of the ideological reform debates – those arguing for more liberalisation and those seeking to resist the private-sector expansion in favour of protecting the public sector – are frequently frustrated by the policy process. For Kochanek (1993: 343), whose arguments place him in the former camp, policy frameworks encouraging liberalisation of domestic and foreign private investment rules have remained necessarily vague and easily open to abuse. Although official policy has opened things up on paper, in practice many of the bureaucratic conditions remain unchanged. He suggests that they continued to embody an antiforeign, proregulation and propublic sector ideology, and that the system retains a "procedural complexity" that produces delay, unaccountability and lack of responsibility.

Although Bangladesh remains a country characterised by continuing mass poverty, the focus of development efforts since the 1990s has shifted away from economic growth towards what is seen as the persistent problem of *governance*, the term that has come to be used by development donors and used more widely to refer to politics, policy and citizenship issues. Two interrelated problems are normally identified here. The first is the problem of partisan politics in which the political system is seen as having become unaccountable, making possible the self-interested use of state power by political parties. The second is the problem of patronage and corruption, which makes it possible for political parties to build rent-seeking alliances with key actors, including the military, business, professional interest groups and the bureaucracy, in order to gain control over public resources. Such is the culture of distrust that competing political parties adopt an "all or nothing" approach in a zero-sum game, in which the successful party gains monopoly control and the losing party sees no choice other than to resort to noncooperation (BRAC 2009).

By the start of the new millennium, the complex and many-sided issue of "corruption" had become a key concern in relation to Bangladesh. The international anticorruption watchdog TI reported in 2002 that corruption among senior government officials had contributed to a loss in economic activity equivalent to close to 4 percent of the GDP in 2001. The issue of corruption was nothing new because there had been widespread concerns voiced by citizens and donors back in the Ershad era and before. As this chapter has argued, the problem has remained part of the historical structural legacy of state formation, with roots back to the East India Company and with a civil service that played a key role in sustaining authoritarian rule during the 1970s and 1980s, and that has remained highly politicised and factionally divided.

## Conclusion: The Patron State

Bangladesh was born out of two significant moments of postcolonial change and rupture during the middle of the twentieth century. The first was the transformation in 1947 of the so-called two nation theory, which had advocated separate Muslim and Hindu homelands in the subcontinent, into a political fact with the creation of Pakistan. This followed an increasing polarisation of Muslim and Hindu politics that had not been the case earlier in the century in Bengal. The second was the subsequent shift of the Bengali Muslim middle classes away from what was termed "communalist" affiliation, which was based on religious difference, towards a secular nationalist identity. Bangladesh broke away from Pakistan, negating the brief heyday of two nation thinking. At the same time, the long history of the exploitation of East Bengal's economy lent the new nation a weak and fragile economic base upon which to build. Coupled with the colonial process of state formation, it is not surprising that Bangladesh remains a country in which the state lacks completeness, political disputes over national identity continue and the viability of the ruling class is questioned.

Under such conditions, the institution of patronage rapidly consolidated itself as a dominant form of political practice within the state, severely hindering the development of an independent professional bureaucracy with the capacity to devise and implement policy. Within patron-client networks, loyalty to the ruling party trumps any real investment in state activity other than its use to further the interests of the party in power, thus contributing to the slowness of capitalist development and to continuing political instability. The result is that Bangladesh has moved during the two decades since democracy was established in 1990 from being a "minimalist democracy" with regular elections, peaceful transfers of government power, a guarantee of basic freedoms and civilian control over institutions and policy to become an "illiberal democracy" (BRAC 2009: xv). Political and legal institutions are subject to partisan politics, and state power is misused for personal and political gain. Politics has become a competition to control the state in order to serve partisan interests within a "winner-takes-all" system. The accountability mechanisms required to provide systemic checks and balances in the system usually fail to operate, so that confrontation becomes seen as a more effective political strategy than negotiation. Problems of weak law and order enforcement, regular defaulting on loans, a deterioration in the quality of administration, the politicisation of the education system and pervasive corruption were all once seen simply as regulatory issues. Today, as Sobhan (2004: 4101) argues, this has now "hardened" into a severe structural problem "embedded in the social and political forces which govern the distribution of power and influence."

5

# Nongovernmental Actors and Civil Society

State building in Bangladesh remains a work in progress, leaving a consider-able amount of institutional space for a wide range of nonstate actors. These range from traditional local-level institutions to more recently established forms of national and international organisation. As we saw in Chapter 4, there is a long history of nongovernmental groups in Bengal, from profes-sional associations to missionary groups, but Bangladesh has more recently become well-known internationally for its extensive "development NGO" sector, in which two Bangladeshi organisations in particular – Grameen Bank and BRAC – have gained international reputations. In contrast to many other developing countries, where international agencies tend to rep-resent the most visible forms of the nongovernmental actor, Bangladesh has an unusually large number of homegrown development NGOs. Although foreign organisations have played important roles in the establishment of many of these local organisations, today the Bangladesh NGO sector dis-plays a strongly indigenous character and can be seen as a local formation of globally determined influences. It is also quite diverse, ranging from many local, small and voluntaristic groups to large-scale organisations that are now some of the world's best-known development NGOs, managing multi-million dollar budgets and occupying high-rise offices. A few of these larger NGOs have become comparable in size and influence to some government departments, bringing fears in some quarters of the creation of a "parallel state."

Apart from the general agreement among most observers that Bangladesh's NGO sector is relatively large, accurate and up-to-date facts and figures are surprisingly hard to come by. One source estimated that there were close to twenty-two thousand NGOs by the turn of the millen-nium (DFID 2000). By 2004, the Social Welfare Ministry had 54,536 NGOs registered and the NGO Affairs Bureau had 1,925. In 2005, a World Bank study cited official statistics stating that there were 206,000 "not-for-profit" organisations in the country and that the NGO sector contributes 6 to 8 percent of Bangladesh's GDP annually (Irish and Simon 2005). The wide range of figures illustrates an important difficulty facing any discussion of NGOs because the label lacks precision and is highly subjective. The definition of what constitutes an NGO is far from clear – for example, although some organisations are formal, many others are not, and although any organisation receiving foreign funds must be registered, there are many NGOs that are locally resourced and therefore do not feature in official statistics.

Some developmentalists have eulogised organisations such as BRAC and Grameen Bank for their grassroots-level efforts to reduce poverty, while critics have suggested that the parallel efforts of the NGOs simply reflects, and contributes further to, the weakness of the state's ability to serve its citizens. Between 20 and 35 percent of the country's population is believed to receive some services, usually credit, health or education, from an NGO (World Bank 2006b). For example, Wood (1997) raised concerns that the extensive roles of NGOs in the delivery of basic services undermine the accountability link that should exist between state and citizen. It constitutes a form of privatisation in which the government delegates its responsibilities out to nonstate actors that have unclear lines of accountability to service users and may often also be mainly foreign funded – an arrangement that he has termed the "franchise state."

Threaded through the dominant narrative of the NGO sector is the idea of a "civil society," which was globally revived during the late 1980s and early 1990s. This old political science concept, which was in reality more of a bundle of often quite different concepts, had been reinvigorated and given new contemporary meaning by intellectuals and citizen activists fighting totalitarian governments in parts of Latin America and in Eastern Europe. It was natural for these ideas to also make their way into the development discourse, finding fertile ground among both the privatising imperatives of neoliberal development policy and in particular as a component of the new emerging discourse of "good governance" and among those activists who argued for the counterhegemonic struggle of grassroots groups and social movements for human rights and land reform. The idea of civil society became one of the main lenses through which the NGO sector in Bangladesh and forms of wider citizen action were viewed, leading to an increased self-awareness among nonstate actors about their roles, as well as to political controversies about the relevance and appropriateness of applying the concept of civil society to a country such as Bangladesh.

## Nonstate Actors in Historical Perspective: Religion, Charity and Resistance

Nonstate actors were important to processes of state formation during pre-colonial and colonial periods in East Bengal. During the Mughal period, the ruling class of *ashraf* Muslims had operated at a distance from wider society, collected revenue and maintained social stability through the subordinate authority of religious leaders such as *mullahs* and *pirs*. These interacted through informal personalised intermediaries with traditional local community groups organised around kin-based institutions (Fernando 2011). As Richard Eaton (1993) has shown, territory was provided to *pirs* by the Mughal state as part of the effort to mobilise the labour effort to clear jungle areas and transform them into land for rice cultivation. The idea of *samaj*, a newly created local community based around the construction of a shrine, helped to create social order among these state-sponsored colonists as they reclaimed and settled these new agricultural lands across the eastern delta. Such land was vested in religious charities before gradually passing into the ownership of a new landed elite. In the latter part of the eighteenth century, local-level political resistance to the revenue-collecting authorities by poor peasants was often organised around *fakirs* (as we saw in Chapter 3). Later, peasant uprisings against zamindars in the mid-nineteenth century were motivated by a combination of class consciousness and religious ideology, as Jude Fernando (2011) argues, and contributed to the reputation of Bengal as the location of rebellious groups and movements.

Various forms of voluntary action have long been a documented aspect in East Bengal, intertwined with traditions of religious charity, philanthropy and self-help. Such action is founded on the basic local village-level institutions that play a central role in daily life, such as *gusti* and *samaj*, which were briefly outlined in Chapter 2. Elders known as *matbars* had traditionally attempted to manage local factions and resolve disputes through the *shalish* village-level council and build public reputations through their participation in mosque and temple committees, such as through the Islamic charitable duty of *zakat*, the payment of one-fortieth of one's income to the poor (Lewis and Hossain 2008). Among Hindus, it has long been customary to provide food to *sadhus* and *faqirs* (Zaidi 1970). During the nineteenth century, Christian missionary work brought additional forms of voluntarist activity, particularly in the education and health sectors, and prefigured some of the "community development" approaches used by contemporary NGOs (Fernando 2011).

Philanthropic activity, often taking inspiration from religious principles, has long been undertaken by better-off members of the community, such as organising schools or mosques, or providing relief for the victims of natural disasters. Such good works may be closely linked with local political processes. Revisiting the Comilla village in 2000 where I had undertaken my Ph.D. research during the mid-1980s, I found many such examples. A local doctor who had left the village many years ago for a successful career in Dhaka, and who had earlier funded the village *madrasa* school, had recently provided funds for an orphanage to be built in the village. Another successful villager, who had become a chief of police in Dhaka, had established a new secondary school in his name and secured municipal funds for its running costs through his relationship with local political leaders in the nearby town. Between the late 1980s and 2000, these efforts had helped to bring the village under the local municipality and connect it with new services, such as a gas supply.

Self-help village-level organisations such as the Palli Mangal Samitis (Village Welfare Societies) were to be found in many districts of Bengal from the 1930s onwards, often encouraged by local colonial administrators in a combination of local good works and in the building of local patronage relationships. During the Pakistan period, a farmer cooperative system had been introduced by charismatic civil servant A. H. Khan whose Comilla cooperative model was later scaled up by the government as a national-level programme under the Ministry of Rural Development and Cooperatives (Lewis 1993). Today, as Richard Holloway (1998: 35) reminds us, associational life is a vital part of the social lives of many people in Bangladesh, who may be members of the Khet Majur Samity (Landless Labourers Association), the national Mohila Parishad (Women's Council) or the Madrasa Teachers Association.

The role of nonstate actors is also highly visible within the history of political struggle between state and society. Both before and after liberation, organised groups of students, lawyers, journalists and cultural activists had constituted a civic force that had helped to build the nationalist vision of a democratic, secular Bangladesh (Hashemi and Hasan 1999: 130). In the 1950s, organised resistance in the cultural sphere in the form of the language movement gradually took on more explicitly economic and political dimensions as a nationalist civil society, rooted in the democratic struggle for autonomy and eventually independence (Rahman 1999). However, after 1971 many of these organisations became absorbed into the state apparatus, gradually narrowing into a more tightly organised political movement under the AL Party, as Mujib used the party organisation to try to "establish state control over society" (Jalal 1995: 90). By 1975, Mujib had secured the "suspension or destruction of rival trade unions, student and youth fronts" and gained control of "pressure groups and potentially alternative points of organised political power" (Jahangir 1986: 44).

The shift towards a militarised authoritarian regime under General Ziaur Rahman generated new forms of popular resistance and opposition, contributing to the emergence of new organisations in the form of pressure groups and NGO umbrella organisations concerned with issues such as civil rights, gender and democracy. The struggles against military rule at the domestic level gradually broadened to include a wide range of secular and religious organisations and viewpoints, including development NGOs funded by foreign donors (Rahman 1999). As the 1980s wore on, these new forms of nonstate actor steadily increased in size and scope, bound by the earlier secular nationalist traditions of Bangladesh's emergence but also increasingly merged with various forms of developmentalist ideology, assisted by the new interest in civil society. The women's movement, for example, had been historically part of the secular nationalist struggle but went on to embrace aspects of both the developmentalist human-rights discourse and opposition to the various forces of Islamisation (Chowdhury 2009). Today, as Sen (2011: 44) points out, progress in the social sphere in Bangladesh such as increased young female literacy rates (now higher than among young males) can be linked to the increasing role that liberated Bangladeshi women are playing in society.

## The Modern Nongovernmental Organisation Sector

### Origins

The combination of the massive postconflict reconstruction effort in 1971 and the devastating cyclone that soon followed created a huge local and international relief effort. This was where the seeds of the modern NGO sector began to take root. Local traditions of voluntary action were deepened and transformed by the experience of resistance, war and natural disaster. The massive international relief effort that followed Bangladesh's Liberation War brought local activists a familiarity with the international "aid industry" and facilitated their access to funds and outside ideas. Continuing mass poverty during the 1970s and 1980s generated widespread disillusionment with government-based rural development work, which consisted of top-down attempts to build formal village cooperatives, a reliance on trickle-down economics for the poor and the constant reorganisation of local government by military regimes that sought to consolidate power by building clientelistic linkages with local rural elites. Relief and development NGOs were, therefore, established by various sections of the middle classes – by sincere members of the reformist elite, former student radicals alienated or restricted by formal politics and members of the new emerging middle class seeking to build socially useful careers in social work or in the professionalising worlds of development aid.

At the same time, despite high levels of local initiative in responding to these problems, Bangladesh was becoming an ever-larger recipient of international development assistance. Many NGOs were initially started up with the help of international development agencies but rapidly took on a distinctive local Bangladeshi identity. NGOs of all kinds quickly became involved in emergency relief work and service delivery across many sectors, from agricultural extension and income generation for the landless, to a range of health and education services. They began to pioneer new forms of rural community organising and an approach to small-scale lending to the poor that became known as "microcredit." Although NGOs had originally begun working in rural areas, by the 1990s many had expanded their programmes into urban contexts. Not all these organisations balanced private action with public spiritedness in equal measure. There were also many NGOs that were started by less scrupulous individuals who saw relatively easy opportunities for the accumulation of foreign funding.

Many NGOs emerged from village self-help societies that had evolved into more formalised organisations on contact with external aid resources and advice. Other NGOs were established by charismatic founder-leaders, individuals who are these days sometimes termed *social entrepreneurs*. For example, F. H. Abed, founder of BRAC was a Shell Oil executive working in the United Kingdom who returned to join the relief effort after liberation. BRAC began as a humanitarian relief organisation in 1972 and aimed to provide assistance to alleviate suffering in the new country. By the 1990s, it had evolved into a multifaceted development agency, undertaking everything from credit and empowerment to health and education work (Lovell 1992). Although it remains inspired by earlier 1970s empowerment approaches, BRAC has gone on to combine a strong social business-management approach to its development work and carefully avoided the political pitfalls that have befallen some of its peers through a continued emphasis on organised growth, innovation and professionalism (Smillie 2009). BRAC, like many NGOs, has run into several areas of controversy, both with the religious right over its highly visible rural female empowerment programmes and with the business sector for its rapidly expanding social business activities (including department stores, a bank and a university that generate income that has helped to make the NGO more or less financially self-sufficient), but it has continually managed to learn and adapt. It has now emerged as one of the world's largest and most successful development NGOs and has gone on to internationalise its activities, initially working in Afghanistan and then later expanding into several sub-Saharan African countries.

Another well-known organisation, Grameen Bank, had roots in work by Chittagong University economics professor Muhammad Yunus, who was experimenting with finding new solutions to local problems of poverty. He developed an innovative approach to microcredit that aimed to overcome the severe problems poor rural people faced in trying to borrow money, including lack of access to formal banks and vulnerability to exploitation by informal moneylenders. The idea emerged from an academic action research project that he first undertook locally in the Chittagong area with colleagues and students. The action research project identified peoples' lack of access to small amounts of capital as a critical factor that perpetuated local poverty. Yunus went on to develop a form of group-based microloans to rural women that was based on collective solidarity instead of formal collateral.

Yunus went on to turn the initial project into the Grameen Bank in 1983. In this model of what was to become the classic microcredit system, means-tested poor rural people were asked to join five-person weekly meeting groups, were given individual loans and agreed to help each other if anyone in the group encountered financial difficulty. The idea was that loans could be repaid weekly throughout the year in small amounts from the household budget. At the same time, people also paid into personal and group savings accounts. As Grameen's activities expanded around the country, it showed that not only were these small loans used productively but also that they were quickly repaid, and the organisation has maintained a loan recovery rate of close to 97 percent, far higher than that achieved by formal banks in the mainstream credit markets in which defaulting is common. By 2004, there were more than four million borrowers, a massive replication effort of the Grameen approach around the world and, from 2004 on, a new Grameen II approach that offered a more flexible range of credit products that better responded to the problems faced by the most vulnerable whose repayment capacity was less regular. By 2010, Grameen had eight million borrowers and was active in every village (Yunus 2010).

As a result of foreign aid and local activism, a new group of nongovernmental relief and development organisations therefore emerged. In the early days, the NGO community was dominated by international NGOs such as

Oxfam, CARE and the Mennonite Central Committee. These organisations initially ran their own projects, which were mainly concerned with emergency relief and reconstruction, but then later began to move to work with local partner NGOs on longer-term development issues. The formation of new Bangladeshi NGOs through a "capacity-building" partnership between these northern and southern NGOs was a formative factor in the proliferation of new organisations around the country.

Under the military governments that followed Mujib's assassination in 1975, NGOs also became the preferred organisational vehicles for many left-leaning activists, who were interested in undertaking development and community-organising work away from the increasingly restricted and degraded political space of formal politics. For example, Proshika was set up in 1976 as a joint Canadian University Service Overseas/Oxfam project by former student activists on the left, influenced in part by the community-level education and mobilisation ideas of radical Brazilian educator Paolo Freire. Its founders were encouraged by activist funders to move forward with the creation of an indigenous organisation in place of a project, and the NGO grew throughout the 1980s and 1990s, linking its grassroots-empowerment politics with a range of service-delivery activities to its groups across the country (Smillie and Hailey 2001). Proshika's name, an acronym drawn from the Bengali words for training, education and action, evolved into one of the country's largest development NGOs.

Initially, the work of many of the major development NGOs was under-pinned by a critical analysis of existing mainstream approaches to rural development assistance by the government and the donors. For some NGOs, it was also premised on the prevailing 1970s "agrarian structuralist" analyses of rural power relations, which emphasised class differentiation based on landownership, tenancy and rural exploitation (Lewis and Hossain 2008). The best known of these critiques was the BRAC-commissioned research study *The Net: Power Structure in Ten Villages* (BRAC 1983). Its findings showed how the landed elites in each village that controlled the local power structure effectively threw out a "net" in which they were able to capture most of the external resources provided by government, donors or charitable organisations intended for the assistance of poor people. The study emphasised patron-client relationships as key contributory factors in the reproduction of rural poverty. This idea led many NGOs to reject mainstream efforts to provide assistance through, for example, giving subsidised loans to village farmer cooperatives. Khan's Comilla cooperative model, which had been seen as a flagship innovation in the 1960s, was now found to be operating more as a mechanism to distribute government patronage in the form of subsidised agricultural inputs than a spontaneous form of self-organisation by farmers (Khan 1989). This new analysis instead justified the need for a new "targeted" NGO approach that organised and empowered the marginalised landless poor. In addition to awareness building, skills training and basic education, the provision of small loans was seen as a way to challenge their exclusion from the formal banking system and their dependence on exploitative elite moneylending by providing a new alternative source of small loans.

### Diversity and Change

From the 1980s, the mainstream international donor community in Bangladesh began to take a more systematic interest in NGOs as "development" actors, in keeping with a global trend in the development industry at that time that saw NGOs as potential "magic bullets" for overcoming problems of poverty. As a result, more and more aid resources became available for their construction and expansion, from \$120 million in 1991 to \$188 million in 1994–5 (World Bank 1996). By the new millennium, it was estimated that NGOs were receiving about 17 percent of the total international-aid flows that were disbursed to Bangladesh (DFID 2000). Nevertheless, the same study reports that of the 22,000 NGOs in Bangladesh, only 1,250 receive foreign assistance, implying that many of the country's NGOs rely on voluntarism, government funds or philanthropy. Of those organisations that do receive foreign funds, the study found distribution is heavily skewed towards a relatively small number of NGOs. More than 85 percent of all funds were consumed by a group of about ten large Bangladeshi NGOs, including BRAC and the Association for Social Advancement (ASA).

These large NGOs have evolved into multipurpose organisations that combine service delivery work (e.g., health care, education, credit and income generation) with activist activity such as grassroots organising and advocacy, the best known of which is BRAC. Others such as ASA have restricted their work to credit, finding that microcredit had the potential to become a form of sustainable poverty-reduction activity. High levels of repayment rates from borrowers ensured that loans could be recovered and recycled, and an administrative charge could be levied to cover organisations' overheads. Another, admittedly smaller, group of development NGOs, such as Nijera Kori (NK) and Samata, rejected the idea of credit services altogether in favour of a more activist approach that remained true to the Freierean tradition. NK takes a distinctive rights-based approach to development work, working with landless men and women, and it remains critical of other NGOs' credit and service delivery approaches that it argues simply "alleviate" poverty rather than addressing its root causes.

GK, set up by the community activist Dr. Zafrullah Chowdhury, developed a cooperative health approach based on the model of an apex hospital at the centre of a group of local health centres staffed by paramedics, who receive regular visits from the hospital's doctors. By reducing the unit costs of health-care delivery, the model aims to deliver a locally sustainable set of basic health services, supported by affordable health insurance and service charges and subsidised by the organisation's own revenue-generation activities through its pharmaceutical manufacturing facilities. In Chapter 4, we saw how the people's health initiative of GK had attempted to challenge the restrictions on people's access to basic medicines. GK campaigned for an essential drugs policy that would limit the importation of costly branded medical products primarily for use by urban elites and produce a list of widely used medicines that could be produced more cheaply locally. However, this had been resisted by the Bangladesh Medical Association, representing a professional medical establishment with strong ties to the international pharmaceutical industry, which stood to lose financially from any tampering with its links with international companies (Chowdhury 1995).

The mass movement that emerged against the first BNP government during the mid-1990s made it clear that some NGOs, through the umbrella organisation Association of Development Agencies in Bangladesh (ADAB), were also seeking ways to become more proactively involved in national politics. During the 1996 national election, ADAB coordinated a Democracy Awareness Education Programme through which fifteen thousand trainers ran awareness-raising workshops across the whole country, contributing to an impressive voter turnout of 74 percent (Ashman 1997).

Although BRAC remains inspired by earlier 1970s empowerment approaches, it has gone on to combine a strong social business-management approach to its development work and carefully sought to avoid the political pitfalls that have befallen some of its peers through its continued emphasis on organised growth, innovation and professionalism. But it has not avoided controversy. In 1994, some of its women NGO field-workers were assaulted in Manikganj and Sitakanda, and later in Brahmanbaria some BRAC schools and staff were also attacked (Rahman 1999). For some observers, this was evidence of a clash between the forces of local religious conservatism and NGOs as purveyors of Western modernity, perhaps best symbolised by growing numbers of female NGO field staff.

## Credit

Credit provision in the form of tiny collateral-free loans, made mainly to low-income women, has become central to the work of most development NGOs. The provision of loans is usually centred on creating a homogenous, solidaristic grassroots group, which in many cases also serves as a mutual savings group. About 90 percent of NGO field offices in a World Bank survey reported that they provided credit services. Although most development NGOs engage in credit provision, just four agencies have come to dominate the sector. Grameen Bank, BRAC, ASA, and Proshika between them lend to 87 percent of the 16.4 million people who borrow from the microcredit NGO sector. A total of close to $1 billion was lent in 2005, and the savings groups that were formed by the microfinance NGOs contained more than half a billion in assets. Such loans by microfinance organisations make up about 5 percent of the overall private-sector credit circulating within Bangladesh's economy (World Bank 2006a).

Grameen's development of this approach in Bangladesh was doubtless innovative as the subsequent global spread of the modern microfinance "movement" attests, but it was also an idea that had roots in various local traditions, such as forms of rotating credit association found in many South Asian societies. Such groups are made up of individuals who contribute to a continually replenished capital fund, which can then be distributed to members by using a principle of rotated access. Many villages also had local social-welfare associations formed by villagers to administer local primary schools, mosques and youth clubs. During the East Pakistan period, establishing village-level cooperatives had also been the cornerstone of the famous Comilla cooperative model (Streefland 1996: 304).

The impacts of microcredit activities on poverty in Bangladesh are a subject of dispute. The World Bank (2006a) reviewed available studies and suggested that the evidence has been broadly positive in four main areas. First, a key benefit to low-income households is in stabilising household income through improved "consumption smoothing." Consumption variability is shown to be close to 50 percent lower than average for Grameen and BRAC members, a finding that is of major importance given the seasonal dimensions of poverty. Second, there is evidence that microcredit may increase the level of household income by between 8 and 18 percent over a period of seven years, though studies differ in their findings as to whether the "extremely poor" benefit to a higher degree than the "moderately poor." Third, there may be impact on aggregate poverty reduction through spillover effects from the economic activities of borrowers. However, this has not yet been effectively quantified, although a few studies suggest only moderate impact is observable. For example, in an eight-year period, one village study found an 8.5 percent reduction among borrowers, but only an 1.1 percent for nonborrowers. Finally, there is a distinctive set of positive nonincome outcomes also associated with women borrowers, who tend to be more able to engage in discussion about family planning with husbands, enjoy a more prominent role in household decision making, gain greater access to economic and social resources, achieve greater mobility, achieve a higher level of enrollment of their children in schools and enjoy better health outcomes.

Critics of the microcredit approach highlight several issues. One is the relatively high cost for small loans charged to borrowers in the form of interest or administrative charge. These are conventionally claimed to average from about 12 to 14 percent, but recent government figures suggest that the lending rate for microloans may range from 20 to 50 percent. NGOs argue that they need to charge an administrative fee because of the relatively high transaction costs incurred in the careful delivery of relatively small loans to low-income borrowers in often-remote communities. Critics argue that microcredit has instead become a sustainable business for NGOs that allows them to charge fees and reduce the need for donor funds, but that effectively passes on the cost to the people in society who are least able to bear these. Further criticism has focused on the oppressive loan-collection practices used by some of these NGOs. Some borrowers respond to the pressure by taking a loan from one NGO in order to repay another. As the World Bank (2006a: 73) points out, such criticism needs to be put in context: poor households do not have the option of accessing a loan from a mainstream commercial bank, and informal moneylenders charge 120 percent per year on average. In 2010, the government's Microcredit Regulatory Authority decided to cap the interest rate on microloans at 27 percent alongside a new regulation that makes a fifteen-day grace period compulsory for repayments, although it remains difficult to see how either will be enforced across the country.

Finally, there are those who see this type of credit as part of the introduction of capitalist relations of production into rural areas previously characterised by traditional social economy, thereby infringing religious sensibilities and damaging the local "moral" economy. Wherever one stands in these debates, what cannot be denied is that credit has become the new development orthodoxy, a catchall solution to problems of poverty leading to a form of unhealthy "microfinance evangelism" (Rogaly 1996). As such, it frequently obscures the need for broader structural reforms such as land redistribution or building more democratic and responsive local institutions. Government was the original credit provider to the poor back in the days of the Comilla approach, and government's role in credit still continues through the work of the Bangladesh Rural Development Board. It also continues through the Palli Karma-Sahayak Foundation (PKSF) set up in 1990 to support and regulate the microfinance sector. PKSF demands that the NGOs it funds should only charge 12.5 percent interest on loans.

### Relations with Government

NGOs compete with government for donor resources and for wider legitimacy because successful NGO work can easily be perceived as government "failure." NGOs' relationship with the government has been turbulent, and has ranged from mutual antagonism to periods of cooperation and partnership. The relationship has required constant maintenance on both sides. In 1989, the government established its NGO Affairs Bureau, which created a "one-stop" service for organisations to register their use of foreign funds. This led to concerns among some of the more critical NGOs that this was less about coordination and oversight and more about creating the means for government to better monitor and control the NGOs. Gradually, however, the government came to see NGOs as an important and permanent feature of the policy landscape. On the NGO side, managing relations with government may also be undertaken through informal networks, and it is quite common for an NGO to employ at least one reasonably senior former government official in order to ensure that problems in working relationships can be solved by using personal ties and channels of communication (Lewis 2010).

The government has gradually become more interested in consultations "with NGOs and civil society" over a number of policy issues. Midway through the 1990s, a GO-NGO Consultative Council was established, with the assistance of various donor agencies, as a committee to build better relations between the government and NGOs. The concept of "partnership" in public management has also been strongly pushed by donors, forming a central part of the neoliberal policy prescription followed in both rich and poor countries from the 1990s onwards. This has led to the government "subcontracting" many of its service-delivery activities to NGOs, including aspects of health care, education and agriculture.

NGOs began to grow more interested in the idea of not just working directly with communities at the grass roots but also with seeking larger-scale change by influencing government policy. During the 1990s, some NGOs began building policy advocacy programmes, in an attempt to influence government policy in favour of the poor. Interestingly, during Ershad's military government, there had been some notable success stories among the NGOs in terms of influencing government policy, from the essential drugs policy mentioned earlier to the creation of a *khas* land-reform law that aimed to redistribute unowned rural land to landless peasants. Wood (2009) argues that it was no accident that development NGOs came to prominence during the period of military government from 1975 to 1990 because Bangladesh's military rulers found NGOs to be useful allies in their search for legitimisation. Both Zia and Ershad aimed to create the transition from military regime to a more legitimate civilian government, and both began building new political parties that they hoped would be seen as legitimate. Working with NGOs had made it possible for government to bypass opposition among displaced political elites and to limit the formation of local-level political opposition to their regimes.

The language of rights and governance began to feature more prominently within the development of NGO discourses through the 1990s. Proshika added a new dimension to its work with the creation of an Institute for Development Policy Analysis and Advocacy (IDPAA). IDPAA and its partners campaigned widely on a variety of social, political and environmental issues. Gono Shahajjo Sangstha began promoting its landless group members as candidates in local UP elections. In Nilphamari, this was met with violent resistance by local landlords, who burnt down the NGO's schools, attacked its staff and members and conducted a house-to-house search to confiscate books and publications (Hashemi 1995). Others sought to explain such incidents as part of ongoing disputes over patron-client relations or land-related conflicts in which NGOs are merely convenient scapegoats. These cases have sometimes been used as evidence that those NGO programmes which challenge local gender norms – female literacy and education, awareness-raising in relation to women's rights – are making an impact in some rural areas.

### Critical Views of Nongovernmental Organisations

Although they were, for a while, the favoured child of donors, development NGOs have met with regular criticism from government and citizens, and to some extent also from the donors. This criticism has taken several forms. The first concerns accountability – in whose name do these NGOs speak and act? Because they are unelected, how convincing is an NGO's link with the communities that it claims to represent? Some also argue that NGOs have grown too rapidly and moved beyond the capacity of their own administrative systems, and that they now lack accountability and legitimacy. The comparatively easy resources provided to them by some donors has encouraged unscrupulous persons to set up "fake" NGOs and over-whelmed organisations that were originally designed for small-scale work. High-profile scandals in recent years have led to the demise of NGOs that were seen as having grown too quickly or as having lacked proper governance or financial accountability systems. NGOs are regulated under old colonial legislation such as the Societies Registration Act of 1860, the Voluntary Social Welfare Agencies (Registration and Control Ordinance) of 1961 and the Foreign Contributions (Regulation) Ordinance of 1982. Concerns about lack of adequate regulation have centred upon the misappropriation of funds and weak governance structures. There is no clearly agreed set of accounting standards for NGOs, as there is now in India (Irish and Simon 2005). Concern among the government and sections of the public about this issue surface regularly in the press, and there have been several well-publicised cases of NGOs abusing their use of foreign funding. For example, in January 2010, there were press reports that the government's NGO Affairs Bureau was investigating allegations that the director of the longstanding NGO Health, Education and Economic Development had provided eleven of his relatives with key positions in the organisation and the board of trustees, and that land was being purchased for private use with the NGO's donor funds.

A second type of criticism is that NGOs are self-serving, and that some NGOs had simply become money-making enterprises for their staff, many of whom enjoy a high standard of material life (such as the use of air-conditioned four-wheel-drive vehicles) and a high-status professional life. Those NGOs that have established business concerns have faced accusations of profiteering for personal gain from sections of the public, and allegations of unfair market competition from groups within the business community. A third area of criticism centres on culture and morality. Some critics portray NGOs as part of an unwelcome apparatus of Westernisation, capitalist modernisation and even as a new form of imperialism. Others make religious objection about the charging of interest on loans because interest is forbidden by Islam, or about the ways that female NGO field-workers have disrupted local gender norms by invading public space. By lending money to women, some argued, the traditional family structure is being undermined by attempting to persuade women that their allegiance to an NGO, or to its repayment schedule, should be stronger than their loyalty to the household patriarch (White and Devine 2009).

Professor Muhammad Yunus of the Grameen Bank has gone further than most in seeking to embrace market-based solutions to poverty. Grameen Bank has never described itself as an NGO, but as a specialised not-for-profit financial institution, with 95 percent of its equity owned by its borrowers and 5 percent owned by the government. Although he acknowledges the importance of charitable organisations and work in the NGO sector, Muhammad Yunus has been more concerned in recent years with the potential of harnessing the transformational power of the market through "social business," an idea that he argues challenges the dysfunctionality that is inherent in conventional "for-profit" business models. In the social business model, the nonloss, nondividend company is a vehicle for addressing social problems and in which benefits are systematically transferred to employees and customers. For example, in 2005 Yunus set up a joint social business venture with the French Danone dairy company to produce an affordable yogurt product fortified with essential micronutrients for children and another with the French water company Veolia to provide affordable, safe drinking water in areas affected by arsenic contamination (Yunus 2010). Yunus came into conflict with the Awami League in 2007 when he tried, unsuccessfully, to start a new political party in an attempt to overcome the deadlock between the two main parties. In 2011, a government investigation into allegations of financial irregularities against the Grameen Bank cleared both the bank and its founder Muhammad Yunus of any wrongdoing, confirming suspicions that the primary reason for such an investigation had been political.

The increasing economic activities of NGOs have sometimes brought them into conflict with the business sector. For example, some NGOs have trading concerns, ranging from small-scale handicrafts businesses to larger enterprises such as printing, clothes or computer services through which some organisations seek to reduce their dependence on foreign aid progressively and mobilise resources locally. BRAC has established its own university, partly in response to the closing off of public space within the old universities that have been paralysed by continuing political violence and partly as a new source of revenue. New private universities for the growing urban middle class are proving highly profitable, tapping a market in which relatively high fees are payable for an education that costs considerably less than the overseas alternative. One highly contentious issue is the income generation activities of NGOs, where there has been a lack of clarity about whether organisations are liable to pay tax. A 2002 court case was settled in favour of BRAC's investment in its new bank because such investment was judged to be permitted by the organisation's charter. Another is the allegation that NGOs that undertake business activities compete unfairly with the mainstream private sector, and this issue has not yet been effectively resolved (Irish and Simon 2005).

Public perceptions of development NGOs began to change partly as a result of what was seen as their conspicuous patterns of consumption and partly because of a more "political" role being played by some organisations. For example, from 1996 onwards, Proshika became more strongly identified in the public mind with the ruling AL political party. When the BNP was reelected in 2001, its leadership began a vendetta against members of the Proshika leadership, whom they accused of having used donor funds to persuade its members and some of its partner organisations to support the AL, under the guise of "voter education" work. Proshika has become destabilised as a result, leading to a leadership crisis that has severely weakened what was once one of the country's two or three leading NGOs (Lewis 2010).

Although internationally respected agencies such as BRAC and Grameen Bank continue to lend credence to the claim that nongovernmental development actors remain key players in Bangladesh, the local landscape is becoming scattered with the debris of failed NGOs. The pattern in which an NGO prospers for a period before falling foul of a leadership struggle or a corruption scandal is reflected in a growing appetite in sections of the media for "NGO bashing." Despite their international reputation, development NGOs remain surprisingly unpopular on the Bangladeshi "street," where they are viewed as self-serving and often criticised for turning helping the poor into a business.

## The Idea of Civil Society

Civil society is usually conceived as the organised sphere of citizen activity beyond the state, market and household. For some, civil society is a "space" between state and market, a public sphere, while for others civil society is a collection of organisations, diverse but committed to a set of normative goals relating to the rights of citizens and the pursuit of the public good, however defined. Civil-society organisations are therefore diverse, with both formal and informal types, and include business associations, self-help groups, cooperatives, religious welfare organisations, philanthropic institutions and development NGOs. To equate only the development NGOs with "civil society," which was a common tendency during the 2000s, is to ignore the range of other forms of organisation and social action that people undertake within the public sphere (Howell and Pearce 2001).

Older traditions of civil society can be traced back to the British colonial period and beyond, in traditions of charitable action, community organising and resistance movements. The long tradition of popular movement and civil protest in Bengal against unwelcome rulers and unjust rule and longstanding traditions of self-help, charity and philanthropy in local communities can also each be understood within the context of civil society. For some citizens, the idea of "civil" society is seen in opposition to the increased dominance of the "military" in society during the 1980s and the need to protect civil institutional space. For many others, the idea of civil society has become firmly associated with the funding activities of international donors and the rise of NGOs. This is particularly the case in relation to those NGOs that undertake advocacy work, taking a rights-based approach or acting in a "watchdog" role to ensure government and business operate within the law. Increasing levels of global networks and linkages also operate, connecting diaspora communities with the home country and linking activists within what some have termed a "global civil society." Two different though interrelated civil-society traditions can therefore be identified, loosely corresponding with pre- and post-Liberation forms of "new" and "old" civil society (Lewis 2004).

There are also substantially different views of civil society in use. What might be termed a mainstream view of civil society, the one taken by donors and government, is essentially a neo-Toquevillian "liberal" view. Here, civil-society groups are seen to articulate a set of socially responsible demands and largely positive public actions that can help to "balance" the tendencies of state and market institutions to overwhelm the interests of citizens. This contrasts somewhat with the "radical" view of civil society that draws on a Gramscian version of the concept adopted by those who instead see civil society as a space in which there is tension and conflict and in which the hegemonic power tendencies of the liberal capitalist state are projected and, to some extent, resisted. In this view, civil society can be seen as a zone of strongly conflicting and competing interests.

Political parties, for example, frequently call for stoppages (*hartals*) and pursue their political agendas outside formal political institutions. The political opposition since 1991 has routinely boycotted the Parliament, lending Bangladesh's democratic institutions a hollow shell quality through which very little "real" democratic process is visible. Harry Blair (1997) suggested that a proliferation of such interest groups within civil society can help create a political "gridlock" that constrains rather than facilitates democratic processes and economic life. It was the dissatisfaction among key elites – and many would argue, elements of the international donor community – that led to the intervention of the military (as another key section of the national elite) to suspend democracy in 2006 and create the eighteen-month period of the military-backed caretaker government.

Popular frustration with the increasing sense of anarchy and lack of law and order in the country, along with the lack of any sense of political progress at the national level led initially to considerable support for such a move.

During the late 1980s, the increasing role of NGOs was met with scepticism by many activists on the left, who saw them as being overaccountable to foreign donors, and as sapping the potential strength of "real" politically organised grassroots movements. As a result, the NGO sector developed a cautious approach to wider public space, remaining isolated from much of society and public life. But during the 1990s, more NGOs began embracing the newly circulating concept of civil society, sometimes as part of their own quests for identity and legitimacy. Some spoke of constructing alliances between different groups in order to mobilise citizens in support of progressive political or social objectives. Civil-society actors came to be seen as vehicles through which people can be seen to be working towards building citizenship rights. Rather than taking citizenship in the Western liberal tradition as something that is conferred from above on citizens by the state, involving rights and responsibilities, Naila Kabeer's (2005) concept of "active citizenship" emphasises the multidimensional, emergent character of citizenship. It is seen instead as an outcome of people's continuing struggles for greater inclusion and encompasses issues of agency, horizontal solidarity and identity. NGOs that see themselves as civil-society organisations are engaged in strengthening peoples' rights as opposed to simply delivering services, and it is in such activities that their effectiveness needs to be judged.

For example, in 1997, the NGO Proshika ran a campaign for propoor financial reforms under the banner of "*kaemon budget chai*" ("what kind of budget do we want?"), which brought a range of individuals and organisations from political parties, trade unions and community groups – including landless rural women leaders – face to face with the minister of finance in 1997 in order to press for a more consultative budgetary planning process. By the beginning of the new millennium, further links between old and new civil society had emerged in the form of such alliances. Some NGOs have, therefore, gained political relevance campaigning for issues such as the right to information, governance reform and the rights of minorities.

Yet civil society remains a highly contested space, as different interest groups, from NGOs to professional associations, seek influence over relevant decision makers within the political system. As with the essential drugs case, NGO efforts to influence government in favour of propoor policies are opposed by other interest groups within civil society (Kochanek 1993). The liberal concept of civil society is normally taken to exclude vertical patron-client relationships and kinship ties. For example, in Robert Putnam's "pure" version of civil society, patronage and kinship are explicitly contrasted with the horizontal ties of trust and reciprocity that he calls "social capital." In Ernest Gellner's (1995) writing, civil society stands in opposition to what he terms the "tyranny of cousins." If one takes on board such ideas of civil society and its necessary relationship to democratic institutions, it is clear that much so-called civil society in Bangladesh is really nothing of the kind. Although NGOs are often taken to be key civil-society representatives, many – particularly those with a local, less professionalised or formal char-acter – can find it difficult to free themselves from the ties of kinship loyalties in their structure and management.

Bangladesh is sometimes regarded as possessing a "strong" civil society. Yet this view oversimplifies, first because, as we have seen, understandings of civil society were quickly seen as needing to go beyond NGOs. The relationship between development NGOs and ideas about "civil society" is therefore not straightforward. By the late 1990s, a new generation of civil society and development writers started to criticise NGOs for not being part of civil society because civil society had now come to be seen as representing a far wider set of organisations. For Ian Smillie (1999: 57), the sudden rise of the civil-society discourse among donors was more a way of justifying NGO support as a strategy for bypassing government:

> Few [NGOs] have ever claimed that they were in the vanguard of civil society. Most do not use that expression at all. It was donors in search of a new label, one that might kill many birds with the same small pebble, who applied it first to NGOs, and as quickly began stripping it off when it no longer suited their purpose.

Second, civil society is clearly subject to influence from the other two "sec-tors" of state and market. The "liberal" conceptualisations of civil society that emerged during the 1990s tended to posit an unrealistically simple dichotomy between civil society and the state, between kinship communi-ties and civil society and between vertical and horizontal social ties (Chand-hoke 2002). As we saw in Chapter 3, patronage relations remain a dominant mode of the exercise of power in Bangladesh. They are the means through which the state seeks to build legitimacy and support, but are also the way society, and particularly its elites, attempt to encroach upon the state. Vari-ous competing interest groups – in the form of different political parties, organised business elites and bureaucratic elites – each seek to have a strong influence on politics and policy. Civil society cannot adequately be viewed as a realm that is separate from or "uncontaminated" by the power of states and of markets (Chandhoke 2002). Although the state seeks to encroach on civil society through the politics of patronage, global market forces have also been formative.

## Globalisation

There is an increasing set of global relationships and linkages that are contributing to the growth and shape of civil society. Globalisation has arguably contributed to an intensification of local grassroots action and helped to facilitate international activist networks, such as those created in the early 1990s around the environmental movement, which had barely existed in the 1980s, but that rapidly gained a high profile in relation to the controversial Flood Action Plan (FAP) (Blair 2001). More recently, links have emerged between Indian and Bangladeshi civil-society groups seeking to challenge the Indian government's Tipumukh dam project (see Chapter 7). At the same time, globalisation has intensified the power and influence of markets in ways that may intensify inequalities and instability in societies like Bangladesh (Lewis and Kanji 2009). In Bangladesh, reaction among citizens to the increased role of markets has created a set of tensions and contradictions between private and public interests, as Jerry Buckland (2003: 146) suggests,

current attention paid to non-governmental organizations, global civil society (or more negatively anti-globalization movement) and grassroots organizations is the result of a dialectical process associated with neo-liberal globalization. These private actors and movements are a logical outcome of economic globalization and segments of these private actors are in tension with it.

These influences have meant that NGOs have become major institutional actors alongside the state and the business sectors. For critics of globalisation in Bangladesh, such as Manzurul Mannan (2005: 272), what is seen as the growing power of multinational companies and international financial institutions threatens to undermine the potential for civil society to evolve into a cohesive and effective space for citizen action, as power becomes more narrowly concentrated.

## Interest Groups and Patronage

As NGOs expanded their work, particularly in credit delivery, new unequal vertical relationships were gradually created between people and the new external service providers (Hasan 1993; Lewis 1993). This process has been political as well as economic. In addition to opening up new political spaces, some NGOs may have also come to occupy more familiar older ones as they – rather than government or traditional moneylenders – become important in distributing resources and mediating with other power structures on behalf of "the poor" (Devine 1998). By the late 1990s, some NGOs started to receive criticism for taking up positions at the interface between the small "p" – politics of local mobilisation and empowerment work – and the large "P" – politics of national political processes – and the increasing politicisation of the country's institutions and processes. It was alleged, for example, that some NGOs encouraged their grassroots group membership to vote for a particular political party in return for continued support. Critics saw this as an example of the new patronage: despite the rhetoric, many NGOs were simply building a "non-democratic clientelistic relationship" with their constituents who were then compelled as clients to act according to the wishes of their patron (Karim 2009: 168).

The government works hard to "police" the line between civil-society organisations and political parties carefully, often attempting to ensure that NGOs do not engage in partisan political activities. Even though there are no formal rules relating to this other than a contested definition of "charity" in the 1860 Act, the "politicisation" of NGOs has become a highly sensitive area. Issues such as lobbying, public education and voter registration are generally seen as acceptable by governments, but there have been periodic accusations that these activities have sometimes become partisan.

Some advocates of civil society have argued that groups such as NGOs are potential microcosms of democratic governance and egalitarian practice, likely to contribute to wider norms of reciprocity and trust. Although NGOs may be different from heavily hierarchical government departments in the ways that people use informal familial terms of address such as *bhai* and *apa* rather than the more formal *sahib* and *sir* found in the public sector, such behaviour also reflects the personalised, charisma-driven power relations within many NGOs. Wood (1997) states that such patron-client relationships then tend to be transmitted from wider society into NGO structures. Despite their appearance of rational bureaucracies, many NGOs rely on such relationships for the recruitment of staff in order to ensure loyalty and reduce risk within a turbulent and often-hostile wider institutional environment.

### Civil Society as a Contested Idea

From the 1990s onwards, the term *civil society* became more commonly used in relation to formal nonstate organisations. In part, this was a  result of its association with the so-called good governance agenda that had been established by the World Bank (and other donors) as part of its policy prescriptions for increasing the effectiveness of development and poverty-reduction work and as part of neoliberal political and institutional development agendas. What Kendall Stiles (2002) calls the "civil society empowerment initiative" became a global phenomenon during the 1990s, with the attempt to promote democratic development through support to organisations active in grassroots development, human rights and democracy building. Central to this agenda was the idea that progress could be made by bypassing unresponsive or ineffective government institutions in favour of NGOs. The idea of civil society (often the English term is used, but it is sometimes translated into Bengali as *shushil shamaj*, literally "gentle society") became a subject of public debate. Some progressive activists tried to co-opt the term within Bangladesh's existing traditions of activism and resistance, while others were more critical – on the traditional left and also sometimes on the right – because they saw this idea of civil society as an unwelcome or irrelevant idea that was being imposed from outside.

In India, Partha Chatterjee (2004) has argued that the concept of civil society is of little relevance to the bulk of the poor because they are compelled to live beyond the reach of the organised worlds of citizenship, pluralism and association. He favours the concept of "political society" that reflects the realities of the ways poor people are made to engage with the state through a forced participation that takes place not through civic organisations but through the highly unruly and uncivil worlds of clientelism, illegality and violence. The mass of India's poor are locked into a set of vertical and unequal relationships that are located far from the horizontal ties, solidarity and gentility implied by the Western liberal concept of civil society and its English-speaking educated elites. Chatterjee's analysis of this type of civil society resonates with the distrust that many ordinary Bangladeshis feel towards what is commonly seen as an elite foreign-aided civil society of NGOs.

### Religion and Civil Society
Civil society has also more recently come to include what have become known, at least in Western civil-society discussions, as "faith-based" organisations. Of the 206,000 not-for-profit organisations documented by the World Bank, 189,000 were described as "religious" (Irish and Simon 2005). Religious organisations may seek to act in pursuit of the public good in

response to local problems. For example, in 2004, a campaign was orga- nised by the Brahmanbaria Islamic Foundation in eastern Bangladesh in which fifty *imams* came together to denounce the un-Islamic practice of "dowry" as a "social vice that claims the lives of hundreds of girls in the country and destroys families." It was reported that the campaign aimed to target the 3,137 mosques in Brahmanbaria through providing antidowry sermons at religious meetings such as *milad* and *waz mahfil,* which were attended by large audiences, where giving and accepting dowry would be stigmatised (Amin 2004). In another example, in the Gopibagh area of Dhaka's Mirpur district in 2001, the leader of one mosque helped orga- nise a community initiative designed to resist the increasing problems of the harassment of residents and street traders by organised crime elements and political party activists. Whistles were issued to local shopkeepers and wooden clubs were given to members of the congregation of the mosque, leading to direct action that successfully reduced the disruption by local touts. A number of those accused were pursued and later beaten to death by a group of angry citizens carrying out a form of "natural justice" (Lewis 2004). According to the liberal seventeenth-century political philosopher John Locke, however, this type of harsh retribution by individuals would be what takes place where there is no civil society, because it is precisely the emergence of a viable state that compels ordinary people to forego the right to take the law into their own hands as a precondition for living within this more enlightened state of civil society.

The liberal view of a "good" civil society has often been contested and remains unstable. Wood (2009) suggests that there was an "unstated secular consensus" in relation to civil society that began to change during the 1990s with the emergence of a new middle class. This new class (mainly in Dhaka, but also in other regional cities) was influenced by the growing economic and cultural influence of the Gulf States on Bangladesh and by the BNP's tradition of leaning towards more Islamic definitions of what it means to be a Bangladeshi. The result was a subtle shift in the secular-religious- nationalist composite that underpinned Bangladesh's cultural and political fabric. This new middle class is increasingly an oppositional formation that is distinct from older established, more secular elites that made up key sections of the intelligentsia, civil service and NGO sector during the 1980s and the 1990s. Although remaining far from the crude dualism implied by Huntingdon's "clash of civilizations" thesis, Wood (2009) argues that the mid-2000s saw signs of a hardening of the contestation between the two main competing traditions that can be broadly termed "secularist" and "fundamentalist" in which the majority occupying the middle ground began to be squeezed out. On the one hand, the presence of JI in the BNP government (2001–6) created pressure for increased control by the government of some of the more secular leftist NGOs and a clampdown resulted during the period from 2004 to 2005. On the other hand, there was a period of violent activity by various terrorist groups, with a series of largely unexplained political assassinations. These groups often made reference to global contexts of Islamic opposition.

### Uncivil Society

There is a strong sense in which "uncivil society" characterises many aspects of life in Bangladesh. Interest groups seek control over almost every area of public space by using increasingly violent methods. The phenomenon of *mustaanism*, the role of "strongmen" involved in criminal business, extortion and rent-seeking behaviour, is firmly tied into politics. *Mustaans* play a hybrid role that combines that of informal leader, local strongman and broker. *Mustaans* may connect underserved individuals, households and communities with political leaders on the basis of delivering vote banks in return for resources, and as such the phenomenon of *mustaanism* can be seen partly as created by politicians and elites. But mustaans also play more parasitic roles, operating on the fringes of criminal extortion and other forms of violence. The "collusive" links among political parties, law enforcement agencies and criminals that operate for mutual benefit form an important component of the structural dimensions of Bangladesh's "malgovernance" (Sobhan 2004: 4108).

Another is the way that the previously progressive tradition of student politics has been transformed. Although earlier student activism helped to animate political transformation from the language movement in the 1950s to the *gono andolon* mass movement of the late 1980s, it now takes the form of an uncivil associationalism based on ever-increasing levels of intimidation and violence. The student wings of the political parties became part of the coercive apparatus of increasingly criminalised patronage politics from the 1970s onwards, culminating in a situation in which university campuses were regularly disrupted by gunfights between student groups and in which students have regularly been required to wait several extra years to complete their degrees. The politicisation of university appointments is commonplace, as groups compete for resources, rents and supporters. Such disruption has become commonplace but reached a fever pitch by 2005 in the period before the military-backed caretaker government took over. For example, in April 2005 ("JCD vandalises RU," 2005) it was reported that at Rajshahi University, rival factions of the Jatiyabadi Chhatra Dal (JCD) student wing of the ruling BNP fought each other and attacked university property over a contested appointment of a new vice-chancellor:

according to eye witnesses, a 30–35 member JCD and BNP backed RU [Rajshahi University] recruits armed with hockey sticks and bamboos attacked the office of the Vice-Chancellor in the administration building at about 10.00am and ransacked his chamber, smashed furniture, window panes, telephone sets and almost everything in the room . . . the same gang then went to the office of the Deans Complex and ransacked 36 rooms by lobbing petrol bombs.

Many aspects of Bangladesh society therefore remain far from the idealised norm of civil society.

Nevertheless, civil-society action can be seen to have made some important contributions to the landscape of politics and citizenship during the postmilitary period. One example of a distinctive civil-society innovation was the idea of the ninety-day neutral caretaker government system that was adopted from 1990 onwards in order to try to ensure fair elections. This arrangement was an outcome of the engagement between citizen groups and the state, in the mass movement (1987–90) mobilised against General Ershad. It has not been universally successful, however. The system operated relatively successfully during the elections in 1991 and 1996, but foundered in 2001 when the defeated AL complained that impartiality had not been maintained due to capture by opposition interests. By 2006, the system had broken down completely, and it was the lack of confidence in the BNP government's willingness to hold the election fairly that led to the imposition of the very different military-backed caretaker government of 2007 to 2008. More recently, a coalition of civil-society organisations loosely led by the Manusher Jonno Foundation helped to promote a Right to Information Act that was formulated under the military-backed caretaker government; it was passed by the new AL government in March 2009 and became law in 2010.

## Conclusion: Creativity and Contradiction

Alongside the state and the market, and intertwined with them, nonstate actors of various kinds have constituted an important though organisationally and ideologically diverse area of the institutional landscape in Bangladesh. Building on long-term traditions of self-help and philanthropy, as well as on the historical roles of social movements, such as that connected with language, modern nonstate actors have crystallised since 1971 around Bangladesh's vibrant NGO sector. This sector continues to play key roles in providing important social services and, in some cases, to innovate new approaches to tackling poverty and advocates in support of citizens' rights. NGOs matter in Bangladesh because they have become a source of creativity and hope within an overall institutional context characterised by poor governance and mass poverty. Two large organisations in particular, BRAC and the Grameen Bank, have impacted upon state and market structures. Bangladesh's NGOs have also become important as wider role models in the world of international development, in which they have helped to advance "the concept of what an NGO should and can be" (Smillie 2009: 217).

Yet even as their international profile has risen, at home in recent years the development NGOs have increasingly fallen from grace as their vulnerabilities have become more apparent. Public concerns about NGO governance and accountability, their implications for the capacity and effectiveness of the still-evolving Bangladesh state, the fact that most are elite run and their overreliance on what is widely seen as the self-serving world of microcredit means that NGOs have become unpopular with the public and the media. Although NGOs do contribute to key particularistic goals in relation to poverty reduction and environment, debates about NGOs are as much about contestations around state power as they are about development effectiveness. For example, in the end NGOs cannot substitute for the need for more effective political parties in the promotion of wider democratic politics. Furthermore, the concept of civil society is unhelpful if it disguises the complex links between state and market that exist in the form of interest groups and patronage relations, and if it merely suggests an overidealised idea of civility that is at odds with the harsh realities of social and political life in Bangladesh. Yet ideas about civil society remain important, whether in their older sense in the form of pre-Liberation movements of protest and nation building that helped to shape the country, or in the newer developmental framings, in which they can illuminate important aspects of citizenship, protest and public action.

# 6

# Economic Development and Transformation

Bangladesh's economy has changed considerably since Liberation. In terms of production and trade, it has seen the rise of nontraditional industrial exports such as the ready-made garment sector and the growth of intensive irrigation-led agriculture. There has been a significant, albeit gradual, shift in economic governance from 1970s-style centralised state planning towards a partially "liberalised" economy with a greater level of integration with the rest of the world. Although the economy had remained heavily dependent on international aid during the 1970s and 1980s, by the 1990s its centrality had become displaced by export earnings from the ready-made garment sector and the rise of remittances from Bangladeshis living and working overseas, particularly in the Gulf States. The garment industry brought important changes in the gender composition of the formal-sector labour force. Investment in infrastructure has helped to facilitate economic growth, but continuing political instability has periodically limited wider economic progress and change, while volatility in international markets has brought increased risk to the economy.

Since the early 1990s, Bangladesh's economic performance has improved in terms of economic growth and gains in poverty reduction. World Bank figures show a jump in GDP growth from an annual average of 3.7 percent during the 1980s to one of 5.2 percent during the second half of the 1990s. Export earnings have increased steadily, from 7 percent of the GDP in 1991 to 18 percent in 2006 (Murshid et al. 2009). However, the economic transformation that has followed from the liberalisation reforms has come at a cost. Despite positive impacts of income growth on poverty, there is a worsening pattern of income distribution. Although most economic change has generally centred on the urban formal sector and the rural nonfarm sector, there has been little impact on the broader farm or urban informal sectors. There are low levels of tax-revenue collection and local resource mobilisation and extensive money laundering for political purposes. As a result, Bangladesh faces the future with an economy that has increasingly globalised elements but also with a large rural sector that remains in place, an extensive "informal sector" and high levels of corruption.

## The Formal Economy since 1971

Similar to East Pakistan during the 1950s and 1960s, Bangladesh had one of the lowest levels of urbanisation and industrialisation in the world. Its primarily rural economy was dominated by agriculture, mainly in the form of rice and jute production. This was to change over the next three decades. By the start of the twenty-first century, the importance of agriculture to the GDP had declined from one-half in the 1970s to just one-sixth, and the services sector had grown from one-third to two-thirds. Industrial production, though it remains relatively low, had also increased from 7 to 15 percent (Rashid 2005). Although the two main drivers of economic growth are migrant-worker remittances and exports, chiefly garments and shrimps, the basic centrality of agriculture to the economy remains.

### Agriculture

Bangladesh's agriculture is usually divided into four main subsectors: crops and horticulture, animal husbandry, forestry and fisheries (Rashid 2005). In terms of crops and horticulture, rice is the dominant crop, produced through three main annual crops known as *amon*, the main rice crop, which may be transplanted, broadcast or grown under deepwater conditions and harvested from October to January; *aus*, harvested in July and August; and *boro*, the previously small winter rice crop, harvested in May through June, which by the late 1990s had expanded with the growth of irrigation technology to reach the scale of the main *amon* crop. Rice from Bangladesh accounts for 9 percent of world production and constitutes approximately 10 percent of Bangladesh's GDP (Rashid 2005). It serves as both a subsistence crop and a cash crop for farmers because even small producers need to sell part of the crop to pay back production loans and to buy basic consumption goods, with the rest being kept for household consumption. The other main food crop grown is wheat, which has grown in popularity among growers since the 1970s, aided by new high-yielding varieties (HYVs) and *boro* irrigation facilities. Other key crops include sugar cane and potatoes.

Successive governments have placed food security at the heart of policy and planning. The need to build food security has dominated government policy and has driven the modernisation of the agricultural sector.

Traditional local rice varieties used in all three rice seasons were previously grown without the use of artificial fertiliser. The 1980s saw a rapid increase in the use of new HYVs of rice and other crops, developed by scientists experimenting with hybrid varieties at the International Rice Research Institute. As part of a new technological package aimed at increasing production, the new seeds were also combined with increased mechanisation of ploughing and irrigation, and with the rise of artificial fertiliser use (Lewis 1991). As a result, there have been impressive gains in domestic food production. Rice production had increased from an average twelve million tons per year during the 1970s to close to eighteen million tons by the 1990s, based mainly on the expansion of the irrigated winter *boro* crop. An extensive food-rationing system that had relied on large-scale imports and disincentivised local farmers was gradually closed down by the government.

By 2000, agriculture was contributing 25.5 percent to the GDP, and the country was close to achieving food self-sufficiency. The production base had become more diversified, with wheat the second-largest food crop after rice. Nevertheless, the unpredictability of the natural environment in terms of floods and drought continued to disrupt the rural economy and meant that Bangladesh found it necessary to continue to import food. But it was clear that these production gains came at a heavy environmental cost. The increased use of chemical fertilisers and pesticides raised concerns about water contamination and public health. The growth of irrigation also depended heavily on the use of shallow tube wells to draw up groundwater, and this led in some areas to the contamination of local water supplies by hitherto unsuspected natural underground arsenic deposits (see Chapter 7). The expansion of *boro* irrigation drew on surface water bodies and, as these were drained, capture fisheries were reduced and access to fish protein particularly for poor people became more restricted (Rashid 2005).

The traditional nonfood crop grown in Bangladesh is jute, an export crop that for decades was second only to rice in its importance and that was the cornerstone of the country's exports. Jute is a fibre that has for centuries been used for making sacks, rope and carpet backing, but its importance as a global commodity has been in steady decline since the 1960s, when close to 80 percent of global jute production came from Bangladesh. From 1973 to 1974, out of total export earnings of US\$454 million, a total of US\$378 million came from a combination of raw jute and jute manufactures (Faaland and Parkinson 1976). Yet by 2004, jute was providing only 3 percent of Bangladesh's export earnings. Global demand for jute declined steadily as synthetic polypropylene products eroded many of its traditional product niches, and a trend towards bulk transport of goods reduced the demand for packaging materials. The economic role of jute, once so very important as an export, has been in almost terminal decline since the 1980s. Even as the popularity of natural fibres such as jute among global consumers has increased, Bangladesh's outmoded and inflexible jute public-sector marketing apparatus failed to capitalise on the opportunities this provided, though these opportunities were not lost on neighbouring India's entrepreneurs and planners. The efforts of a small number of NGOs to keep alive the sector through the production of small-scale jute handcrafts have had little impact on this decline.

Livestock farming underpins crop production because most farmland is still ploughed with animal power. The sector is made up of cows, buffalo, goats and sheep, though despite its importance, there are still relatively poor livestock management knowledge and practice prevailing in this subsector. Forestry forms the third subsector. The three areas of Bangladesh that contain extensive forests are the CHT, Khulna and Sylhet, while smaller forest areas remain in parts of central Bangladesh in Dhaka, Tangail, Mymensingh and Jamalpur. As Rashid (2005: 87) explains, during the period since the 1970s, the forests have been undermined by extensive felling, and although poor households are conventionally blamed for the destruction of forests, "it is the affluent who support and execute large-scale felling, both legal and illegal, often through mechanized operations."

Finally, Bangladesh's extensive rivers and other water bodies provide the basis for fisheries, which is the last important subsector. Fisheries production is estimated at close to two million tonnes annually from three main sources of fishery – open water, closed water and marine (FAO 2007). Fish has long represented an important source of animal protein and other key nutrients for the people of Bangladesh and is estimated to provide close to 70 percent of the country's protein requirements. Fishing is also an important source of employment, with close to one million people estimated to be involved in fishing full time and a further eleven million engaged in fishing on a part-time basis in order to supplement their basic livelihoods (Rashid 2005). Yet the fisheries sector is highly vulnerable. The potential for building on Bangladesh's natural resource base for intensifying fish production has long been undermined by a relative lack of investment. The consumption of freshwater fish declined by 38 percent between 1995 and 2000 among the poor living on the wetlands, and open-water fish stocks are believed to be in decline. Only in the shrimp sector has there been significant production growth, aiding exports, but at a high cost in terms of social and environmental factors. Although official figures show steadily increasing fisheries production levels, other studies point to a decline, which seems plausible given a range of problems arising from irrigation and drainage infrastructure, the problem of overfishing and pollution from the increased use of agrichemicals (Rashid 2005). Despite this, many argue that water is a long-underutilised resource, and that the fisheries subsector could potentially become a more important source of animal protein for people in Bangladesh than it has been to date, if the means can be found to manage this important natural capital in more sustainable ways.

*Infrastructure*

A visitor who knew Bangladesh in the 1980s would be struck by the considerable improvement in Bangladesh's transport infrastructure today. A network of metalled roads that can be used all the year-round has revolutionised travel for many people. Navigation of the waterways has been made easier by the availability of cheap diesel engines, which have been fitted to boats whose sails used to be a regular and spectacular sight on the rivers up to the late 1980s. This has increased people's physical access to almost every subdistrict, aided by the widespread construction of new bridges. No longer are most long journeys across the country punctuated by the long wait for slow ferries. Of particular significance was the completion in 1998 of the 4.8 kilometre Jamuna Bridge, which at last linked the two halves of the country together with a direct road and rail link. The bridge cost three-quarters of a billion dollars, was funded primarily by the Japanese government, the World Bank and the Asian Development Bank and reduced – for example – the travel time from Dhaka to Bogra from twenty to six hours (Map 2).

The country's telecommunications network, which had long been costly and inefficient, was superseded by the new mobile-phone technology from the mid-1990s onwards. The government and Grameen Phone introduced an effective cell-phone network that rapidly provided information access to rural households by creating network coverage across the whole country. Grameen Phone was established in 1996 by Muhammad Yunus, the founder of the Grameen Bank, as a joint venture with Telenor, Norway's largest telecommunications company. By 2009, it was Bangladesh's largest taxpaying company, with more than twenty-five million subscribers. To widen access further, Grameen Bank borrowers were encouraged to start small-scale telephone businesses at the village level, selling access to telephone service to those without phones of their own. People were able to rent a cell phone or

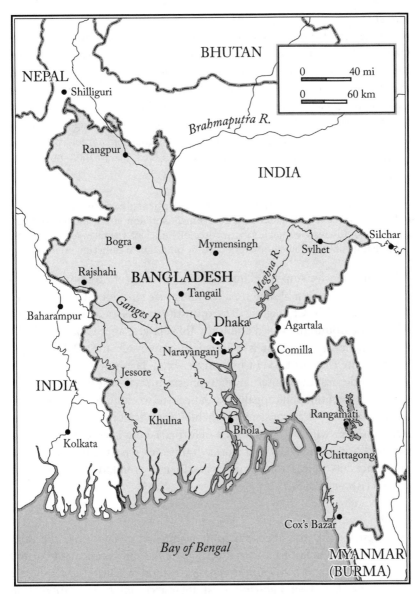

Map 2. Map of Bangladesh

SIM card (subscriber identity module) from these small-scale entrepreneurs, whose businesses were funded by loans from Grameen Bank. As Yunus (2010:18–19) describes, there are now four hundred thousand such service providers known locally as "telephone ladies."

## Industry

New industries have emerged alongside the changing rural and urban land-scapes of Bangladesh. Since the 1980s, the ready-made garment industry has grown to become the major economic actor in the country. Employing mainly women, the rise of this garment industry has also been a force for far-reaching social change, with close to one million women gaining entry to the industrial workforce in the cities of Dhaka and Chittagong in chal-lenge of longstanding restrictive social norms that had largely prevented women's participation in the formal economy. As Kabeer (2000: 69) points out,

it took market forces, and the advent of an export-oriented garment manufacturing industry, to achieve what a decade of government and non-government efforts had failed to do: to create a female labour force of sufficient visibility, and on such a scale, that it could no longer be overlooked by official data gathering exercises.

A labour-intensive ship-breaking industry, another nontraditional enter-prise, has become established on a ten kilometre stretch of the coastal area of the Sitakund in Chittagong. The industry specialises in breaking large ships from around the world and is the third largest after Gujarat in India and Shanghai in China. It is believed to employ up to 200,000 people and generate close to US$114 million per year. The industry is, however, attracting domestic and international concern from labour rights and green activists on account of its appallingly dangerous working conditions, use of child labour and disastrous environmental impacts. It is a largely informal sector business with little application of formal labour laws regarding work-ing conditions. One NGO that works in this area reported that in the five years since 2000 at least forty workers lost their lives and five thousand were injured (Ahmed 2005).

## Energy

The energy sector has also seen some significant change since the early 1970s. A major area of industrial activity is the development of natural gas production and distribution systems. Although natural gas and coal deposits had long been known to exist, their accessibility and exploitation did not begin to take place until the second half of the 1970s. By 1977, half the country's electricity was produced using natural gas, and this had risen to 89 percent of electricity by the end of the 1990s. At the same time, the country's power infrastructure has remained inadequate. During the 1980s, the Rural Electrification Board had set up a network of electricity consumer cooperatives known as Palli Biddut Samities, to improve access to power in rural areas by providing supply to newly connected areas on a not-for-profit basis. However, many consumers face a situation in which they are made to pay for an irregular service. Frequent electricity supply interruptions and voltage fluctuations remain commonplace, and these act as a debilitating brake on the process of industrialisation (Rashid 2005). In 2006, in a village called Kansat in the northern district of Chapainawabganj, a protest took place among residents who resented paying for electricity that they did not receive. Shockingly, for perhaps the first time in Bangladesh's history, the police opened fire on ordinary villagers, killing twenty people and injuring many more. In 2009, it remained the case that only 45 percent of households had an electricity connection. The low level of contribution of the electricity sector to the GDP had remained more or less constant for the decade, from 1.27 percent in 2001–2002 to 1.35 percent in 2006–2007 (Hossain 2009).

### Foreign Aid

The role of foreign aid in the formal economy has also shifted since 1971. One of the key economic stories of the past two decades has, therefore, been the relative decline of Bangladesh's dependence on foreign aid. International aid flows have long been an important component of Bangladesh's economy, in terms of resources and of the ideological influences foreign aid brings through its conditionality and selectivity. As we saw in Chapter 4, the new state had been initially cautious about taking on the commitments and obligations that would come as part of foreign aid. But by the early 1980s, General Ziaur Rahman had increased Bangladesh's use of foreign aid and pursued a measure of economic liberalisation that cemented the country's relationship with Western donors. This trend continued and intensified under General Ershad, and foreign-aid receipts continued to grow. As it would turn out, at 7.6 percent of the GDP, aid in 1990 had reached its high point at the end of the military government of Ershad. By 2001, it had fallen to less than 2 percent. This may have been because, as donor conditionality had grown more strict and overall global aid flows had declined, new priorities had emerged and led to reallocations elsewhere than Bangladesh. Also, because a large proportion of aid had been provided primarily to finance food provision, as domestic food production increased, such aid became redirected. There were also other, perhaps more subtle, reasons for the reduction of international aid to Bangladesh, as Hossain (2005: 13) explains,

It is possible that aid flows declined in Bangladesh in the 1990s in part because donors felt they had less need or scope to intervene. They may have felt less need to intervene because, for the first time under democratic rule, economic policy remained broadly in line with donor preferences, and growth and poverty reduction were steady, if unspectacular. Donors may also have had less scope to intervene because the problems of development in Bangladesh were increasingly being diagnosed as political (or "governance") problems, rather than the familiar problems of resource constraints and technical deficiencies.

Despite the relative decline of the quantities of aid to Bangladesh, its importance has been immense in shaping the direction of Bangladesh's economic and political transformation, both in terms of the institutional and political culture that is built at the interface of aid negotiations between donors and government and by the content of donors' general promotion of a promarket set of policies. Although the quantity of aid has decreased, there have been significant changes to the ways that aid is delivered. These have included the attempt to create better-coordinated donor approaches, the idea of direct government "budget support" in which aid is delivered not through projects but directly into ministries in order to try to build improved "ownership" of reforms, and the joint development of "poverty reduction strategy plans" that aim to set out comprehensive and shared government and donor policies for reducing poverty. Although there are many useful gains from these more systematic coordinated approaches to aid relations, such changes have also served to increase the power of donors to influence government.

However, as Hossain (2005: 14) also points out, donor support has not always been confined to "mainstream" forms of market-based policies. A group of "like-minded donors" that has included the Scandinavian countries, the Netherlands and Canada have attempted to "push for more radical policies than governments have been willing or able to deliver" on issues such as agrarian reform and poverty reduction. The composition of aid has also changed over time. Between 1972 and 2006, a total of $45 billion was received, of which 45 percent was in the form of grant aid and the rest was loan. The proportion of loans has increased steadily as a share of total aid, with grants representing only 26 percent of the $1.3 billion of foreign aid received annually between 2004 and 2006. Although debt-service payments for loans has increased from $108 million in 1980 to $644 million in 2006, the country's debt-service liability has, however, declined as a proportion of exports, from a peak of 24 percent in 1988 to close to 6 percent in 2006 as exports and remittances have increased (MHHDC 2008).

Despite the overall decline in aid flows, the past two decades have been characterised by a growth in the "nongovernmentalisation" of official aid.

A higher proportion of the aid that has been given has been focused on nongovernmental actors (see Chapter 4). During the 1990s, there was an increasing move by donors towards providing more support to development NGOs, which were seen as organisations that promised more impact than traditional government or donor-led "projects" on poverty reduction. NGOs acted either through the direct delivery of services or through the indirect policy route of propoor advocacy. A key economic element of this shift to funding NGOs can be found in the rise of the credit and development approach, discussed later in this chapter.

### Economic Governance

As we saw in Chapter 3, in 1971 the country inherited a large public sector and a wide-ranging set of regulations governing industry, trade and financial markets, and this was consolidated by Mujib, who further extended public ownership in the years after 1971. This began to change during the 1980s, as General Rahman's accommodation with foreign aid opened up new space for rethinking policies in light of the new Western trends towards privatisation, free markets and liberalisation, and there was also a growing awareness of the limitations of existing institutional arrangements. Bangladesh began on a path as a "reluctant liberaliser," responding to both its own official reassessment and reflection and to pressure from aid donors, but failing to develop a systematic approach to the overall reform process in terms of planning or sequencing. The results have been characterised as neither "planned gradualism nor shock therapy," with an uncoordinated mix of unfolding reforms taking place in varying ways and at different paces across different sectors (Islam 2005: 380).

Agriculture was one of the earliest sectors to face liberalisation of both its inputs and output markets, and this has been relatively successful. At independence, Bangladesh, like the other countries of South Asia, had been left with a highly centralised system of institutions and practices that gave the government strong control over the production, supply and distribution of food crops. Liberalisation was mainly donor driven, with, for example, the continuation of large-scale food aid made conditional on changes to the existing system of food rationing and subsidies, much of which was inefficient and "captured" by the nonpoor. Public control over food became liberalised under the influence of the World Bank and other donors. What was once a vast, subsidised public food system was dismantled relatively rapidly during the 1980s, when the government legalised the private importation of food grains and removed restrictions on private stockholding and marketing. The consumer subsidies provided by the rural and urban food-ration system were withdrawn, and the ration system replaced with targeted forms of "in kind" benefits such as food-for-work schemes. The reform of the food market took place without the violent protests that have been experienced in many other developing countries (Ahmed and Haggblade 2000: 15).

Trade liberalisation made possible increased importation of improved agricultural technology such as mechanised irrigation equipment. The deregulation of the domestic market led to an increased demand for private-sector distribution of nationally produced fertiliser and pesticides (Nurul Islam 2004). The potential shock of this change was balanced by increased agricultural production, which prevented a corresponding increase in the cost of food as subsidies were withdrawn. Nevertheless, the global food crisis that was experienced in 2008 still resulted in outbreaks of rioting in Bangladesh that were widely reported and became an important factor in the loss of confidence in the military-backed caretaker government during the second half of its two-year rule. Next came moves towards liberalisation in financial services, industry and international trade. During the 1980s, private banks, both domestic and foreign, were allowed to compete with the dominant nationalised banks, and to set their own interest rates. Yet a high incidence of default on loans remains a chronic problem and the sector lacks an effective regulatory system (Islam 2005). Today, the government retains a 51 percent stake of the shares of the country's four state-run commercial banks. In the 1990s, there was a wide-ranging reduction of tariffs, the removal of most restrictions on foreign investment and the introduction of current account convertibility. Imports also grew, as the growth in exports and remittances created higher levels of demand. This was the outcome not only of the liberalisation of import restrictions but was also aided by the growth of GDP and the increased availability of foreign exchange from international aid and rising remittances. As agricultural production increased, the growth of marketable surplus meant that more farm products were being distributed and marketed within and between rural and urban areas, and this fed an increase in domestic trade.

Since 1990, successive AL and BNP governments cautiously continued with the policy of liberalising the economy in order to stimulate growth through increased market-based activity. This has meant a reduced role for government and a range of efforts to stimulate private-sector activity. The first BNP government introduced value-added tax (VAT) in place of the existing sales tax as part of its efforts to broaden the revenue base, and made efforts to improve broader revenue-collection systems with the result that public revenues increased. The domestic resource component of the Annual Development Plan increased from 10 percent in 1990 and 1991 to 40 percent in 1996 and 1997, which also contributed to a reduction of dependence on foreign aid.

The AL government that followed (1996–2001) continued this trend with a set of reforms that attempted tighter tax administration and a loosening of import duties. However, during this period the visibility, if not also the extent, of widespread administrative mismanagement and corruption increased, and this brought negative implications for government revenue and expenditure. When the second BNP government was elected in 2001, liberalisation policies continued, and in 2003 the exchange rate was floated. The publicly owned Adamjee Jute Mill at Narayanganj near Dhaka, the largest in the world and employing twenty-five thousand workers, and a potent national symbol but that had long been a largely unproductive public-sector asset, was closed down in 2002. Despite a 17 percent increase in revenue collection during 2002 and 2003, levels of mismanagement and inefficiency seemed to be increasing, and Bangladesh was regularly flagged by TI as heading the international corruption league tables.

A key problem remained the weakness of Bangladesh's institutions, which tended to provide more incentives for smuggling than for legitimate trade and which rewarded trade over productive economic activity. The result was a set of perverse incentives that leaves capital accumulated mostly in nonproductive activities and in which "industry provides the greatest risk and the least reward" (Kochanek 1993: 346). A study by Uddin (2005: 178) of the performance of privatised companies found that privatisation had largely failed to improve accountability and transparency within business or to increase contributions by companies to state coffers, and it had simply created a system of "family capitalism" characterised by "personalised budgetary systems" and increasingly coercive forms of control over workers and managers.

Another key area of the liberalisation policy has been the introduction of new government policies to stimulate export growth. Bangladesh's first EPZ had been constructed in Chittagong during the early 1980s and had become a centre for the expanding garment industry. Businesses established within EPZs are provided with a wide range of concessions. They are permitted the duty-free importation of capital and raw materials, to retain their foreign currency earnings, and to hire expatriate and nonunionised workers. They are entitled to ten-year tax holidays and are given preferential status in gaining utility services. Another EPZ was opened in Dhaka in 1993 specialising in high-technology companies, and this was followed by further EPZs that were constructed in Chalna, Comilla, Ishwardi and Uttara. By 2002, the EPZs were generating more than $1 billion in export revenue per year and employed more than one hundred thousand workers. South Korea emerged as the leading foreign investor, followed by the United States, Japan and the United Kingdom.

Economic growth therefore increased during the 1990s and into the 2000s, driven by external and internal factors. By the end of the 2000s, the Bangladesh economy had consistently sustained impressive growth rates of close to 6 percent per year. The AL government elected in 2008 began its term with indications that its economic management policy might take some new turns, combining some areas of renewed government control with continuing use of a private market–based policy. For example, it has planned a series of public-private partnerships in relation to the construction of new infrastructure, such as the new Dhaka-Chittagong highway project, two proposed new coal-fired power stations and a new deep-sea port for Chittagong. At the same time, the AL is subject to political pressure to reopen some of the government-run mills and factories that were closed previously. The government has also stated that it will return to the FYP approach to planning in place of the Poverty Reduction Strategy Paper (PRSP) approach adopted at the behest of the World Bank and other donors in 2002.

## Bangladesh in the International Economy (1): The Rise of Nontraditional Exports

### Garments

The rise of the ready-made garment sector has been central to Bangladesh's industrialisation process and its export strategy. In 1990, Bangladesh was exporting $0.64 billion worth of garments, which by 2001 had increased to $4.86 billion. By 2009, garments constituted three-quarters of total exports and were worth nearly $11 billion a year. The industry employs nearly two and a half million people in its factories, 90 percent of whom are women, and creates further employment in related services such as transport, insurance and banking (Murshid et al. 2009). Although Bangladesh had long been known as a historical centre of quality textile production, there is little if any connection between this past and its modern ready-made garment sector. Today the garment sector is an industry in which all fabric, patterns, thread and fasteners and most other components are simply foreign-produced inputs brought in for manufacture by low-cost labour. As a result, there are few backward production linkages into the local economy that could help to stimulate local production beyond assembly. Nevertheless, the ready-made garment sector has quickly grown to become central to Bangladesh's economy.

The sector's origins can be traced to the late 1970s, when a handful of factories began producing clothes for Western markets as a consequence of the Multi-Fibre Arrangement (MFA). The MFA was put in place in 1974 by developed countries in order to protect their clothing manufacturers from growing quantities of cheap imports from developing countries. The MFA subjected poor producer countries to strict export quotas. Although the MFA was primarily designed to protect European and North American producers, it also provided opportunities to very poor countries such as Bangladesh. Under the agreement, it became possible for established garment-producing countries to activate the unused export quotas of nongarment-producing poor countries in order to extend their production base. In the case of Bangladesh, where there was no existing export garment industry, it was the South Korean capital, whose quotas were already filled, that acted as the catalyst for the start-up of the Bangladesh ready-made garment sector. This process of expansion was ultimately driven by the need for Western retailers to seek new countries in which they could source garments in order to "get around" the quotas.

The European Union (EU) now imports just more than half of the country's garment exports, with the remainder going mostly to the United States, with small markets also in Japan, Mexico and Canada. What explains this dramatic rise? According to Shahpar Selim (2008), three sets of factors had influenced the rapid growth of this industry. First, as we have seen, the wider external trade environment has favoured Bangladesh through the international quota system. Second, factor costs have been highly advantageous. Wage rates in Bangladesh have remained among the lowest in the world, and entry to the labour market requires little in the way of formal education or capital requirements. Bangladeshi garments are 40 to 100 percent cheaper than Chinese counterparts in European markets and 30 to 70 percent cheaper in U.S. markets. At the same time, investors face low infrastructure costs and factory space can be rented very cheaply. The third main influence has been domestic policy reform, chiefly the liberalisation of trade, which has included measures such as the back-to-back letter-of-credit system and bonded warehouse facility which have helped to support and facilitate the growth of the sector. The sector includes both woven and knitted garments, and enterprises take diverse forms, though out of more than four thousand listed firms, it is estimated that only about fifteen large companies dominate production.

Yet Bangladesh's international comparative advantage remains limited to that of being a source of cheap labour and of low-cost, mass-produced basic products. Within the value chain, most of the garment producers deal with intermediary "buying houses" rather than directly with Western retailers. Nor, according to Selim (2008: 119), is there much management innovation in evidence within the overall production setting:

> [the] majority of firms are risk averse, poorly trained, passive actors with a low interest in active marketing, have little opportunity for direct bargaining and have weak strategies to cope with upcoming supply chain challenges at the firm level.

Nevertheless, the industry's reliance on a largely female workforce drawn from rural areas has contributed to far-reaching social changes in the cities and the countryside. A World Bank (2008: 6) report on gender found that the garment industry has been a key driver of the "empowerment" of women observed by many agencies within the country since the 1980s. The new factories primarily drew on the labour of village women who had learned traditional sewing skills as young girls within rural households, with the result that a generation of young women was able to challenge the constraints of kin and patriarchal social norms and shape new identities in new settings beyond the village.

These women report that they value the chance to earn their own living, gain a measure of independent purchasing power, be able to save and remit money to their families in the village and secure more control over their choice of partner and date of marriage. Female participation in the wider labour market has been a major economic factor driving social change. At the same time, these positive aspects of social change also need to be set against the generally harsh lives faced by garment workers in terms of the lack of labour rights, poor working conditions and high levels of violence against women (Kabeer 2000).

Although production remains concentrated mostly at the level of basic items at the cheap bottom end of the market, there are some signs that some producers are moving up the value ladder to produce higher-quality goods. In 2005, the end of the MFA, and therefore of Bangladesh's protected quota, led some people to fear for the future of Bangladesh's garment exports in the face of increased competition from China and Vietnam. Yet the international competitiveness of Bangladesh's low labour costs, and some measure of adaptation among factory management, apparently ensured that the industry survived the international policy shift with relatively little damage. The easing of EU's rules of origin for least-developed countries from 2011, making duty-free access to European markets allowable for garments with a far higher proportion of important components than previously, is expected to be highly beneficial for the sector.

*Shrimp*

The second export growth area has been shrimp. Rising global demand for shrimp offered Bangladesh new export opportunities within the international agrifood system. In 1993, the government began the promotion of semi-intensive shrimp farming, and between 1993 and 1994 and 1994 and 1995, the value of fish and shrimp exports increased by 30 percent. By 2005 to 2006, the fisheries sector was contributing 4.9 percent to Bangladesh's GDP and represented 4.4 percent of the country's exports. Frozen shrimp and fish exports had doubled in the decade since the mid-1990s to become worth $460 million. Shrimp and prawns have, therefore, become an extremely important source of export earnings for Bangladesh, constituting 25 percent of total exports (if the ready-made garment sector is excluded) and more than 70 percent of primary product exports. By the early 1990s, the export of shrimp had become a major growth area of the economy – and highly controversial. About one-half is small-scale, relatively labour-intensive freshwater prawn (*golda*) farming, while the rest is larger-scale and more capital-intensive brackish-water shrimp (*bagda*). The supply chain, from the collection of larvae in the rivers to the factories that process the final product, employs close to one million people, the majority of whom are women (Carr and Ito 2010). In the southern areas of the country, the cultivation of shrimp within polders flooded with saline water had become common, though the practice led to criticism that small farmers were losing farmland to these large-scale shrimp entrepreneurs, and that the intrusion of saline water onto agricultural land was leading to serious environmental problems.

Shrimp farming, however, has not only brought negative environmental impacts but also worrying social implications as it has expanded. NGOs such as NK have been active in organising resistance among poor households evicted from land by local elites engaged in intensive shrimp cultivation, and there have from time to time been violent clashes between "shrimp lords" and local rural communities. Meghna Guhathakurta (2003: 296) finds that the shrimp cultivation monoculture has begun "to disarticulate the organic link between people and environment" in terms of changing land use, class and gender relations and environmental impacts. The state, keen to benefit from the foreign exchange, has helped facilitate the rapid increase in shrimp by offering incentives in the form of loans to entrepreneurs, many of whom have come from outside the area.

The shrimp business demonstrates the need to confront a difficult trade-off between the livelihoods of poor people, and the issue of increased integration into global export markets. A key challenge for Bangladesh's aquaculture exports comes from the food safety and traceability require-ments established by Europe and North America and adopted by the World Trade Organization because these may be used as arbitrary barriers to trade and impact negatively on livelihoods. In 1997, the EU, Bangladesh's major market, banned shrimp imports from Bangladesh after it was alleged that it did not comply with regulations, leading to $15 million in lost revenue between August and December of that year.

The government's PRSP set out a strategy for increasing shrimp exports and improving compliance, but this policy favoured *bagda* farming, which it saw as easier to regulate, but which brings less opportunities for employment for the rural poor and has a greater negative environmental impact than *golda* farming. Although globalisation may offer Bangladesh important eco-nomic opportunities, nontariff trade barriers such as the Hazard Analysis Critical Control Point regulations adopted by most rich countries (apart from Japan) impacts negatively on countries such as Bangladesh in the form of lost export earnings and creation of bias towards *bagda*. Although the government continues to work on improving compliance, some devel-opment projects and NGOs are experimenting with linking poor farmers with niche markets in Europe for "organic" prawns and with a growing domestic middle-class market (Carr and Ito 2010).

### Remittances

The third area of international economic integration is the remittance econ-omy. The subject of migration is dealt with in more detail in Chapter 7. Remittances from Bangladeshis working overseas have grown steadily, from close to $500,000 in 1985 and 1986 to $1.5 billion by 1997 and 1998. In 1991, Bangladesh's current account was, for the first time, pulled out of deficit as a result of the growth of private transfers from those of its citizens working abroad.

Remittances remain essential to the country's macroeconomic stability and help to counteract regular deficits in other areas of the economy such as trade, services and other income. The past ten years has seen a rapid growth of remittances, which increased from 3 percent of the GDP in 1995 to close to 9.5 percent in 2009. It is estimated that about five million Bangladeshis are resident abroad, and although initially this was concentrated in the Middle East, this population has become more geographically diverse in recent years (Murshid et al. 2009). By 2007, the total contribution of Bangladesh's overseas remittances amounted to about $7 billion, but the real figure was probably much higher – because official figures do not include private or informal transfers.

After 2001, the balance of remittances shifted from the Middle East towards countries such as the United States, which during 2006 and 2007 became the second-largest source after Saudi Arabia, with a greater proportion also now coming from individuals in the United Kingdom. This shift was the result of Western governments' new post-9/11 international money-transfer restrictions designed to address the rise of money laundering and terrorism. Close to half of worker remittances are believed to be sent by using the traditional informal system of money transfer known as *hundi*, a system developed in the Islamic world using broker intermediaries who move money based on an honour system.

### United Nations Peacekeeping

A final area in which Bangladesh has successfully developed a nontraditional "export" is in relation to the growth of its role in UN peacekeeping. This business has provided the army and the government with an important new source of income. In 2006 and 2007, Bangladesh received more than $200 million from the work of more than nine thousand of its service personnel across ten UN peacekeeping missions. This has also arguably contributed to the reduction of the army's role in politics during the period since 1990. By the 2000s, the country had become the second-largest provider of soldiers, police and observers to the United Nations in what amounts to an innovative variation on the country's efforts to export its key resource of people.

The expanded international role for the army has also recently impacted domestic politics. Concerns that the army would be providing security for the planned 2006 national elections (that were widely believed to be flawed) led the United Nations to question its international legitimacy and to imply in a public statement on January 11, 2007, that its future peacekeeping contracts might be adversely affected. This was believed to be the catalyst that led Army Chief of Staff General Ahmed to order the president to declare a state of emergency immediately, cancelling the forthcoming election and establishing the military-backed caretaker government that was to remain in place until elections finally took place in December 2008.

## Bangladesh in the International Economy (2): Global and Regional Issues

Although the rise of nontraditional exports has been impressive, Bangladesh's level of integration into the global economy remains highly uneven, with negative and positive implications. Although there is a need for increased foreign investment on terms favourable to the development of Bangladesh's economy, the lack of integration in many areas may have served to protect it from of the turbulence affecting the global economy from 2008.

### Energy and Investment

Bangladesh's position as a source of unexploited natural resources has begun to attract more attention from international capital-seeking opportunities to exploit natural gas reserves and coal deposits. Although these reserves have been identified for many years, they were traditionally viewed as difficult and costly to access. Only with recent global energy shortages have prices increased to the extent that there is now a stronger economic logic for exploiting these resources. The government estimates that there are nearly thirty trillion cubic feet of gas reserves, of which two-thirds are believed to be recoverable – providing the capacity to meet the country's domestic needs for the next three to five decades. Half of the current supply is used for electricity production, 90 percent of which is produced from gas, with the rest used for fertiliser manufacture, household use and other commercial and industrial purposes.

Because Bangladesh lacks capital and technology of its own to undertake gas exploitation, the government opened the sector to foreign investment during the mid-1990s. A total of eight production-sharing agreements were signed with foreign companies in different parts of the country, including with the U.S. company Rexwood Oakland, for the Sangu gas field in the Bay of Bengal, and the U.S. company Occidental, for the Bibyana and Moulavi Bazar fields in Sylhet. The UK-based company Cairn Energy was awarded production-sharing rights in another Bay of Bengal area, while the Irish exploration company Tullow Oil located another gas field in an area close to Dhaka. The Bibyana gas field began production in mid-2007 on the basis of a joint venture between Chevron and the government's Petrobangla company, aiming to supply two hundred cubic feet of gas per day.

Energy shortages remain an important problem in Bangladesh. It is estimated that close to 85 percent of the country's households have access to electricity, but that only 60 percent of the electricity that is produced is actually paid for, with "system loss" (a popular euphemism for accounts for theft and corruption) accounting for 30 percent of the power that is generated. The government is wary of further popular unrest after the 2006 incident at Kansat. In April 2010, the threat of protests among middle classes about the growing electricity shortages in Dhaka became so pressing that the government agreed to fast-track an attempted solution. This was a plan for the rapid construction by foreign companies such as the U.S. company General Electric to set up a series of small diesel-driven power plants on government land or on floating units close to harbours in an attempt to alleviate the pressure.

Bangladesh's energy reserves, and in particular its abundant stocks of natural gas, have recently become an area of political contention. The question of supplying gas to India is highly controversial for many Bangladeshis, and strong anti-Indian feelings have left the government unwilling to cede the political value of portraying India as Bangladesh's giant hostile neighbour for the opportunity to earn scarce foreign exchange. Pressure on the government to change its stance is increasing, as foreign investors begin to find the domestic market insufficient to recover their investment, and donors such as the World Bank increasingly argue for the need to generate new revenue streams that could improve the balance of payments.

The government has also been interested to exploit coal in order to reduce dependence on gas, although many members of the population remain unconnected to the gas supply. Coal has, therefore, also become of more interest to foreign investors. An ill-fated 2005 Tata investment plan (see following text) was to have included rights to the coal deposits in Barapukaria in the Dinajpur area of northwest Bangladesh, as part of a $3 billion combined investment package to develop gas, coal and steel production. The UK-based Asia Energy's plan to exploit an area of high-quality coal in Phulbari, also in the north of the country, ran into resistance in 2006 in the form of local protests against the proposed environmentally destructive "open pit" mine and was subsequently deferred.

## Relations with India

Bangladesh has the problem of a longstanding overall trade deficit, has traditionally been financed through a combination of foreign aid and remittances and the challenge of expanding the country's exports remains important. India is Bangladesh's logical trading partner, but compared with India, Bangladesh has liberalised more rapidly, largely due to its higher level of dependence on the World Bank and International Monetary Fund. Bangladesh cannot easily export to India because there is little that Bangladesh produces that India does not produce more cheaply, but its domestic market is open to, and in many areas dominated by, Indian goods. Furthermore, although a South Asian Free Trade Agreement is now in place, providing duty-free access in theory for many of Bangladesh's goods, a range of nontariff barriers – such as strict product-testing certification and labelling requirements – create major obstacles for Bangladesh's exports. For example, although India's trucks can enter Bangladesh, the reverse is not possible. There is widespread smuggling through the porous border between the two countries. This works in favour of India where most goods tend to be cheaper and undermines the potential of small businesses to grow in Bangladesh. At the same time, India has long been requesting transit facilities by land and rail through Bangladesh in order to give it better access to the northeastern states (Islam 2004).

Immigration issues and concerns about terrorism have further contributed to the lack of progress in moving forward the economic relations between India and Bangladesh. Bangladesh's border with India is 2,500 miles long, making it the fifth longest in the world. Ranging from hills and dense forest in India's northeast to the *sundarban* mangrove creeks and waterways that border with West Bengal, it is extremely porous, with poorly patrolled and irregularly maintained barbed-wire fencing and sentry posts. Regular skirmishes take place between the border guards of both sides, often causing fatalities. India has recently become more preoccupied with border security and in 2006 began constructing a new two-and-a-half-metre-high steel fence at a cost of more than $1 billion. In India's northeastern states, there are fears that insurgent groups are using Bangladesh as a safe haven, and that large numbers of incoming migrants from Bangladesh may alter the religious composition of these Indian border territories. Also underpinning India's stance is the fear that the world's third-largest majority Muslim country is vulnerable to a shift away from its generally tolerant tradition of moderate religion and secular politics towards stronger Islamist tendencies. Few people believe, however, that such an infrastructure would do much in practice to deter economic migration from the region's poorest country, and the fence remains incomplete.

Investment is also needed to develop Bangladesh's ports, railways, communication systems and electricity supply, on which the country's future industrial expansion and growth will depend. As mentioned earlier, a large-scale investment plan by the Indian Tata company was proposed in 2005. It aimed at exploiting the large natural-gas reserves in Bangladesh and also included a steel mill, fertiliser factory and power plant. The plan ultimately failed to materialise, with the government unable to secure a deal in relation to the sharing of Bangladesh's precious natural resources that would satisfy both the strong nationalist sentiments of interest groups with the demands of the private sector and national energy needs. At an estimated value of $3 billion, the proposed Tata initiative would have dramatically altered Bangladesh's regional trade position.

The period of the military-backed caretaker government (2007–8) saw an improvement of relations with India as compared with the previous BNP-led coalition government. Two areas of progress were negotiated during this time. First, in April 2007, a passenger train link was established between Dhaka and Kolkata. Then in 2008, India agreed, despite an export-ban policy and rising food prices, to allow rice exports to Bangladesh. The election of the AL government in 2008 continued the signs of a thaw. In January 2010, Hasina made a four-day official visit to India for what some observers saw as a potentially important India-Bangladesh summit. Although it was symbolic rather than substantive, the visit was a potentially defining moment in the shaping of Bangladesh's regional position. The key issues of contention between the two countries were discussed – border disputes, migration and trade imbalance, as well as the long-running water-sharing problem, in which downstream Bangladesh is highly vulnerable to India's upstream water-control policies. A new agreement was made that promised $1 billion in Indian investment in infrastructure, the supply of 250 megawatts of electricity, the removal of import restrictions on almost fifty items from Bangladesh and an agreement by Hasina to deal with the problems of Indian rebel groups using Bangladesh's border areas as bases for cross-border attacks. Maritime and land-boundary issues and water sharing were not addressed, but the meeting has arguably set the climate for more constructive negotiations to follow in the future.

### Relations with the United States and China

Trade relations with the United States have grown closer during the past decade, with a rise in bilateral trade and a substantial amount of direct investment mostly in power generation and natural gas exploration. The United States has now become the largest importer of Bangladesh's ready-made garment sector. It was quick to provide a tacit recognition of the military-backed caretaker government when it took power, a stance that reflected concerns that political instability might lead to a consolidation of power by still-disparate Islamic extremist elements in the country.

Economic ties with China are also growing. In 2005, a visit of the Chinese premier Wen Jiabao marked the thirtieth anniversary of the establishment of diplomatic relations between the two nations and raised hopes of closer economic ties. In particular, the agriculture, transport and telecommunication sectors were singled out for future cooperation. In 2010, it was reported that Chinese aid to a value of $9 billion was to be provided to Bangladesh in order to increase the depth of Chittagong's deepwater port facilities and construct a road link through Burma to China.

## Poverty and Economic Change

Bangladesh remains one of the poorest countries in the world. At the end of 2009, the Economist Intelligence Unit (EIU) ranked Bangladesh 106 out of 160 countries in its "quality of life" index, which takes into account income poverty, life expectancy, levels of corruption and the condition of a country's institutions – the least favourable ranking among the South Asian countries. Income level per head in Bangladesh is one of the lowest anywhere in the world, and more than half the population live below the World Bank's poverty line, which it defines as living on less than $1.25 per day (EIU 2009). About one-third of Bangladesh's poor people live in what has been termed "extreme poverty," a category that encompasses particularly vulnerable groups such as elderly poor people, people with disabilities, destitute persons and socially excluded ethnic or religious groups (MHHDC 2008).

Despite this negative picture, the situation has improved during the past two decades, with Bangladesh ranked 127th in the EIU's 1989 index. Change has been driven by the rise of the textile-export industry, the growth of remittances and increased agricultural productivity. This has meant that the GDP per head has almost doubled from $733 in 1989 to $1,307 in 2009, calculated by EIU at constant 2006 purchasing power parity (EIU, December 2009). In contrast to the negative views held during the 1970s and 1980s, Bangladesh came to be seen as a "success story" by development agencies such as the World Bank (2008). Its figures indicate that the incidence of poverty has fallen from 57 percent of the population in the early 1990s to 49 percent in 2005 as a result of the country's steady economic growth. Rural consumption patterns have changed over time, with increased household-consumption expenditure on nonfood items such as clothing and footwear (Hossain 2010).

However, these positive trends are unevenly distributed across the econ-omy as a whole. There has been considerable variation in progress with poverty reduction in different parts of the country, due to the uneven avail-ability of economic opportunities and to higher levels of vulnerability to natural disaster in certain areas. Overall income distribution has worsened, mainly as a result of the contrast between the relative dynamism to be found in the urban/formal sectors as compared with the more static rural/informal sectors and in the rural nonfarm sector as compared with traditional agri-culture (Ahmed and Mahmud 2006). The Gini coefficient (the measure of income inequality) has increased substantially from 38.8 at the national level in 1992 to 46.7 in 2005, indicating a more rapid rise of inequalities within urban populations as compared to rural (MHHDC 2008). S. R. Osmani's (2005) data shows that an increase of income inequality has taken place in rural and urban areas, widening more sharply during the 1990s. In the 1980s, the Gini for consumption expenditure for urban areas went from 0.30 to 0.32 between 1983 and 1984 and 1991 and 1992, but by 2000 had increased to 0.38. In rural areas, the Gini was constant staying close to 0.25 during the 1980s but had risen to 0.30 by 2000.

The modest reduction in poverty has been achieved through a variety of different economic processes and intervention strategies. One of the most important has been the increase in agricultural production achieved since the 1970s, which has produced a decline in the real price of rice. From the mid-1970s to the early 1990s, particularly as the growth of irrigated *boro* winter rice expanded, the real price of rice fell by 34 percent (Dorosh 2000). It is also widely accepted that an important contribution to the decline of poverty has been made by the extensive microcredit programmes conducted by government and the NGOs that have made it possible for borrowers to improve their livelihoods through acquiring small-scale assets such as livestock (see Chapter 5).

Receiving less attention, but equally if not more important, has been the growth of innovative "social protection" schemes. A range of unconditional and conditional cash transfers are provided to poor people in the form of relief and food-for-work and school feeding programmes. The Vulnerable Group Development programme, for example, is a longstanding government initiative, implemented in partnership with the NGOs. It provides welfare-based food transfers to the poor, while also offering recipients access to microcredit services in order to strengthen their assets and livelihood options in more sustainable ways. More recently, there have been new initiatives that also aim to transfer assets directly to the very poorest people. Since it was established in 2002, BRAC's Challenging Frontiers of Poverty programme has attempted to break with the welfare approach and with the dominant microfinance orthodoxy of "self-help" through credit. Although recognising that effective social protection requires that people are given cash and food, BRAC argued that because this is consumed, it is insufficient to help people move out of poverty. Instead there must also be support to people's ongoing efforts to build their livelihoods by strengthening material and social assets. BRAC's approach is to provide both cash payments and an asset, such as a cow, along with functional education, health-support services and rights awareness building. The programme has been very well evaluated and has responded innovatively to a range of challenges, including the need to build coalitions with nonpoor groups in areas where there may be common interest in challenging the status quo. The result has been the creation of new grassroots "poverty reduction committees," which have had some success in enlisting the support of the local nonpoor to improve conditions for the very poorest, for example by contributing to building improved village sanitation facilities (Smillie 2009).

Although economic poverty statistics still dominate the development world, and are central to the UN MDGs, these often fail to convey either the full complexity or the human dimensions of poverty very well. Money-based poverty measures tend to convey little of the world in which ordinary people live. In Bangladesh, a household's poverty goes beyond only the lack of money to include struggles with ill health, everyday rights, access to basic services and the discrimination people face on the basis of age, gender and disability. For example, for the non-Bengali "tribal" populations in the CHT and other areas of the country, levels of poverty and social deprivation are higher than for the population as a whole (MHHDC 2008).

In a smaller-scale study designed to gain a detailed insight into household experiences with poverty, David Hulme (2004) describes how Maymana, a widow, and Mofizul, her disabled son, try to deal with their deteriorating situation in a rural household. They try to use family and neighbour networks and to access a range of government and NGO services that are available. Like the majority of rural households, they have become effectively landless and, as in the case of 15 percent of households, they are headed by a female. They possess a minimal asset base – a mud hut and a tiny homestead plot, but during the past decade, the household's situation and their asset base has been slowly eroded. During the early 1990s, they had been relatively secure, originally living in a five-person household (Maymana, her husband Hafeez, two daughters and a young son) and owning an acre of farmland along with three cycle rickshaws that they rented out. But Maymana's husband Hafeez died in 1998 after a long period of ill health, and they had to sell one of the rickshaws to pay for health-care services. Maymana's father-in-law then took over ownership of the farm plot, leaving her to depend on her two married daughters for support. She depends on this small income because Mofizul, her young, disabled son is frequently unwell and requires costly medical services, and Maymana is unable to find regular work. Such household "life histories" provide an important glimpse into many people's constant struggle to secure their well-being and avoid slipping into destitution.

Progress with poverty reduction has also been geographically uneven. The World Bank's figures show that there are severe disparities between the eastern and western parts of the country, with Dhaka, Sylhet and Chittagong experiencing far greater progress with poverty reduction than other districts in western parts of the country. Natural disasters also produce regular setbacks to processes of economic change and transformation and cause widespread hardship and destruction. Although there had been an upbeat mood among donors and policy makers during the mid-2000s, this positive mid-decade picture was severely interrupted by the twin shocks of the heavy 2007 floods and cyclone and the sudden global food crisis, which starkly highlighted the country's vulnerability to food-import price volatility.

There is now a more coordinated approach to tackling poverty in the form of the PRSP. Designed and guided by the World Bank, the PRSP approach was intended to build a national consensus around the antipoverty policy, based on an inclusive process of public discussion and consultation between government, donors, civil society and the private sector. Critics have pointed to the way that the PRSPs also provide an effective means for donors such as the World Bank to shape the overall policy process in the country better. Nevertheless, the resulting document was widely seen as more consultative and demand-driven than much earlier government policy, though considerable doubts were raised about the capacity of the government to implement an ambitious plan that seemed to recognise the importance of the multidimensional causes of poverty and the seriousness of the obstacles standing in the way of poverty-reduction policy (Bhattacharya 2005).

From a political economy perspective, an additional problem is that recent poverty-reduction efforts have preferred to focus on individualised approaches that seek to strengthen what Sobhan (2007: 1) calls "the agency role of the poor," at the expense of structural issues such as unequal land ownership or producers' adverse incorporation into value chains. Microcredit and social-protection efforts may form an important component of an antipoverty strategy (Sobhan 2007: 3–4), but they only go so far:

Access of a poor woman to micro-credit to buy a cow does not address the problem of who controls the milk market or the distribution chain or value addition associated with the processing of milk. Investing milk cow owners with a sense of agency to seek a better price for their milk may help to improve the price they receive from milk traders. But the primary producer still remains at the bottom of the value chain for milk products and enhancement of their agency role, within a market driven system, will not significantly enhance returns on their supply of milk. It is only when the woman as an agent can graduate into the position of a principal, as a possible shareholder in a milk processing enterprise, that the original microcredit beneficiary will not only be able to enhance their income but also acquire a stake in an important industry and share in its growth.

Since the 1980s, there have been some attempts to challenge structural poverty, with an ongoing effort at implementing small-scale land reform. In an unstable environment, as rivers change their course and coastlines become eroded, new areas of land appear and others become submerged over time. This process regularly raises questions of land ownership as new tracts of *khas* land emerge and are claimed for farming. As a result of a concerted NGO campaign in the latter stages of the Ershad regime, a new land-reform law was passed that required new *khas* land to be redistributed to landless households (Devine 2002). Some NGOs have long been active in trying to help landless people to formalise their rights over this land and begin cultivation because local landowners often occupy it illegally and achieve de facto ownership in defiance of the reform. In 2008, a new research report on the *khas* land situation indicated that the total amount of *khas* land amounts to close to 1.3 million acres, of which about three-quarters of a million acres have at least nominally been redistributed to poor households. However, the report finds that 54,873.8 acres of *khas* land is illegally occupied, while a further 28,884.6 acres of *khas* land remains eligible for lease. In the *haor* water body areas of the country, the report found that more than half those people who had received redistributed land from the government faced serious problems holding on to it, including illegal occupation by, or unlawful distribution to, nonpoor people and problems with corrupt officials within the local land-settlement offices (Hossain 2008).

The real challenge, Sobhan (2007) argues, is to transform the patron-client relationship that structures relations between individual poor people and the elites who control their livelihoods through their ownership of key assets. Only when garment workers gain more of a stake in their industry, in the way that the Grameen Bank is now mainly owned and partly controlled by its female borrowers, will more substantive poverty reduction take place. Yet the process of "declientelisation" that has been called for poses enormous problems for a society in which patron-client relationships, often politicised, dominate most areas of life.

## Urbanisation

Bangladesh is experiencing a very high rate of urbanisation. The population of Dhaka was just 0.4 million in 1951, increased to 1.4 million in the mid-1970s and had risen to 10 million by 2001, placing Dhaka in the top ten of the world's "mega-cities." Bangladesh's second city, Chittagong, grew in the same period from four hundred thousand to four million. By 2007, Dhaka's population was 31.1 million people and the United Nations predicted that it will reach 16.8 million by 2015 (Alam and Rabbani 2007).

Haider Khan (2008) cites data that indicates that, although just 8.8 percent of the population lived in urban areas in 1974, this had risen to 23.4 percent by 2001. The percentage of the population urbanised is currently more than 25 percent and is increasing by a rate of more than 3.5 percent per year. In Dhaka, the largest city, there are 3.4 million poor people, constituting 35.4 percent of the population according to official figures (Banks 2008).

Bangladesh's rapid process of urbanisation may have started from a relatively low base compared to many less predominantly rural developing countries, but it has been spectacular nonetheless. The main "pull factor" for rural to urban migration is the perception of an increasing difference in earning potential between the agricultural and nonagricultural sectors. Those who migrate to urban areas will find it difficult to find a well-paying industrial or service job in the formal sector and are likely to enter the urban informal sector instead, in which there might be relative ease of entry into the labour market but low pay, high levels of job insecurity and exploitation (Khan 2008). A rapid yet unplanned process of urbanisation has combined with a period of impressive but unregulated economic growth to create a serious crisis in Dhaka and other cities, where essential services are "on the brink of collapse" (Siddiqui et al. 2010: 344).

One consequence of this urbanisation is that the distribution of poverty is changing, with a shift becoming noticeable from rural to urban areas at the end of the 1990s. Official figures suggest that the percentage of poor people living in urban areas increased from 46.7 percent in 1991 to 52.5 percent in 2000, with the proportion in rural areas falling from 47.6 percent to 42.3 percent during the same period. This has led to a large gap between rural and urban areas, as well as between the two main cities of Dhaka and Chittagong and Bangladesh's other urban areas. The two major cities receive as much as half of the total overall investments, with the rest characterised by "benign neglect" and the consequent draining away of their human capital to the two large cities (Rashid 2005: 20). The unplanned movement of largely unskilled and poor rural people into rural areas has created large urban slum areas, where the provision of basic services generally remains beyond the capacity of the authorities (Rashid 2005). For example, Dhaka faces a large number of severe infrastructural and environmental problems including flooding, lack of compliance with national planning regulations due to poor implementation and lack of resources, surface-water contamination, inadequate sewage management, transport congestion and poor utility services such as electricity and gas – all of which impact negatively on the livelihoods of the poor (Alam and Rabbani 2007).

Urban populations of poor people lack access to the same level of social services as their rural counterparts, such as vaccination programmes, food-for-education schemes or old-age stipend services. Furthermore, within urban areas there is a wide gap between slum dwellers and those people who then move to more secure urban dwellings. The urban poor, therefore, face a distinctive set of disadvantages as compared with the rural poor, who may remain better off in relation to several key social indicators. For example, primary school enrollment for rural children aged six to ten in one study was found to be more than 83 percent, while for urban children it was only 60 percent (Afsar 2010).

Urban slum dwellers face tough conditions on several levels (Wood and Salway 2000: 670), including the arduous physical conditions of settlement density and the loss of control over their environment, poor labour standards and conditions of work and insecure contracts and trying to access informal labour markets that are usually mediated by *mustaans*. Usually people try to adapt by attempting to re-create forms of community and social solidarity with fellow migrants from their part of the country or social group. But without the personal ties that help to organise relationships in the village, recently urbanised people face conditions of "less trust on which to construct longer-term, multi-period and multi-dimensional transactions," and "unfamiliar codes of honour and obligation." They are also more vulnerable to insecurity, theft and violence, particularly against women. Urban environments are, therefore, high-risk settings for poor people recently arrived from rural areas.

Although the rural poor have long been seen as a key priority for government and donors, there is now an increasing need to focus policy efforts in order to assist poor people in urban areas. Despite the extent of urban income poverty being lower in absolute terms than in rural areas, this is now increasing proportionately as the rate of urbanisation has grown. The need for increased priority to be given to urban areas for antipoverty interventions and improved infrastructure is increasingly recognised by the donor community (World Bank 2006c: v). Organisations such as the Coalition of the Urban Poor, a network of fifty-three NGOs working on urban poverty, and Basti Basheer Odhikar Surakha Committee, a network of grassroots committees within low-income settlements, are active in collective mobilisation of the urban poor at the grassroots level. The aim is to try to improve their participation in urban governance through lobbying local ward commissioners as a way of influencing urban policies (Banks 2008: 366). Such activities operate within the local-level clientelistic face-to-face politics that prevail across Bangladesh, with formal and informal dimensions. This means that the poor have to deal not only with formal local-level officials and NGOs but must also interact with local *mustaans* and corrupt police if local problems are to be solved. The city corporation is split into ninety wards, each with a democratically elected commissioner, with considerable room for manoeuvre in order to implement policy and allocate resources as they see fit. Yet the urban poor, assisted by these civil-society groups (see Chapter 5) face widening opportunities for old and new forms of participation in municipal governance through voting in city elections and, in some cases, through building accountability links with a responsive ward commissioner, which can help improve people access, for example, to water and electricity (Banks 2008).

## Conclusion: Cautious Optimism?

Bangladesh continues to face a set of formidable obstacles to economic progress: its large and increasing population, its vulnerability to frequent and devastating natural disasters, its less than adequate infrastructure and the historical weakness of its political institutions. There are significant potential risks to the country that remain to be addressed in relation to environmental sustainability and the global HIV/AIDS crisis. Although there is a continuing lack of institutional efficiency and high levels of corruption, consistent GDP growth rates of 6 percent annually have been sustained through the past decade and seem set to continue for the foreseeable future. Agricultural production growth and the rise of the garment industry provide evidence that many economic challenges can be addressed. Despite continuing high levels of mass poverty, international agencies such as the World Bank now report that Bangladesh has a good chance of meeting several MDG targets, such as the eradication of extreme poverty and hunger, securing universal primary education and reducing child mortality. In April 2010, it was reported that UN Secretary General Ban Ki-moon had praised the Bangladesh government for the progress that has been made and suggested that many other countries could learn from what it has achieved in relation to the MDGs, microcredit and disaster preparedness ("Achieving MDGs," April 22, 2010).

Bangladesh's economic performance continues to present a puzzle to many observers. The extremes of optimism and pessimism that have characterised earlier debates are unhelpful in assessing Bangladesh's difficult path ahead, and a more balanced view of cautious optimism is called for. As Kochanek (1993: 344) puts it, Bangladesh is "neither a basket case nor a potential tiger." Yet Bangladesh's position in the global economic order carries some contradictions. Although it has attained relatively high levels of global economic integration in terms of increasing migrant remittances and rising exports of garments and shrimp, it has a far lower degree of linkage with international financial capital. For example, Bangladesh's capital account has not been liberalised, so the country is less vulnerable to sudden capital flight. This helps to insulate Bangladesh from the volatility of global market forces. The worst global financial crisis since the 1930s struck the international economy in 2008, when the financial system became affected by the spread of so-called toxic assets originating in U.S. mortgage markets. The crisis highlighted Bangladesh's low level of integration, and it appeared less affected by the crisis than many other countries in the region. Nevertheless, there are concerns that exports, remittances and imports could become entry points for negative economic fallout during the coming years. Ultimately, the case of Bangladesh suggests that actual forms of capitalist transformation may take more diverse forms than those implied by the narrow predictions of some economic-development theorists. Bangladesh's less predictable, nonuniform pattern of change that combines a surprising economic and social dynamism with the relative dysfunction of many of its political institutions challenges the "modernisation" idea of development with its fixed trajectory of Western-style change and deviates from the model of stagnation in the "periphery" that was predicted by the radical "dependency" theorists of the 1970s.

# 7

# Population, Natural Resources and Environment

This chapter examines the relationship between political and economic change, and broader demographic and environmental factors. It begins with a discussion of Bangladesh's ecological setting. The country's location within a highly fertile but ecologically unstable river-delta system is central to an understanding of its population and economy. As we saw in Chapter 6, agricultural production has increased since the 1980s through the spread of modern farming techniques and the rapid expansion of irrigation technology, but production gains have come at the expense of heavy environmental costs. These include the depletion of soil quality through the overuse of artificial fertilisers, increased pollution from the use of chemical pesticides, the problem of saline intrusion and, in some areas, the contamination of groundwater and crops by arsenic, natural deposits of which have been disturbed by the drilling of new irrigation wells.

The next part of the chapter then moves on to a discussion of population issues. The delta has long attracted large numbers of people who come to farm its small areas of highly fertile land, leading to longstanding concerns about "population pressure" as a negative factor that affects development. Bangladesh is a country not much larger in area than England, but it now faces a population that is estimated at 162 million, and is one of the most densely populated areas in the world. For example, although Bangladesh has historically been a country of small farmers, population pressure on available cultivable land combined with long-term land fragmentation through inheritance practices means that more than half of the rural population has been functionally landless for the past few decades. The idea that high levels of population growth need to be brought down has long been an important priority among government policy makers and international development agencies. Yet people nevertheless remain one of the country's key resources.

The nature and extent of poverty was briefly discussed in Chapter 6; but in this chapter we go on to consider a broader range of "social development" indicators, such as those relating to health and education, and people's rights as citizens and then place these in the context of the region. Finally, we look at the efforts of Bangladeshis to manage these pressures through migration. Longstanding internal, regional and international traditions of migration are central to the livelihood strategies of many households, and remittances have grown to become a mainstay of the economy. At the same time, illegal migration by Bangladeshis has become a sensitive issue for India, and there are several unsolved problems relating to refugees and the forced movement of people. Recently, climate change has brought a new dimension to policy discussion of migration.

## Natural Resources and Ecology

Bangladesh forms the end point of the Ganga-Brahmaputra-Meghna river system, the second-largest river system in the world, which drains vast areas of surrounding China, Nepal and India (Map 3). Its land is almost entirely low lying, with close to three-quarters less than ten metres above sea level. Large areas of the country are subject to annual flooding, with flood water originating from three different sources: rainfall, rivers and the sea. In the northeastern area of Sylhet, there are tectonic depressions known locally as haors that act as sinks for the river Meghna and its tributaries as they begin rising each year from early April, bringing water from the Assam Plateau. In the central and western areas of Bangladesh, large tracts of low-lying land are flooded by the Ganga and Brahmaputra Rivers each year. Furthermore, Bangladesh is located within a delta that is still continuing to be formed, making its rivers constantly subject to changes in their courses. There are a series of oxbow lakes known as *beels* in the western region that have been created by the eastwards shift of the main course of the Ganga, where large quantities of water accumulate each year over these areas of heavy clay soil with poor drainage. Finally, the eastern coastal areas contain lowlands that are prone to annual river flooding and to the intrusion of sea water. These areas are less than two metres above sea level and are therefore highly vulnerable to abnormalities in both river and sea levels (Bradnock 1984).

The country's tropical climate is an important asset that makes intensive high-yielding agriculture possible, with crops grown throughout the year drawing on extensive sunshine and abundant water. Good soil is found on

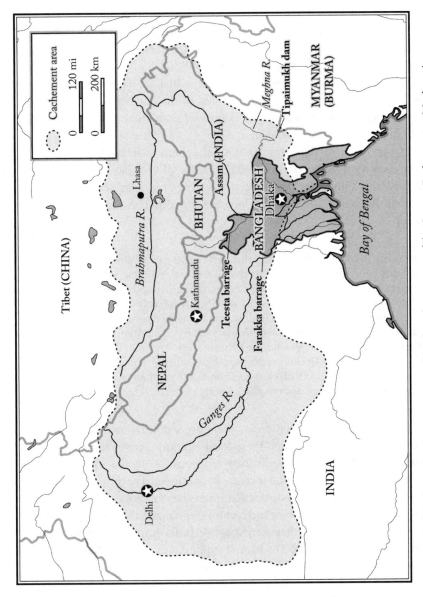

Map 3: Bangladesh as a riparian country: combined catchment area of the Ganges–Brahmaputra–Meghna river systems (from Adnan 2009).

about one-third of Bangladesh's cultivable land, an unusually high proportion for tropical countries (Rashid 2005). The flatness of the land is also an
asset, with a far higher proportion of Bangladesh's overall land available for
cultivation – four-fifths – than is the case in other mountainous rice-growing
countries such as Korea or Japan. Finally, the quantity of water available to
Bangladesh through rainfall and the flow of its rivers is an important asset,
despite the many problems it causes. Without this, Bangladesh would be as
dry as the Sahara and Arabian deserts with which it shares its latitude on
the Tropic of Cancer. The mountain chain of the Himalayas acts to block
the trade winds, and this produces extensive rainfall that prevents the land
from drying out for half the year.

Yet very little in this complex natural system is straightforward, and
much is yet to be understood. The causes of the natural fertility of
Bangladesh's alluvial soil is a matter of controversy, as agricultural scient-
ist Hugh Brammer (1990:164), a longstanding observer of the region, has
noted:

It is widely believed in Bangladesh that "silt" deposited by floods improves and
maintains soil fertility. Farmers and others are mistaken in that belief; most floodplain land is flooded by clear rainwater and even where rivers deposit new alluvium,
it often is relatively infertile for several years before it has "ripened." However, the
farmers are correct in associating fertility benefits with seasonal flooding, especially
with deep flooding. The fertility flush observed by farmers apparently is derived
from nitrogen-fixing blue-green algae living in the water, from decomposing, submerged, plant remains (including the lower leaves of deep-water rice and jute), and
from the increased plant availability of phosphorous and other nutrient elements
in the chemically reduced, submerged top-soils.

In the southwestern coastal areas, there are extensive mangrove forests
known as the *sundarbans*, and these form a unique ecosystem. Here, local
communities have forged a distinctive way of life in the forests that is
increasingly threatened by the increase in commercial shrimp farming and
the destruction of local fish stocks. The forests serve as important protection
against disaster, such as floods and cyclones, and may have helped to protect
Bangladesh and the southeastern coast of India from the impact of the
devastating 2004 tsunami. The habitat supports much wildlife, including a
population of tigers, though these are now increasingly threatened. Amitav
Ghosh's novel *The Hungry Tide* (2004) offers a vivid portrayal of this unique
area, where boundaries seem to dissolve between land and water, India and
Bangladesh and the different religious and ethnic communities that try to
make a living in the *sundarbans*.

As a result of its unique location at the junction of this complex system, the country possesses a rich heritage of biodiversity, within a distinctively evolved ecosystem that contains an unusually wide variety of animal and plant species. The population is heavily reliant on the management of the natural resources found within the floodplain system, the forests, mangroves and hill tracts for their livelihoods and for basic survival. It is estimated that 70 percent of the population depends on the country's main natural resource endowments of cultivated wetlands and forest resources. Rural poverty remains extensive, so it is clear that anything that threatens biodiversity levels and natural capital availability will impact negatively on income, nutrition and food security.

Geography is simultaneously Bangladesh's blessing and its curse. In his classic overview of Bangladesh's economic geography, Haroun er Rashid (2005: 13) challenges what he sees as the standard "superficial" view of the country as "poor in natural resources," arguing instead that its open ocean access, fertile soils, tropical climate and seasonal abundance of rainfall and river flow are "major natural assets." Although agriculture has long provided the economic backbone of the country, some of these other attributes may hold the key to its future. Its extensive coastline provides Bangladesh with access to oceanfront resources such as fish and other living marine resources as well as salt, fossil fuels and minerals. Ocean access through the Bay of Bengal provides Bangladesh with links to the Indian Ocean and to international shipping lanes that greatly aid its trade potential and avoid the many problems Paul Collier (2007) has associated with "landlocked" developing countries. The main port of Chittagong is usefully positioned on the boundary of south and southeast Asia, giving it a unique strategic importance. The idea of building on the geographical comparative advantage and improving "connectivity" is rapidly becoming a key idea for conceptualising the future economy and society of Bangladesh. For example, its geographical position as a potential bridge between south and southeast Asia and the potential to build links with other small countries in the region such as Bhutan, with which Bangladesh recently has signed a trade deal, alongside developing links with India and China, are increasingly seen as crucial for the future (Zafar Sobhan 2010).

### Natural Hazards
Tropical storms and cyclones occur each year between late October and December, due to a complex set of meteorological factors. Robert Bradnock (1984: 42) explains that each June, the westerly jet stream moves to the north of the Himalayas and Tibetan Plateau, while the equatorial westerlies

also intensify, creating an airstream conducive towards the formation of cyclones. These develop and move towards Bangladesh, drawn to the area by high late-autumn sea temperatures in the Bay of Bengal, and form a humid core of warm air that drives the development of cyclones. Because the bay is far north of the equator, it is subject to the Coriolis force that moves air across the earth, and this fans the core into the circular wind pattern that characterises cyclones. If a cyclone reaches the coastal tip of Bangladesh, the result is the "funnelling" of water up against the coastline, leading to an increase in sea level that can be as high as three metres. Winds of up to 250 kilometres per hour then propel these storm surges across the land to produce heavy flooding, the destruction of infrastructure and, in many cases, severe loss of life.

Although the floods constitute a major natural hazard, it is perhaps ironic, as Bradnock (1984:43) points out, that the country effectively owes its existence and its viability to the propensity of its rivers to flood. It is the silt brought down by the rivers that has created the delta, and the silt ensures that the fertility of the land is regularly replenished. Without this flooding, the soil would never have been able to sustain such a high level of continuous agricultural cultivation and would become exhausted. The Bangladesh delta area is, therefore, inherently dynamic: the water is a force that gives life but also takes it away.

### Human Impact

Bangladesh's susceptibility to natural environmental hazards and their impact on its people are well-known. But events within the natural environmental system also need to be seen as phenomena that are strongly influenced by various forms of human activity, within the borders of Bangladesh and beyond. A wide range of important environmental problems afflict Bangladesh, some old and some new, and these arise from the complex interplay of people, policies and natural environment. For example, the major rivers and tidal regimes are constantly changing their configuration as a result of the interplay of natural factors such as earthquakes and forms of human interference such as the creation of large-scale upstream river barrages, as well as the many small-scale embankments that are built by government and farmers. This can, at times, make it difficult to isolate the precise interplay between natural processes and human interventions within a dynamic and complex system (Brammer 1990:164).

Nevertheless, it has long been clear that the environment has been put at risk by a series of environmentally unsound development policies, a weak regulatory framework that has neglected issues of sustainability and conservation and the substantial pressure created by population growth. According to USAID's Web site, accessed June 29, 2009:

95% of Bangladesh's natural forests and 50% of its freshwater wetlands are lost or degraded. Bangladesh now has among the smallest areas of protected and intact forest in the world, consisting of 1.4% of its landmass. Many terrestrial wildlife species have been lost during the last 100 years. In addition, the World Conservation Union (IUCN) in 2000 classified 40% of Bangladesh's freshwater fish species as threatened with national extinction.

Bangladesh's ecology is highly fragile and precariously poised. One potentially devastating and largely unforeseen issue that has received enormous attention during the past decade is the problem of arsenic in the water supply. In some areas of the country, natural arsenic deposits have entered the drinking water as increased numbers of tube wells have been introduced in order to irrigate paddy fields and provide clean drinking water. There are also concerns that arsenic is entering the food system in larger quantities. A recently reported Bangladesh University of Engineering and Technology study by Badruzzaman and Ali reported that rice grown on land that had been irrigated by arsenic-contaminated groundwater could deliver 0.3 milligrams (300 micrograms) of arsenic per kilo of paddy. The health risks associated with arsenic include cancers of various kinds as well as vomiting, abdominal pain and diarrhoea, and these disproportionately affect children and the elderly. Yet the health implications of Bangladesh's arsenic problem are not yet fully known. The WHO guidelines set out in 1967 specify a safe limit of 2.14 micrograms/kilograms of body weight per day (Mosquera and Rahman 2010).

## The International Politics of Water Management

Water-sharing disputes have dominated and regularly strained Bangladesh's relations with India (see Chapter 6). Bangladesh is highly constrained in terms of its "room for manoeuvre" in order to manage its water needs. The combined basins of the three enormous rivers cover about 80 percent of Bangladesh's land area, while only 8 percent of their drainage area lies within the country's own territory, leading to a situation in which "more than 90 per cent of the area is subject to the sovereign control of other co-riparian states" (Adnan 2009: 106). As a lower "riparian" country, it is therefore heavily vulnerable to the downstream effects of India's water-management efforts.

The main longstanding area of conflict has been India's Farakka barrage. The Ganges River runs across India into Bangladesh, and during the dry season it is a vital source of irrigation water for crops. In 1974, India constructed a barrage at Farakka that was designed to divert water into a tributary feeding the increasingly silted port of Kolkata. The barrage was neither an effective engineering solution to the problems of Kolkata port nor a deliberate attempt to undermine Bangladesh's economy, but the scheme quickly became a source of political tension between the two countries (Crow 1995). A provisional agreement between the two countries was signed in 1977, but this soon lapsed. The problem continued to fester until 1993, when Bangladesh raised the issue at the UN General Assembly, and in 1996 the two countries signed the thirty-year Ganges Water Treaty, which stated that they would share water equally whenever the water flow fell below an agreed amount of seventy thousand cubic feet per second. A second dispute relates to the Teesta, the fourth major river that flows from India into Bangladesh, which provides an important source of irrigation water in the northwest. A barrage built by Bangladesh in 1990 began to operate during the 1990s, but an Indian barrage constructed upstream has hampered its operation. The resolution of the subsequent long-running dispute has also proved elusive, but a new draft proposal tabled in March 2010 after a five-year hiatus has reopened the door to a treaty similar to the Farakka one. This opportunity followed from Hasina's visit to India earlier that year.

More recently, India's new Tipaimukh hydroelectric dam project has attracted opposition from Bangladeshis, who see it as another example of Indian interference with Bangladesh's water rights. The proposed Indian government project, due to cost $1.35 million, involves plans to build a 164-metre-high dam near the confluence of two rivers – the Barak and the Tuivai – in Manipur, just sixty miles from the Bangladesh border. Many local activists in India also fear that it will have an adverse environmental impact on local indigenous communities, fisheries resources and wildlife. Activists argue that eight villages will be totally submerged and another ninety will be affected, with as many as forty thousand people losing their land. Some links between activists from both countries already exist, and the increased efforts to build regional civil-society cooperation on such issues across national boundaries will be an important trend in the coming decade.

### Flood Control

Although annual flooding is an essential component of Bangladesh's agro-ecological system, there has been a long history of flood control efforts that have aimed, largely unsuccessfully, to try to mitigate the negative impacts of abnormal flooding on communities. These have been primarily centred on public engineering works to construct embankments along rivers in order to prevent overflowing. In 1922, a devastating flood affected the northern part of Bengal. A subsequent government report into how to improve mitigation of flooding by Kolkata Professor Prasanta C. Mahalanobis (1927) argued that the building of embankments as a flood control strategy would be ineffective due to problems of rapid siltation because they would simply raise the river beds. Nevertheless, this finding had been forgotten by the time the Pakistan government began its multimillion dollar flood control master plan in 1964. This was centred on the construction of precisely such infrastructure, was assisted by international donor funds and met with mixed results.

History repeated itself once again in 1989, when the FAP was launched in response to the heavy flooding that occurred during 1987 and 1988. These were the final years of Ershad's military government, and the plan, which was estimated to require $5 to $10 billion, was agreed by an unelected government and a multidonor group with little if any public debate. An attempt was made to consult local people as a concession won after a campaign involving local activists, researchers and international civil society. There was also resistance to the plan from some local communities, such as a well-documented mobilisation in Beel Dakatia (Adnan 2009). It was clear that FAP essentially rested upon the same set of technical assumptions that had been regularly discredited during the period since Mahalanobis's perceptive but largely ignored report more than half a decade earlier (Adnan 2009). After Ershad's removal in 1990, the caretaker government launched a task force to investigate viability. By 1993, despite already having spent millions of dollars of aid money, FAP had been shelved.

Local people who live with floods and outside officials have always tended, perhaps not surprisingly, to see the problem very differently. The key issue at the root of flood control is a contested view of floodplain management between those who favour a "dryland scenario" – normally outsiders and policy makers – and those who see the floodplains as "wetlands," which is the indigenous view of a complex farming system in which diversified, sustainable agricultural cropping, livestock and fisheries management activities are all possible under conditions of normal flooding (Adnan 2009: 107). The idea of the dryland proponents is that agricultural production can be increased by keeping flood water out of the fields during the monsoon season, but

this official view is at variance with the social and cultural perceptions of the floodplain dwellers, and largely ignores the views of concerned professional experts on agricultural and environmental issues . . . the dryland scenario may be regarded as the product of a technocratic culture in which scientific principles and skills are marshalled to address a narrowly defined "problem," without adequate concern for the wider picture.

The FAP became a case study of the way development experts have a tendency to conceive of problems in an overly technical way and seek to impose top-down solutions, rather than engaging locally with the perspectives and ideas of people who deal with such problems on a daily basis – in order to subordinate and apply scientific knowledge as effectively as possible to social needs. There is a danger that this pattern will repeat itself during the coming decade in relation to the problem of climate change, which has rapidly come to dominate the policy and development landscape.

### Climate Change

In 2007, the Fourth Assessment Report of the Inter-Governmental Panel on Climate Change predicted that average global temperatures could rise by close to three degrees centigrade by the end of the current century, and that sea levels could rise by fifty-nine centimetres, causing increased flooding due to higher rainfall and the melting of Himalayan snow and glaciers. Although Bangladesh has long been accustomed to the destructive power of cyclones, climate science now suggests that extreme weather events such as 2007's devastating Hurricane Sidr could be increasing in frequency. In 2009, Cyclone Aila hit southwest Bangladesh with even more force than its predecessor, fortunately with less damage to people and food crops, but it still caused serious loss to shrimp production. More frequent periods of heat wave and heavy rainfall are also now being predicted (Alam 2008). As a result, climate change has moved to the centre of the policy agendas of many of the main development agencies. For example, USAID now characterises Bangladesh as "the most vulnerable country to climate change impact," with rising global sea levels that are already altering local ecosystems and adding to economic hardship among the population. It is predicted that the coming decades will create a high level of additional distress:

By 2050, 70 million people could be affected annually by floods; 8 million by drought; up to 8% of the low-lying lands may become permanently inundated. In addition to direct inundation of a large population, the sea level rise will certainly result in increased frequency and severity of flooding along the major estuarine rivers. Saltwater intrusion problems will also be exacerbated in coastal aquifers. Some impacts manifesting in erratic weather patterns and unexpected extreme climatic events have already been evident.

There is an increasingly pessimistic diagnosis of Bangladesh's situation: as sea levels rise, land is lost from the coastal areas, and as the flow of river water down into the delta from the melting Himalayan glaciers increases, more land will then be lost through increased rapid soil erosion. Climate change is becoming a problem for communities in rural and urban areas. As we saw in Chapter 6, nearly a half of Dhaka's population lives in slums and squatter settlements. This has long been a city that is highly vulnerable to monsoon flooding, causing great human suffering and economic loss. Poor drainage due to poor infrastructure and management means that floods regularly affect at least half the city's area. Climate change is also predicted to affect Dhaka through increased heat stress, due to the fact that the city's temperatures are slightly higher than those of the surrounding areas (Alam 2008).

The Bangladesh government has been quick to respond to the local and international climate change agenda, becoming the first to produce a National Adaptation Plan of Action in 2005, after a range of consultations were organised with local communities and civil-society groups (Ayers 2011). In November 2007, the government announced that it would incorporate the impacts of climate change into all of its development activities. It adopted World Bank recommendations regarding climate change impacts into a new twenty-five-year water-sector plan, coastal zone-management programmes and disaster-preparedness plans. A joint UK DFID and government of Bangladesh meeting was held in London in September 2008 in order to prepare for the Copenhagen UN Summit meeting on global warming. The result was a pledge by the United Kingdom for £75 million additional funding over the next five years in order to help fight climate change through adaptation, technology transfer and mitigation and to assist Bangladesh's efforts through further international resource mobilisation. The government also announced that it would add $45 million of its own resources during 2009 and outlined plans for a Multi-Donor Trust Fund, a basket-funding mechanism for adaptation resources. In September 2009, the government produced its *Climate Change Strategy and Action Plan* based on six "pillars for action": food security, social protection and health; comprehensive disaster management; infrastructure, research and knowledge management; mitigation and low carbon development; and capacity building and institutional strengthening (MoEF 2009). At the 2009 Copenhagen summit, despite its disappointing outcome, a delegation of 150 people from the Bangladesh government and civil society attended and played an active role. The wide range of climate change adaptation experiments currently underway has led one observer to suggest that "rather than pitying Bangladesh, [we] may end up learning from her example" (Beit 2011).

Climate change is clearly a pressing issue for Bangladesh, but there are growing concerns about the ways responses to this highly complex problem are unfolding. Perhaps unhelpfully, international media coverage of climate change issues in Bangladesh increasingly draws on a "crisis narrative." The headline of a Reuter's news agency article dated April 14, 2008, proclaimed that "Bangladesh faces climate refugee nightmare." There is increasing talk of the plight of internally displaced "climate change refugees" who are being forced to leave coastal and river areas in search of more secure environments. Johann Hari, writing in *The Independent* newspaper (June 20, 2008), reported on coastal villagers' accounts of increased problems of saline drinking water, farmland that has become too damaged to grow crops and coastal seas that have become too treacherous to fish. On one island near Cox's Bazaar, he reported that two-thirds of the land has disappeared and found a community whose population has fallen from thirty thousand to eighteen thousand in twenty years. He drew attention to fears that growing pressures on resources brought about by climate change could fuel increases in disorder and religious intolerance. Linking Bangladesh's crisis with the need for the world's wealthy countries to take action on the causes of climate change, he concluded with the apocalyptic message that "if we carry on as we are, Bangladesh will enter its endgame."

Although climate change constitutes a major crisis, the invention of new terms such as *climate refugee* sits uncomfortably within long-term narratives of poverty and livelihoods issues in Bangladesh. It implies a recent climate-driven break with past behaviours, rather than the continuation of and adaptation within people's long-term survival strategies. As Betsy Hartmann (2010) points out, the term *climate refugee* replays an earlier idea from the 1990s about "environmental refugees," which in turn recycles unhelpful colonial stereotypes of environmentally destructive peasants. The result is that the economic and political causes of environmental problems run the risk of being obscured and the demographic pressure for migration overemphasised. Bradnock and Saunders (2002) argue that we may apply overly simplistic understandings of the interplay between environment and human activity at our peril. Ideas about "environmental change" are as much socially and politically constructed as they are derived from formal scientific knowledge and data. Rivers have regularly changed course, and coastal areas are constantly being eroded. For many people, the need to migrate as a result of Bangladesh's unstable river and coastal ecology is not new, but rather has always been a part of the harsh livelihoods that were fragile long before climate change issues began to engage the minds of policy makers. The intensification of livelihood pressures is perhaps a more helpful diagnosis, especially if it can help to stimulate action that avoids the mistakes of past interventions like the FAP.

## Population

Over time, Bangladesh's fertile lands have attracted many people to its deltaic ecosystem. During the British period, the province of Bengal was already understood to be the most densely populated area in India. By 1901, the population of present-day Bangladesh was 28.9 million and had risen to 44.2 million by 1951 and to 129 million in 2001. Between 1901 and 2001, population density has increased from 200 to 896 people per square kilometre. Current (2009) estimates put the population at 162.7 million people. Some projections indicate Bangladesh will have a population of close to 250 million by 2050.

The delta's "success" in terms of its capacity to support a large population is due to three main sets of factors, as Kamal (2008) argues. First, the area is highly suitable for agriculture. The richness of the deltaic soil combines with high rainfall levels to create arable land of exceptionally high fertility. East Bengal was long considered among Indian states by the colonial authorities to contain prime rice-growing areas, such as the Mymensingh district, and by the start of the twentieth century, farming was the primary occupation of 87 percent of the population with rice, jute and cotton as the main crops. Second, the eastern part of Bengal benefits from a riverine environment with good drainage to the sea, and this helped to prevent the growth of the malaria-bearing mosquitoes that have thrived more successfully in the slower-moving rivers of present-day West Bengal. The third factor is that of religion, because it has long been observed that Muslim fertility has tended to be higher than Hindu fertility within the subcontinent. Population density, though uniformly high, is nevertheless uneven. When the notorious 1970 cyclone hit the coastal area, it caused maximum damage because it affected the islands at the mouth of the delta where farmers had migrated and concentrated in large numbers for the cultivation season. If it had hit the coast two hundred kilometres to the west in the *sundarbans*, where population density is much lower, it would have been less destructive and caused far lower loss of life (Bradnock 1984: 43). The urban population constituted 24.6 percent of the total population in 2006 and has been increasing at approximately double the rate of the overall population (EIU Country Report 2009).

## Population Growth and Family Planning

Concerns about population growth have a long history. During the British period, the authorities viewed the increase of population in what was already seen as a densely populated territory as a contributing factor to famine. During the early Pakistan era, the establishment of a FPA by social workers gradually led to the introduction of a family planning policy as part of Pakistan's First FYP (1960–5). The idea that food production and population growth was a trade-off became established, bolstered by the global neo-Malthusian discourse of the time.

At Liberation, Bangladesh quickly attracted considerable attention from the global, but predominantly Western, "overpopulation" lobby. This perspective was carried over into the First FYP of Bangladesh (1975–80), which gave family planning equal emphasis to food production, bringing in several ministries across different social sectors to combine it with maternal and child health initiatives and public-education efforts to form a broad-based family planning programme. By the end of the millennium, the fertility rate had declined from 6.3 births per woman from 1971 to 1975 to 3.3 (Barkat-e-Khuda 2005). In 1971, the annual population growth rate had been 2.5 percent. Since then, population control and family planning interventions have been extensively undertaken by government and NGOs supported by internationally funded initiatives. Over time, the government's family planning programme also came to include private-sector social-marketing organisations in a multiagency "partnership" approach. Overall, there has been considerable success in bringing down the population growth rate, which has declined from 2.2 percent in 1991 to 1.3 percent in 2006, according to official data from the Bangladesh Bureau of Statistics. Contraception use has widened, and the total fertility rate (the average number of children that a women bears over her lifetime) has dropped from 6.4 in 1970 to 2.9 in 2006. In 2006, UN data indicated that there was a crude birth rate of twenty-six per one thousand and a crude death rate of eight per one thousand.

There has been little religious opposition to family planning in Bangladesh (Barkat-e-Khuda 2005). Although many religious leaders favour a conservative interpretation of Islam, the Department of Family Planning's education workers have provided religious leaders with family planning messages based on religious messages, as well as health-education messages on breast-feeding and mother and child health, and *imams* are encouraged to speak about these issues at Friday prayers. Many *imams* favour the Hanafite school of Islam, often regarded as one of the liberal Sunni traditions, in which it is acceptable in some areas of life to make religious rulings in accordance with local circumstances. As a result, Bangladesh's Muslims have come to believe that – providing a wife approves – contraception is allowed because she has the same equal rights to a child as the father does.

The "success story" of population growth reduction was driven in no small part by the Malthusian impetus towards population control that was influential in domestic and international development policy from the 1970s onwards (World Bank 2008). After the UN Population Conference in Cairo in 1994, there was a shift from the international policy rhetoric of "population control" to one of "women's reproductive health," reflecting women's struggles over reproductive rights and choices. Nevertheless, Hartmann (1995) draws attention to the ways that global population control programmes can be seen as an additional burden placed by rich countries on poor people and as programmes that draw attention away from more equitable and effective solutions to the pressing economic, political and environmental problems many countries face.

Some argue that family planning services in Bangladesh are now losing momentum as donor and government priorities shift into other areas. Despite the gains made in the early 2000s when the growth rate was 1.59 percent, it was reported in 2006 that this figure had again increased to 2.9 percent, making the government's target of reducing the population growth rate to 1 percent by 2010 look unobtainable (Hasan 2006). At the same time, infant and child mortality has decreased due to a successful immunisation effort, and life expectancy has also risen dramatically, from forty-four years in 1970 to sixty-two years in 2003. UNICEF figures indicate that child mortality improved from 248 per thousand in 1960 to 69 per thousand in 2003, and infant mortality (under one year) from 149 per thousand to 46 per thousand during the same time period. The population growth rate remains a controversial issue.

Rashid (2005: 38) argues that Bangladesh is a good example of a country that remains poor in part because it has not yet been able to develop its human resources adequately:

Lack of natural resources has not hampered nations from achieving a relatively high standard of living, as witnessed in South Korea, Thailand and Malaysia. On the other hand the roster of less-developed countries is replete with nations rich in minerals, fuel and water resources and yet with a low average standard of living. The crucial factor, the catalyst one might say, is the human factor.

Although there have been some important achievements in developing the capacities and rights of Bangladesh's people in areas such as primary education and access to family planning services, quality of life for the majority of the population is threatened by the persistence of large-scale deprivation in many areas of social development. This remains a crucial challenge for the future.

## Migration and Refugees

Geographical mobility has long characterised the lives of many of the region's people, who have moved within Bengal and beyond. During the twentieth century and before, forms of "internal migration" took place from East Bengal, to other areas of the subcontinent and elsewhere within the British Empire. There was an internationalisation of migration during the Pakistan period, and this has grown into the "global" migration that occurs today (Knights 1996). In view of the often-harsh economic conditions under which the majority lives in Bangladesh, it is unsurprising that a strong tendency has existed for people to move in search of better opportunities (Naher 2002: 267). A complex mix of factors and incentives drives migration processes. For some poor rural people, a set of "push" factors contribute to seasonal migration as people travel to other areas as labourers in order to help with harvesting or with construction work, and also fuel the growing trend for rural to urban migration. Most people in Bangladesh also value education highly and search out educational opportunities that will give access to better-paying and higher-status jobs. A set of "pull" factors also operate in the cities, particularly Dhaka, where there may be the promise of economic opportunities that are unavailable in the countryside.

International migration from Bangladesh since the 1980s (short- and long-term, and within and beyond the subcontinent) is creating growing numbers of people in a so-called Bangladeshi diaspora. International migration has created many positive economic impacts, such as the growth of overseas remittances upon which the government now depends to balance its books. It has also brought political impacts, in the way that the immigration discourse has become a problematic issue with India, which accuses Bangladesh of not doing enough to curb illegal movements of people across its border. Immigration has also contributed to cultural changes in recent decades. These range from global Westernised *deshi* youth cultures to conservative religious traditions from the Gulf countries that have been brought back to Bangladesh by returning migrants. Today, the idea of international migration has also become a highly visible part of the cultural fabric of society, where large crowds of people can often be seen outside foreign embassies in Dhaka queuing for visas, and where the press has advertised citizenship lotteries in which millions of people apply for a tiny allocation of opportunities to begin a new life in a foreign country such as the United States or Canada.

The politics of migration has also been a visible feature of Bengal's history. At partition in 1947, there were large-scale movements of people across the new borders, and these continued for some time after. There has been far more focus on "Partition-in-the-West" than on events in Bengal (Rahman and Van Schendel 2004: 217). Bengal's partition was relatively peaceful by comparison with that in Punjab, and a process of "unregulated migration and everyday mobility" continued across the newly drawn border for many years afterwards (Ludden 2002: 226). Nevertheless, periodic unrest also contributed to various movements that took place during the period after the first migrants moved to East Pakistan in 1947, as Rahman and Van Schendel (2004: 217) describe in relation to one border area close to Rajshahi:

In 1950, riots in several parts of East Pakistan and India led to a new influx of settlers. The next marker occurred in 1952 when passports and visas were introduced, prompting some newly arrived settlers to return to India, and inducing some Muslims in India to cross the border and become Pakistanis. A one-day riot in Rajshahi town in 1962 was followed by similar riots across the border, leading to a renewed exchange of population. And finally, in 1965, war broke out between India and Pakistan, after which immigration into East Pakistan declined sharply.

The position of the hundreds of thousands of non-Bengali Urdu-speaking Muslims who had fled to Bangladesh from other parts of India – such as Bihar – in 1947 became problematic in 1971 when their outsider status was cemented through their support for Pakistan during the Liberation War. Although many have subsequently managed to migrate to Pakistan through legal or illegal means, others remain in refugee camps in Bangladesh. Some of these have successfully integrated into Bangladeshi society, but many others, particularly the older generation, still face discrimination and exclusion.

## Migration, Conflict and Refugees in the Chittagong Hill Tracts

There has also been the movement of Bengali settlers, often state-sponsored, into the CHT, where incomers have intruded upon and displaced non-Bengali *jumma* (shifting cultivator) hill peoples. The displacement of non-Bengali groups has led to longstanding conflicts over rights and citizenship. The CHT in the southeast of Bangladesh was made a protected area for "tribal" groups during the British period, and nontribal people were not permitted to own land. In 1962, the Kaptai Dam was built by the Pakistan government in order to provide power for the Karnaphuli hydroelectric power station, which provides 5 percent of the country's electricity. The ponding of water resulted in the displacement of one hundred thousand people, few of whom received proper compensation, and the loss of substantial area of cultivable land (Parveen and Faisal 2002). From the 1970s, there was an influx of Bengali settlers in the CHT, often encouraged by the state, and this quickly brought resistance from the Chakmas and other tribal communities, who quickly saw that they lacked full citizenship rights within the new Bengali state.

As a result, the Parbatya Chattagram Janasaghati Samity (PCJSS) Party was formed in 1972, with a military wing (known as the Shanti Bahini, or Peace Force). The CHT issue had long been complicated by regional politics. In 1956, Pakistan had used Chittagong as a base for proving covert support to India's Naga dissidents, and it was later used by factions of the Burmese Communist Party and by Rohingyas (Arakani Muslims) organisations in their struggles against the Burmese government in Rangoon (Ali 1993). By the 1970s, Bangladesh was accusing India of giving support to the groups that emerged to resist the oppression and further marginalisation of these non-Bengali communities. As many as twenty-five thousand indigenous people had died in the guerrilla war before the peace accords were signed in December 1997. The treaty promised a political solution to the issue, and a number of new steps began to be taken. Although a Regional Council Act had been passed in 1988 in order to provide a limited form of decentralised government, an interim CHT Regional Council was not established until 1999. Following the treaty, there was a phased return of weapons from PCJSS members who were compensated with Tk 50,000 each (close to US$700), and a start was made with the return and rehabilitation of hill refugees from Tripura. In 2001, the CHT Land (Disputes Settlement) Commission Act was passed and a Land Commission set up in 2004. A total of sixty-four PCJSS members and close to two hundred repatriated refugees were reinstated to their former government jobs, and 675 members were appointed as police constables.

However, by 2009, both CHT community members and many Bangladeshi human-rights activists were arguing that much still needed to be done in order to address fundamental issues underlying the internal conflict: settlers are still active in taking over hill peoples' land, the return of land to repatriated hill people and those dispossessed has not been carried out, the CHT Regional Council and the three elected district councils are not yet functioning and lack an adequate budget and the army has withdrawn from only a fraction of its hundreds of military camps in the CHT.

*International Migration to the United Kingdom, the Gulf and Elsewhere*
In the 1920s, small numbers of Bengali sailors, who had long served with
the British merchant navy, began to settle in the United Kingdom. They
were mainly from the northeastern area of Sylhet, which was then part of
Assam. The reasons as to why people from landlocked Sylhet district should
have developed this historical link with seafaring is somewhat obscure, but
there has been conjecture that it is the result of various factors – "the watery
landscape of Sylhet, the blood of wandering Arabs, or just the desperate need
to earn a living" (Adams 1987: 13). After the Second World War, during
which many of these Sylhetis had contributed to the British war effort, more
left their ships to settle in British cities such as London or Birmingham. Many
found employment in the new "Indian" restaurant trade.

During the 1950s and 1960s, these small populations were able to grow
further as UK labour-recruitment initiatives offered new opportunities
(Gardner 1992). Immigration restrictions were introduced in the United
Kingdom during the 1960s and 1970s, but family reunion rules made it
possible for numbers to increase up to the 1980s, with a strong geographical
bias continuing towards those from the initial Sylheti areas, rather than
from Bangladesh more widely. Emigration to the United States, Canada
and Australia also took place at this time. There are "permanent and semi-
permanent" and "short term, precarious" forms of migration (Knights
1996).

In the 1970s, a second set of international migration opportunities
opened up as increased oil prices created a new demand for labour in the
Middle East to support its industrialisation. Much of this labour was sourced
from south and southeast Asia and from north Africa. The Bangladesh government, eager to access the potential of international remittances provided
by migrant workers, established a Wage Earners' Scheme in 1974. This
scheme provided favourable rates of exchange for workers on temporary
contracts to remit their earnings through official money transfers. As a result, large numbers of temporary workers from Bangladesh began working
in the Middle East. As competition increased among the contract labour
travel agencies that quickly emerged, a set of new destinations was added,
including Malaysia, Singapore, Hong Kong, South Korea, Morocco and
Taiwan. Malaysia's economic boom, in particular during the 1990s, provided
many job opportunities for Bangladeshis in oil, rubber and other industries.
However, all these tended to be short-term, relatively insecure migration
opportunities and were vulnerable to periodic disruption by political tensions in the Middle East. The tough working conditions and fluctuating
wage levels and exchange rates often made the lives of many such migrants

extremely harsh. By 1996, it was estimated that seven hundred thousand Bangladeshis were working in Saudi Arabia, the majority of whom worked in manual labouring jobs and earned less than counterpart workers from Pakistan or India, on account of their lower level of skills and training.

In the 1990s, official figures indicated that 250,000 workers were leaving Bangladesh each year, and by 2007, it was estimated that four million Bangladeshis were working abroad, but in both cases the real figure was probably much larger. There is still much to be learned about the experiences of this large-scale movement of people as they travel abroad for jobs, the impacts of the money that they send home and the social changes associated with their return. Rashid (2005: 10) is correct when he suggests that issues of migration in relation to Bangladesh still await proper documentation – "a story largely untold and under-researched."

### Bangladeshis in India

More recently, migration by Bangladeshis into India has received considerable commentary in the Indian media. This has been a contentious issue since the 1950s because Indian politicians have been found from time to time to be building political support by registering and providing services to outsiders. For example, elements within Assam's Congress Party have been accused of encouraging immigration from Bangladesh in order to increase its ethnic Bengali Hindu voter base (Karlekar 2005).

There have been two major strands to immigration debates in India – the scale of illegal immigration and the potential threat of terrorism. In 2001, a Group of Ministers report suggested that there were fifteen million illegal Bangladeshi immigrants in India. Within the atmosphere of the so-called war on terror, there has been growing anxiety in India about the possibility that Bangladesh is now a safe haven for Islamic militant groups to launch attacks against India (Karlekar 2005).

### Bangladesh beyond Its Borders

Bangladesh is a geographically bounded country and a community, real and imagined, that increasingly exists at a global level. Today, it has become commonplace to point to the increasing networks of transnational connections that link migrants from Bangladesh and such networks have grown in scale and intensity.

Bangladesh has long been influenced by sections of its population located outside its borders. During the period immediately before 1971, its new government operated as a government in exile from India, although there was also support forthcoming from communities of migrants in places such as Britain. As Delwar Hussain (2007:201) documents, members of the UK Bengali community organised support for the effort to force the Pakistani leadership to cede power after the 1970 election, sending some of their members to fight, and then went on to mobilise resources to assist their side in the conflict. For example, the London branch of the AL held fundraising events in many UK cities, lobbied members of Parliament, raised public awareness and sent supplies for the war effort. This challenged the popular stereotype of passive, marginalised immigrant communities and highlighted instead their connection and commitment to reshaping the postcolonial world. At the same time, and in more international elite circles, Ravi Shankar and George Harrison organised the Concert for Bangladesh in New York City, which was held on August 1, 1971, that raised international awareness of the refugee crisis and donated a still-disputed sum of money for UNICEF's relief work with children.

For many years afterwards, and up to the present day, unresolved issues from this period have continued to influence the politics of Bengali communities both in the United Kingdom and Bangladesh. Members of the JI political party, who were branded collaborators and war criminals after 1971, found sanctuary in East London and the JI Party's UK mission was established in the East London Mosque (Hussain 2007). British Bangladeshi politics and organisations continue to reflect and reinforce historical and political debates "at home." Local government councillors in London's Tower Hamlets area (where there is a large Bangladeshi community) are frequently simultaneously members of the AL or the BNP and members of British parties. Institutions such as Shadinata Trust try to assert broader Bengali secular and cultural traditions, while the East London mosque often serves to reinforce the idea that local community initiatives and educational work should be primarily informed by Islamic ideas and traditions instead (Hussain 2007).

Today, it appears that many of the younger generation in the United Kingdom now express their Bangladeshi identities with stronger reference to global Islamic revival than with the nationalist tradition. For many of the younger generation, there is declining interest in what appear as distant national historical issues far removed from the problems of inner-city deprivation and a renewal of interest in religious identities that seem to offer more possibilities for dealing with today's problems. One of Sarah Glynn's (2006: 28) informants from the Nirmul Committee admitted that his was often quite difficult work:

If you ... talk to [the] younger generation [of] the Bengali community ... if you say "what is '71, what's happened? There was a war between Bangladesh and who?" [They will say] "Oh, maybe the British or something." People don't have a clue.

The committee, originally set up in Bangladesh by Jahanara Imam in 1992 to revive the unfinished business of bringing 1971 war criminals to justice, serves in London as a local pressure group to educate young people about the spirit and history of 1971. But as Glynn (2006) has argued, such efforts increasingly compete somewhat unfavourably with the attraction of Islamic ideology. As migrant communities have moved into second and third generations, the idea of Bangladesh is under constant review and reconstruction and may diverge from those found among people in the country.

Bangladesh's large and rapidly growing diaspora has taken root in recent decades in a variety of locations. Remittances from this migration have been particularly important in contributing to economic growth and the provision of new infrastructure, particularly in Sylhet and in areas of eastern Bangladesh such as Comilla. By the late 1990s, the volume of remittances to Bangladesh had overtaken that of international development assistance flows.

## Well-Being and Capabilities

The human development index (HDI) designed by the UN Development Programme aims to provide a measure of development trends that moves beyond one that only looks at economic indicators. It combines the GDP with a country's achievements in health and education in order to assess social progress. Although Bangladesh has made good progress in the years between 1995 and 2005, its HDI remains the second lowest among the seven South Asian countries (MHHDC 2008).

### Social Protection

*Social protection* is the term used for policies that are designed to address problems of poverty and vulnerability and is taken to include not only government measures implied by the older term *social security* but also the wider nongovernmental, private and informal forms of social and economic support. World Bank (2006c) describes how the government of Bangladesh has attempted to "complement" the three stands of its overall development policy thrust (growth-centred economic policies, governance and institutional reforms and the development of physical and human capital) by putting in place a set of social protection policies and programmes. These aim to safeguard the well-being of the most vulnerable sections of the population and are often termed *safety nets*.

The main forms are cash-based transfer programmes, and these take a variety of shapes and cater to different sections of the population. For example, there are cash-for-work programmes that are open to many poor adults, payments given as stipends to poor children to enroll in school, cash transfers made to the elderly and pensions provided to special groups, such as civil servants. Other schemes involve food and other in-kind transfers, ranging from rapid-response food-assistance programmes to address the needs of vulnerable people in the aftermath of a natural disaster, to food transfer programmes to poor people combined with micro-credit programmes. These seek to enable recipients to set up small businesses in order to reduce their vulnerability in the medium to longer term. Such schemes are administered by government line ministries such as the Social Welfare, Food and Disaster Management, and Women and Children's Affairs ministeries, and many involve partnership arrangements with NGOs.

The impact of these policies and programmes is decidedly mixed. There is some evidence for the short term "alleviation" of poverty and vulner-ability through assisting peoples' access to consumption goods and to the process of "consumption smoothing," which is the need to cover temporary shortfalls in household incomes, for example, due to seasonal fluctuation in wage rates or labour availability. However, coverage remains limited. It remains the case that, out of the sixty million people who are poor in Bangladesh, only between four and five million people receive assistance through such safety net programmes. Also there is less evidence that these policies are contributing to the long-term creation of employment or asset accumulation, and therefore there is little chance that such interventions can contribute to overcoming the structural barriers that help to reproduce poverty. A third problem is that of "targeting" the right people. Schemes that use landownership as a criterion for selection may be increasingly outmoded because low levels of landholding are increasingly common to poor and nonpoor people. Also, where social protection includes micro-credit provision, selecting only those who are capable of repaying loans may exclude others who are the most vulnerable. Finally, there is a persist-ent problem with the misallocation of resources, which ranges from 10 to 50 percent of resources for food-based interventions and 5 to 25 percent in the case of cash-based programmes (World Bank 2006c).

Furthermore, government expenditure on safety net programmes remains low and has declined, despite the fact that population growth means that the number of poor people has remained close to the sixty mil-lion mark. Social assistance expenditure reached a peak of about 8 percent of public expenditure in 1998, but by 2004 was close to 2.5 percent (World Bank 2006c).

## *Health*

There has been good progress with improving life expectancy and with reducing fertility and child mortality. In many other areas of health provision,
the picture is less positive. Extensive malnutrition exists in Bangladesh, and
almost half of children under six years of age are stunted or underweight
(World Bank 2006c). There has been slow progress made with increasing the
levels of sanitation available to its population. During the ten years between
1994 and 2004, sanitation only increased by four percentage points, while
the percentage of the population with sewage connections fell from 12 to
7 percent (MHHDC 2008). Bangladesh faces rising levels of tuberculosis,
and the HIV/AIDS epidemic remains a serious potential threat to public
health. In the government's 2004–5 survey, HIV prevalence among intraven-
ous drug users in the central area of Bangladesh was found to be 4.9 percent
and increasing (Ministry of Health and Family Welfare 2005). A range of
noncommunicable diseases such as heart disease are on the increase. Despite
some progress with immunisation, it seems that the earlier momentum has
not been successfully sustained, and after a five-year absence it was reported
by UNICEF that polio had reappeared in some areas.

Successive governments have attempted to build on the rudimentary
health system that was inherited in 1971, initially through the extension of
public provision. Most people's health needs were mainly met by traditional
healers and other informal, often unqualified, providers. From the mid-
1980s to the mid-2000s, investment in public-health services led to some
impressive progress, at least at the formal level. For example, in 1990, the
government launched a national-level primary health-care policy to equip
each union with either a Union Sub-Centre or a Health and Family Welfare
Centre (HFWC) in order to provide a health complex for every *upazila* and
to build a general hospital or tertiary facility for each district. By 1995, it was
reported that 92 percent of unions and 95 percent of rural *upazilas* had these
facilities. In 1979, the government established its Expanded Programme
of Immunization in order to reduce vaccine-preventable morbidity and
mortality, and the initiative soon achieved significant gains. According to
UNICEF, it has become the most successful public-health intervention in
the country: for example, while in 1986 there were 41 neonatal deaths due
to tetanus per 1,000 live births, this had dropped to 2.3 per 1,000 live births
by 2000.

At the same time, the continuing large gaps in public provision grew
more populated with growing activities of numerous NGOs, local-level
philanthropic initiatives and new private-sector providers such as diag-
nostic centres. Taking the total health sector as a whole (and not just the

government sector), by 2000 there were two and a half times as many hospitals, double the number of beds as there had been in the mid-1980s, with ten hospitals per million people, and one hospital bed per three thousand people. The number of doctors increased from 105 to 241 per million people, and registered nurses from 34 to 136 per million people (Osmani 2006).

The New National Health Policy established in 1998 produced a large-scale Health and Population Sector Programme (HPSP), with aims that included putting a full-time doctor and nurse in each HFWC, constructing thirteen thousand new community clinics (1 per 6,000 persons) and offering an Essential Services Package in order to ensure proper primary health and basic reproductive health services. A new Client Bill of Rights to improve accountability was promised but did not materialise. According to Osmani (2006: 206) when the programme was evaluated it was found that little had changed: "people's right to health remains jeopardized by the lack of essential drugs in government facilities," and that poor households "feel that government services discriminate against them and treat them with disrespect." Progress has proved much more elusive in broader public-health provision than in family planning services. The HPSP was a major sectorwide programme aimed to promote universal access to health care, develop better-quality health services and reduce population growth to replacement level (2 children per couple) by 2005 (Barkat-e-Khuda 2005). Despite the increased public investment in public services it was found that services retracted overall, due to poor management of facilities leading to increased waiting times and lack of availability of medicines. Those rating government health services as "good" fell from 37 percent to 10 percent during the life of the programme, and it was found that the public preferred "unqualified practitioners over government services" (Cockcroft et al. 2007). The HPSP was succeeded by the five-year Health, Nutrition and Population Sector Programme that aimed to improve basic health services in cost-effective, equitable and accessible ways, but, as recent studies have indicated, major problems continue (see, e.g., Sida 2010).

Investment in public-health infrastructure has unfortunately been offset by two factors. The first is the problem that many public facilities remain inactive due to lack of adequate staff, medicine or equipment. The second is that there is inequality of access because, in practice, it is necessary to access government doctors doing private work, which only the better off can afford. As in many other parts of South Asia, the health-care system continues to be characterised by weak delivery systems based on "an underfunded and inefficient public sector and an unregulated and expensive private sector" (MHHDC 2008: 197). In general, a low priority is given to public health by policy makers, and those funds that are allocated are frequently mismanaged. The result has been a massive growth of private provision. For example, in 1980 there were 510 government hospitals and 39 private, and by 1998 there were 626 private hospitals and clinics and 647 government ones. Recent observation suggests that a preference for private providers increasingly characterises even the very poorest people seeking health-care services (Sida 2010).

The system today consists of a mix of public-private provision, in theory overseen by government, but in practice largely unregulated. A diverse set of practitioners draws upon a range of different levels of formal and informal knowledge. Low-income people are faced with complex choices, which they seek to manage the best that they can by using the limited information and resources that they have (Sida 2010). For example, if a rural woman seeking obstetric care faces complications, she has various formal and informal local service options, from using home remedies provided by a *dai* home-birth attendant to a range of *kabiraj* indigenous healers, such as herbalists or folk psychotherapists, to accessing formal-sector medical professionals, either in the bazaar or the hospital. A key factor in these choices will be cost because traditional services will tend to be less detrimental to a household's long-term livelihood, than if a procedure at a hospital or clinic is required that may require sale of an asset such as a cow or the incurral of a long-term household debt if a loan is taken to cover the cost of treatment (Muna et al. 2002).

There has been undoubted progress during the last two decades in improving health services, including expanded health-care facilities, a large-scale immunisation programme, greatly increased access to clean drinking water and improved food security. The consequence of all this has been a decline in infant mortality and an increased life expectancy. But in practice, the public-health system provides only the barest level of service for most of the population. Also, from a rights perspective, there continue to be some serious problems. There is a pronounced disparity of access to basic services between rich and poor, low-quality services and unsociable behaviours displayed towards service users by health personnel, low levels of participation by ordinary people in the design and implementation of programmes and a general lack of local and national accountability. Real change requires not just building more infrastructure and employing more medical personnel but also major policy reforms, which go beyond the health sector to include education, decentralisation, civil society and judiciary (Osmani 2006).

## Education

Bangladesh's constitution (Article 17) recognised the right of every person to an education and defined a state responsibility to provide basic education. At that time, education services were provided by a diverse range of private and charitable schools and by *madrasas* (Muslim religious seminaries) that offered various types of religious education. After Liberation, the government nationalised the thirty-six thousand private schools that existed in diverse forms across the country, although opposition to the conversion of teachers into public employees in some areas meant that the nationalisation was only partial. The *madrasa* sector presented a particular challenge because the dominant, privately funded and more conservative Qomi *madrasas* drew on orthodox Islamic texts and included the teaching of Urdu, which made them less suited to preparing young people for life in post-Liberation Bangladesh. The government has therefore promoted a system of publicly funded alternative Aliya reformed *madrasas*, and this effort has been reasonably successful. The Aliya schools combine secular subjects with religious teaching and constitute more than 30 percent of secondary school students, but have not displaced the centrality of the Qomi *madrasa* tradition (Bano 2008).

The national planning process has gradually increased its focus on primary education. In the First FYP (1973–8), only a low priority was given to primary education, but with the Second FYP (1980–5), a universal primary education project was established as part of a stronger commitment to primary education. This was strengthened in the Third FYP (1985–90), and the universal primary education project continued. By the Fourth FYP (1990–5) it was well established and a general education project was created, designed to increase primary education enrollment and ensure that five years of education was completed. The emphasis now was on providing new buildings and free textbooks, and this gradually shifted towards improving the quality of curriculum, teaching approaches and teacher training (Askvik 2000).

It was not until the 1990s that systematic government attention was given to increasing school enrollment rates, and these quickly began to increase, reaching 100 percent by the end of the decade. In 1992, a Task Force on Primary and Mass Education was created by the new democratic government aimed at addressing the problem of mass illiteracy. The education reform process had always been highly political. Mujib's education nationalisation programme was primarily designed to help create a support base by filling local key positions with his supporters and had been resisted in some areas. The decision to make primary education compulsory was also an essentially populist decision that had first been suggested by Ershad and then later introduced by Khaleda Zia. But for the first time, primary education now began to feature as a key national issue that was above party politics.

At this time, the idea of "nonformal education" also began to enter the policy mainstream, driven primarily by the NGO sector, which aimed to target children adolescents and adults (Askvik 2000). Nonformal education deemphasised the more "academic" concerns of the curriculum, bringing a focus on training programmes and targeting education towards poor people. It uses a truncated model with the more limited aims of teaching only basic writing, reading and calculation. Central is the idea of applying more up-to-date pedagogical techniques such as using examples from local village life to illustrate classes, relying more on participation, experimentation and flexibility than on the in-depth training of teachers. Initially government was sceptical of NGO ideas, fearing that their reliance on donor funds might divert international resources from the main education system, but government eventually began to include NGOs and set up a separate directorate to look after nonformal education, even if many in the government mainly viewed NGOs as providers of literacy training rather than "proper" primary education (Askvik 2000: 5)

Although much has been achieved, civil-society organisations such as Education Watch have regularly drawn attention to quality issues within the primary education that is provided, a finding that is more recently echoed by the Sida Reality Check Approach initiative (Sida 2010). Furthermore, although there may have been an impressive increase in access to primary education, access remains unequal at the secondary and tertiary levels: "only 24 percent of expenditures at the secondary level, and only 17 percent of expenditures at the tertiary level accruing to the poor" (World Bank 2006c: ii). School management committees had first been set up in 1981 to try to involve the local community in schools, and parent-teacher associations were established in 1984 to give further stimulation to parent involvement, but neither has met with much success. A key challenge has been that of creating workable channels for citizens to demand better services from schools. A central problem is that the parents of "first-generation learners" are unlikely to be confident enough either to get involved or to question or challenge teachers and education authorities.

The privatisation agenda has gained ground in the education sector primarily at the university or tertiary level. In 1992, the government passed a Private University Act that made it possible for the University Grant Commission to approve private universities alongside the twelve public universities that have existed for many years. The oldest public university, Dhaka University, had been established in 1921. By 2006, more than fifty new universities had been approved, and many have become significant and highly profitable institutions, proving opportunities to the new middle classes seeking to avoid the instability found in the public sector and the prohibitively high costs associated with seeking an education overseas.

In June 2010, the government approved a new National Education Policy that aims to bring all students in Bangladesh under a single unified system that includes general, *madrasa* and vocational education. All students will also be required to study religion and ethics. The new policy introduces nontraditional subjects such as information and communication technology alongside "Bangladesh studies," in an attempt to broaden its practical relevance and remain consistent with the spirit of the country's history.

## Conclusion: People, Nature and Resources

Bangladesh's geography has been a blessing and a curse. It has offered fertile agricultural land, provided plentiful water resources and made possible ocean access via the Bay of Bengal through the country's Chittagong port, which is at a strategic position on the boundary of south and southeast Asia. At the same time, the Bengal delta is an environmentally unstable area that is vulnerable to a wide range of natural hazards, and these have been worsened by intensive human cultivation and settlement and by the forces of global climate change. The people of the Bengal delta have long sought to manage a uniquely difficult set of resource pressures, through ever more ingenious and intensive strategies for organising whatever economic and environmental resources available to them. Long-standing internal, regional and international traditions of migration remain central to the livelihood strategies of many households, with remittances growing to become a mainstay of the economy. Government strategies to develop and protect the well-being of Bangladesh's people will be central to a sustainable future, with education and health remaining key priorities for government and nongovernmental agencies. These remain pressing and difficult areas of social policy and are still sectors that are extensively underwritten by international development donor funding.

The interplay between Bangladesh's people and its wider environment is set to become the dominant policy theme once again for national-, regional- and global-level discussions of Bangladesh's future. The neo-Malthusian concerns about overpopulation that began during the 1970s and the flood control discourses of the 1980s and 1990s have, by the second decade of the twenty-first century, begun to evolve into and link with the new "climate change" narratives. It remains to be seen how far the framing of Bangladesh within these emerging climate change ideas will offer productive new ways to safeguard the future well-being of its people, or whether these simply lead back to earlier unhelpful forms of top-down intervention. This framing will most likely lead some observers to continue to predict apocalyptic scenarios of social and environmental breakdown and mass international migration. However, it seems that the government at least has made a good start with making climate change a central element of its current and future policy agenda.

8

## Conclusion

## Bangladesh Faces the Future

This account of Bangladesh's state, economy and civil society began by considering the situation of the garment industry workers, many of whom once again took to the streets during 2010 in pursuit of higher pay and improved working conditions. The protests provided an entry point into an analysis of the country's political economy and as a microcosm of issues arising from its precarious location at the periphery of the global economy. In considering the "past of the present," it has been necessary to explore the historical factors that continue to influence contemporary Bangladesh, alongside the more familiar and well-documented worlds of the international aid regime – including struggles over land and tenancy, an incompletely institutionalised postcolonial state, the dominance of social and political patronage relationships, the country's fragile ecological interdependence with its neighbours and the pluralist religious traditions in society that have long characterised the Bengal delta.

The concluding chapter draws together the main ideas and discussions of the earlier seven chapters and assesses the key dilemmas for the future in relation to building a more inclusive politics, securing economic growth while addressing rising inequalities, operating on a rapidly changing international stage and dealing with increasing environmental challenges. An important motivation for writing this book is the fact that Bangladesh has received far less attention from researchers, policy makers and the media, particularly in Western societies, than it deserves. The case of Bangladesh should be of central concern to anyone interested in at least four important sets of wider contemporary issues: the ways that processes of economic globalisation are impacting upon low-income countries; the challenges of improving international development policies and practices; the need to understand how a stable "moderate Muslim majority" country addresses the threat of extremism within an international context in which Muslims are increasingly demonised as global terrorists; and peoples' struggle to build viable and sustainable livelihoods under the environmental threat of climate change. In the second part of the chapter, each of these themes is discussed further.

## Dilemmas in an Age of Neoliberalism

First, there is the need to reinvigorate democratic institutions in ways that can build more inclusive politics, while safeguarding society from risks brought by growing forms of intolerance and "uncivil society." Chronic problems remain within the current political system. In the prevailing "winner takes all" political culture, the loser is left with few incentives to carry on political opposition and resorts instead to confrontation. The confrontational political style is also an outcome of weak authoritarian political parties that lack either discipline or accountable organisational structures. Institutions that were designed to provide control, oversight and accountability, including the bureaucracy, judiciary and local government, are effectively "politicised," not in the sense that they are made to serve any particular ideology but because their interests are aligned with the private money-making agendas of politicians (Sobhan 2004). Partisan politics, in which the ruling party seeks to establish control over public resources, can only be challenged by the creation of more effective institutions that can enforce a clearer boundary between public and partisan interests.

It has become common to refer to Bangladesh as a failing state, yet, in some areas, the state has operated surprisingly effectively under extremely adverse circumstances. It has successfully mobilised resources towards national social priorities such as universal primary education, intensified agricultural production to build a level of food security and, most recently, is taking the initiative at the global level to develop a climate change policy agenda well before most other countries (Ayers 2011). Nevertheless, stronger forms of organised citizen action will be needed if government and institutions are to be made more responsive and accountable. Within civil society, hierarchy and patronage mostly mitigate against creating horizontal alliances among subordinate classes for collective action. Yet, within local communities, some NGOs are beginning to find ways for coalition building between poor and nonpoor groups to take action without confrontation over local issues such as water and sanitation in ways that benefit the poorest (Lewis and Hossain 2008). Such approaches may also bring potentially significant outcomes in terms of gender equality because face-to-face interaction between grassroots organisations and their constituencies generates opportunities to challenge norms and rules governing women's subordination (Kabeer 1994). The 2010 Right to Information Act may open up new possibilities for a strengthening of citizenship rights. Yet the "civics" approach will not be sufficient on its own; it needs a thoroughgoing political reform process that challenges "the underlying dynamic of political behaviour and the interests involved in the competition for power" (Sobhan 2004: 4101).

Second, Bangladesh needs to build on its recent economic growth in ways that check rising inequalities and to ensure that sufficient benefits are harnessed for its still-large rural population and not just for the urban middle classes. Driven by the liberalisation policies initiated by its military leaders in conjunction with the international donor establishment from the late 1970s onwards, an increasing role has been played by market forces. Agricultural production has increased and more than a million new formal-sector jobs have been created in the garment industry. At the same time, it is clear that the gap has widened between people engaged in traditional rural livelihoods and those who have been able to move into new opportunities for more formal employment. Attempts to privatise large-scale nationalised industries, such as the jute mills, have met with extensive resistance from workers, trade unions and political patrons, leaving this once important industry severely depleted. Behind impressive levels of economic growth, there is also the hidden reality of a "rotten foundation" of growing illegality and lawlessness, embodied by the *mustaan* culture and signs of rising economic inequalities (Devine 2008). Shortages of energy in Dhaka and other urban areas are beginning to create major challenges for the government. Electricity shortages, in particular, feed unrest especially in urban areas and impact negatively on garment exports.

At the same time, as Sen (2011: 44) has argued, Bangladesh has made some impressive gains compared to India, despite the latter's economic dynamism, on the basis of government policies and civil-society initiatives. Although India has far stronger economic indicators than Bangladesh (a GNP per capita of US$1,770 compared with US$590), this economic advantage does not translate across into other key social indicators in which Bangladesh has made stronger progress. For example, life expectancy is 66.9 years compared to India's 64.4 years, the child under five mortality rate is fifty-two per thousand compared with sixty-six per thousand in India and mean years of schooling amount to 4.8 years compared with 4.4 years in India.

Third, Bangladesh will need to manage effectively the new strategic context of global terrorism that it now finds itself in, with domestic and international implications. At the height of the rhetoric of the so-called war on terror during the mid-2000s, it became commonplace among Western governments and think tanks to suggest that Bangladesh's society and politics were becoming more Islamist in character. For example, Maneeza Hossain (2006) wrote alarmingly of "the rising tide of Islamism" in Bangladesh and raised the possibility of the country becoming a failed state. When the BNP formed a government in alliance with JI in 2001, a series of terrorist incidents began occurring over the next few years. Many people feared the rise of a new Islamic politics and saw these events as a key threat to political stability, as extremists became emboldened by a growing public disillusionment with the dysfunctional political status quo. Yet there have been no terrorist attacks in the country since 2005. The government has been proactive in banning Islamist groups, and it has pursued a useful policy of greater cooperation with India in order to tackle the activities of such groups on either side of each country's border.

Finally, the market-based intensification of agriculture across most areas of the country and the rapid expansion of shrimp production in ecologically precarious areas has significantly added to pressures on the natural environment. A key effect of Bangladesh's efforts at deregulation, liberalisation and market reform is to attract forms of international capital that emphasise only short-term gain, leading to an increasingly unfavourable interaction between economy and environment (Rahman and Wiest 2003). Environmental degradation contributes to a shift away from small-scale agricultural and artisanal livelihoods in the informal sector towards a greater dependence on formal, though highly volatile, types of employment in growing export-oriented industries, such as garments and shrimp. Economic change impacts on human ecology and livelihoods, because people are forced to move from their original rural communities as a consequence of higher levels of market integration, urbanisation and environmental degradation. The result is an ever-growing set of economic, political and social problems, intensified by the process of rapid, unplanned urbanisation. If the process of global integration deepens, ordinary people may find that they have even less control over change. The environmental dangers Bangladesh faces will during the coming years need to be grasped and tackled, primarily through national and local initiatives, but they will also require extensive support at the international level.

## Wider Issues

### Responding to Rapid Global Change

Bangladesh has long experienced the fact that areas of the developing world are increasingly polarised between small countries and their more powerful neighbours. Globalisation has helped strengthen Bangladesh's powerful neighbour India. Bangladesh now faces the increasing power of China and India as BRIC countries. The BRICs concept usefully encapsulates an important shift in Western thinking that recognises that globalisation no longer equates with U.S.-style economic change. China is becoming more involved with Bangladesh, as indicated, for example by the announcement in 2010 of the Chittagong deepwater port project. The challenge for Bangladesh will be to secure benefits for itself as it increasingly becomes an arena of competition between the two BRIC neighbours. Bangladesh's growing presence within international institutions, including a well-publicised role in UN peacekeeping forces since the 1990s, will assist with this.

Globalisation has led not only to the rapid rise of nontraditional exports but also to large numbers of global migrants and the new centrality of remittances to the GNP. Emerging interest among international capital to exploit the country's newly important gas and other fossil fuel reserves is also likely to intensify. Oil and gas deposits in the Bay of Bengal have come to be seen as major economic assets by Bangladesh, along with India and Burma, and the demarcation of international boundaries and securing investment for the exploitation of these resources will be key areas of contention over the next decade. The 2008 global financial crisis highlighted aspects of Bangladesh's relative lack of integration with global markets and suggested that this may have worked largely to its benefit. It also made it clear that a balance will need to be achieved between building higher levels of domestic resilience and further integration with international capital. The financial collapse came hard on the heels of the global food crisis, which highlighted the need for the government to ensure a firmer grip on ensuring the population's access to affordable, domestically grown food. The crisis also indicated a higher-level step change in the global economy in the form of new recognition that greater regulation of markets and financial institutions was needed. Perhaps the postneoliberal world has now become a little closer.

*Improving Development Relationships*

The development industry has supported incorporation into global systems in several sectors of the economy. For example, the introduction of water-seed-fertiliser technologies has restructured agricultural production and distribution networks and has created new links with international agribusiness. The expansion of rural infrastructure, including extensive road building and the construction of new bridges, has helped to integrate Bangladesh's villages more fully into wider markets. Despite this, and the rise of remittances, garments and the shrimp industry, much of Bangladesh's economy remains relatively marginal to global capital. In terms of production and employment, the country is still dominated by the informal economy. Yet power is becoming more narrowly concentrated, and the possibilities of an oppositional civil society may fade as its cohesion is undermined by the overdominant influences of state and market.

Although aid is less important in overall financial terms than it was a decade ago, Bangladesh remains an important country in terms of the changing ideas and policies of the international development industry. Bangladesh has come to be seen as a development success story, both in terms of its policy progress towards the MDGs and the profile and contribution of its NGO sector. For Amartya Sen (2011: 44), Bangladesh's progress can be understood as a result of the "committed public policies" of the government and the "imaginative activism" of the NGO sector. At the same time, development discourse remains an important structural matrix that helps to influence, if not actually determine, many of Bangladesh's policy choices. Judgments about Bangladesh's progress and "success" are still made visible and understood predominantly through developmentalist frameworks, such as those created by the MDGs or TI's *Corruption Perceptions Index*, or through the growing international reputation of the larger NGOs. Yet *development* is a term that means different things to different people, from the range of prescriptions provided by professional foreign experts to the villager who speaks of *unnayan*, meaning a combination of general progress and locally determined modernity.

Since the 1980s, various forms of the neoliberal policy agenda have dominated international donor policies towards Bangladesh, and these have, to varying degrees, been incorporated into government thinking. These changes have favoured less government regulation, a reduced public sector and the delegation of many state services to other forms of providers in the nongovernmental and private sectors. In some areas, such as agricultural input liberalisation and the removal of restrictions on export industries, such as ready-made garments and shrimp, there has been significant economic impact. In others, such as public-sector reform, progress has been extremely limited. In other areas, such as the privatisation of certain state-owned industries, the effects have been negative, concentrating the control of assets in a few hands and compounding inefficiencies. Continuing pressure to "chip away" at the state may, as Cooper (2002: 202–3) has argued in relation to Africa, further undermine the positive potential of both state and markets to improve governance and protect citizens:

keeping a market economy functioning requires more state capacity than maintaining a centralised economy; the latter may work badly, but it functions in the interests of the rulers. Shrinking government may do less to shrink the capacity of bad rulers to steal than to weaken the basic institutions that permit workforces to be trained and to stay healthy, or to provide the predictable services which domestic and foreign investors need.

The case of Bangladesh offers an important international example of the need to balance state and market.

The world of aid relationships has long been rife with sets of unresolved tensions between aid donors and recipients (Hossain 2004: 25). The history of aid in Bangladesh provides valuable insights into the local and international power relationships that have influenced state, economy and civil society since 1971:

Aid is less important in Bangladesh than before, but the goodwill of donor countries is still needed. In the classic client manner, Bangladesh needs patronage in the international system, for favoured trading or immigration status, for recognition, protection from more powerful neighbours.... Accepting aid may be part of the price of gaining donor countries' goodwill. But this also suggests that if the costs of aid are too high – in terms of unpalatable conditions, administrative time and effort, and the discomfort of the personal experience of being a recipient – aid can be declined or stalled.

Today, Western aid is undergoing rapid change, within its own systems and the wider context in which it operates. There is an emphasis on more aid coordination, harmonisation and local ownership; there is a global recession that is already reducing the resources that it has at its disposal; and there are new aid entrants such as China with levels of resources that seem set to reshape the world of aid. Such changes are already presenting the government and people of Bangladesh with new opportunities and impetus to address the inequalities that have traditionally characterised aid relationships.

### Stability within a Moderate Muslim-Majority Country
The "idea" of Bangladesh will always be one that is diverse, and one that is maintained and contested inside and outside its geographical borders. This has become even more the case as the forces of globalisation highlight and accelerate the ways that Bangladesh is constructed and understood, transformed into a nation containing identities that exist well beyond the territoriality of its borders. The idea of Bangladesh is sustained, in many different forms, within a set of diverse and dispersed migrant communities around the world.

Although it seems unlikely that the problem of terrorism has retreated more than temporarily, Bangladesh's long history of multiple religious traditions offers at least some safeguard against the level of problems that have become observable in Pakistan. Few countries that emerged from the decolonisation process into independence have the cultural and linguistic coherence possessed by Bangladesh, and this has helped to shape national identities and provide a counterweight against such instability. Although a *wahabi* influence has grown through inflows of religious assistance to the Qomi *madrasa* sector, and as cultural backwash from migration by Bangladeshi workers to Saudi Arabia, a more tolerant set of syncretic, Sufi- and Hindu-influenced traditions remains alive:

> Visions of community in precolonial Bengal were not necessarily based on a simple designation of Hindu and Muslim. The many diverse people of Bengal oriented themselves in a number of categories, such as *ashraf* and non-*ashraf* status. Muslim rulers were not simply Muslims but were Turk, Afghan, Habshi, and Arab. . . . Group identity was asserted in a number of complex ways that during the colonial period were reduced to "Hindu" and "Muslim." The conflation of the numerous visions of community into two categories became the source of religious nationalism in the twentieth century. (Uddin 2006: 180)

Diverse religious and cultural histories of early Bengal remain instructive and important for understanding how a complex cultural, linguistic and religious identity helps to hold together today's Bangladesh, and they challenge any simplistic binary notion of religious ideology and practice. At the same time, tensions around religious and cultural identities regularly surface, much as they do in any other society. In April 2011, for example, an organisation of *baul* singers holding a peaceful two-day cultural event in Rajbari were attacked by local activists who claimed that the event was "anti-Islamic," and this was followed the next week by a human chain protest organised by *baul* supporters outside the National Press Club in Dhaka ("Bauls' Human Chain Protests," 2011).

### Environment and Climate Change

Images of environment, nature and landscape have long been central to the ways Bangladesh is experienced and imagined, both by locals and outsiders. There is a long history to the romantic vision of a premodern, classless rural society of Bengal that presented the delta as being populated by picturesque villages, dramatic rivers and opulent paddy fields, whose ripening rice each year turns a golden colour at harvest time. Such imagery became an important symbolic element of the nationalist vision of the new country. Rabindranath Tagore's 1906 song "Amar Sonar Bangla" ("My Golden Bengal"), which was to become Bangladesh's national anthem, had originally been written to inspire the struggle for reunification after the 1905 partition of Bengal by the British.

The complexity of Bangladesh's environment and ecology has never been particularly well understood by scientists. Many of the agricultural and natural resource predictions made about Bangladesh have proved incorrect. For example, the potential of the country's agricultural system to adapt and expand was underestimated during the 1970s, and the achievement of rice self-sufficiency two decades later was met with surprise (Bradnock and Saunders 2002: 52). The same may also be true of the "crisis narrative" of destructive environmental change that is now being circulated in the development field and the global media:

the vicious circle of global warming, sea level rise and coastal inundation has such common-sense logic and apparently severe human consequences that the name of Bangladesh has become synonymous with flooding, mass death and migration on a globally threatening scale. In the process Bangladesh has become one of the most potent symbols in the arguments surrounding climate change and global warming.

Today it is the destructive power of nature that now dominates this romantic tradition, where cyclones and floods periodically wreak destruction on people in a country that has been made even more vulnerable by the forces of climate change, accelerated by the effects of economic transformation far away in the industrialised world. The government of Bangladesh has been one of the first to respond to the challenge of climate change. Although there is unpredictability about the future trajectories of environmental, economic and social change, the resilience and adaptability of Bangladesh's people remains an important beacon of hope.

# Glossary of Bengali Terms

| | |
|---|---|
| *adivasi* | indigenous people of the Indian subcontinent |
| *ajlaf* | a term used for lower social orders |
| *amon* | autumn rice crop |
| *apa* | sister |
| *ashraf* | higher-status title, sometimes indicating a claim of descent from the family of the Prophet Muhammad |
| *aus* | early summer rice crop |
| *bagda* | brackish water shrimp |
| *bazaar* | marketplace |
| *bediya* | river gypsies |
| *beel* | floodplain water body |
| *bhadralok* | respectable people |
| *bhai* | brother |
| *bhasha andolon* | language movement |
| *boro* | winter rice crop |
| *char* | river land, often shifting when rivers change course |
| *dalaal* | broker or intermediary |
| *dargar* | shrine |
| *deshi* | general term referring to a person from or product of the subcontinent |
| *dharma-nirapeksata* | neutrality in religion |
| *diwani* | right to collect land revenue |
| *fakir* | religious medicant |
| Faraizi | early nineteenth-century Bengali Muslim reformist movement |
| *golda* | freshwater prawn |

| | |
|---|---|
| *gusti* | lineage group |
| *hat* | weekly or biweekly market |
| *imam* | mosque leader who conducts the prayers |
| *ghat* | river port |
| *gherao* | collective attempt to gain redress by surrounding an employer's office |
| *gono andolon* | people's movement |
| *gram* | village |
| *gram sarkar* | village government |
| *gusti* | patrilineage |
| *haor* | a form of lake |
| *hartal* | strike or stoppage |
| *hoirani* | harassment |
| *jama'at* | congregation of worshippers (Muslim) |
| *jamdani* | a high-quality muslin cloth |
| *jawan* | enlisted man |
| *jotedar* | rich tenant farmers |
| *jumma* | shifting cultivator |
| *khas* | land that has been newly formed by changing river courses, or confiscated from landowners in breach of land-reform legislation, that becomes state-owned land legally reserved for redistribution to landless households |
| *lakh* | one hundred thousand |
| *madrasa* | Muslim religious seminary |
| *matbar* | village leader or elder |
| *mazar* | tomb or mausoleum |
| *mukhti bahini* | freedom fighter, term given to the forces that fought against Pakistan in 1971 |
| *mullah* | Muslim religious leader |
| *mustaan* | person involved in organised crime, hoodlum |
| *nawab* | a title given to a ruler or noble |
| *para* | neighbourhood of a village |
| *paribar* | family |
| *parishad* | council |
| *paurashava* | municipality |
| *pir* | saint, holy man |
| *purdah* | Muslim or Hindu norm of gender seclusion |

| | |
|---|---|
| *rakkhi bahini* | defence force, a paramilitary group formed by Mujib in 1975 |
| *razakar* | means volunteer, but refers to informal paramilitary forces organised by Pakistan army in 1971 |
| *sadar* | headquarters |
| *salish* | traditional mechanism for village dispute settlement, less formal than the village courts |
| *samaj* | local residential community, society |
| *samity* | NGO-formed grassroots group |
| *sarkar* | government |
| *shushil samaj* | civil society, literally "gentle society" |
| *swaraj* | self-rule |
| *taka* | Bangladesh currency (Tk) (approximately US$1.00 = Tk70) |
| *thana* | old subdistrict, literally "police station" |
| *unnayan* | development or modernity |
| *upazila* | new subdistrict, coined by Ershad |
| *waz mahfil* | lecture by Islamic scholar |
| *zakat* | Islamic duty to pay one-fortieth of one's income to the poor |
| zamindar | originally intermediaries who collected revenue from farmers, later a loosely used term for landlord |
| *zila* | district |

# Bibliography

"Achieving MDGs: UN Chief Terms Bangladesh a Model Country," *The Daily Star*, April 22, 2010, http://www.thedailystar.net/newDesign/news-details.php?nid= 135359 (accessed May 16, 2011).

Adams, Caroline. 1987. *Across Seven Seas and Thirteen Rivers: Life Stories of Pioneer Sylheti Settlers in Britain*. London: Tower Hamlets Arts Project.

Adnan, Shapan. 2009. "Intellectual Critiques, People's Resistance and Inter-riperian Contestations: Constraints to the Power of the State Regarding Flood Water Control and Water Management in the Ganges-Brahmaputra-Meghna Delta of Bangladesh," in *Water, Sovereignty and Borders in Asia and Oceania*, ed. Devleena Ghosh, Heather Goodall and Stephanie Hemelryk Donald. London: Routledge, 104–24.

Afsar, Rita. "Poverty, Inequality and the Challenges of Pro-Poor Governance in Bangladesh," *Journal of South Asian Development* 5, no. 2 (2010): 187–219.

Afzal, M. Rafique. 2001. *Pakistan: History and Politics: 1947–1971*. Oxford: Oxford University Press.

Ahmed, Rasiuddin and Steven Haggblade. 2000. Introduction to *Out of the Shadow of Famine: Evolving Food Markets and Food Policy in Bangladesh*, ed. Rasiuddin Ahmed, Steven Haggblade and Tawfiq-e-Elahi Chowdhury. Baltimore, MD: Johns Hopkins University Press, 1–20.

Ahmed, Reaz. "Ship Breaking Industry Remains Largely Ignored," *The Daily Star*, February 26, 2005, http://www.thedailystar.net/2005/02/26/d50226011513.htm (accessed May 16, 2011).

Ahmed, Sadiq. 2006. "The Political Economy of Development Experience in Bangladesh," in *Growth and Poverty: The Development Experience of Bangladesh*, ed. Sadiq Ahmed and Wahiduddin Mahmud. Dhaka, Bangladesh: University Press, 93–148.

Ahmed, Sadiq and Wahiduddin Mahmud. 2006. Preface to *Growth and Poverty: The Development Experience of Bangladesh*, ed. Sadiq Ahmed and Wahiduddin Mahmud. Dhaka, Bangladesh: University Press, ix–xxii.

Ahmed, Salahuddin. 2004. *Bangladesh: Past and Present*. New Delhi: A. P. H. Publishing.

Alam, Mozaharul. "Floods in Dhaka," *id21 Insights* 71 (January 2008), http://www.eldis .org/go/topics/insights/2008/climate-change-and-cities/floods-in-dhaka (accessed May 11, 2011).

Alam, Mozaharul and Mohammed Golam Rabbani. "Vulnerabilities and Responses to Climate Change in Dhaka," *Environment and Urbanization* 19, no. 1 (2007): 81–97.

Alam, S. M. Shamsul. 1995. *The State, Class Formation, and Development in Bangladesh.* Lanham, MD: University Press of America.

Alavi, Hamza. 1972. "The State in Postcolonial Societies," in *Imperialism and Revolution in South Asia*, ed. Kathleen Gough and Hari P. Sharma. London: Monthly Review Press, 145–73.

Ali, S. Mahmud. 1993. *The Fearful State: Power, People and Internal War in South Asia.* London: Zed Books.

Amin, Aasha Mehreen. "Imams against Dowry?" *The Daily Star Magazine*, July 16, 2004, http://www.thedailystar.net/magazine/2004/07/03/human.htm (accessed May 16, 2011).

Anam, Tahmima. 2007. *A Golden Age.* London: John Murray.

Anisuzzaman, M. 2001. "The Identity Question and Politics," in *Bangladesh: Promise and Performance*, ed. Rounaq Jahan. London: Zed Books, 45–63.

Ashman, Darcy. "The Democracy Awareness Education Program of the Association of Development Agencies in Bangladesh (ADAB)," *Discourse: A Journal of Policy Studies* 1, no. 2 (1997): 31–47. Dhaka, Bangladesh: Institute for Development Policy Analysis and Advocacy, Proshika.

Askvik, Steinar. 2000. "Modernization, Mass Education and the Role of the State in Bangladesh." Paper presented at European Network of Bangladesh Studies Workshop, Oslo, May 14–16.

Ayers, Jessica. "Resolving the Adaptation Paradox: Exploring the Potential for Deliberative Adaptation Policy-Making in Bangladesh," *Global Environmental Politics* 11, no. 1 (2011): 62–88.

Bangladesh Rural Advancement Committee (BRAC). 1983. *The Net: Power Structure in Ten Villages.* Rural Study Series 2, BRAC, Dhaka.

————. 2009. *The State of Governance in Bangladesh 2008: Confrontation, Competition, Accountability.* Institute of Governance Studies, BRAC University, Dhaka.

Banks, Nicola. "A Tale of Two Wards: Political Participation and the Urban Poor in Dhaka City," *Environment and Urbanization* 20, no. 2 (2008): 361–76.

Bano, Masooda. 2008. "Allowing for Diversity: State-Madrasa Relations in Bangladesh." Religions and Development Programme, Working Paper No. 13. University of Birmingham, United Kingdom.

Banu, Razia Akter. 1992. *Islam in Bangladesh: International Studies in Sociology and Anthropology.* Leiden, The Netherlands: E. J. Brill.

Barkat-e-Khuda. 2005. "Fertility Decline in Bangladesh: Role of Family Planning Programme and Socio-economic Changes," in *Islam, the State and Population*, ed. Gavin W. Jones and Mehtab S. Karim. London: C. Hurst and Company, 218–32.

Barua, Tushar Kani. 1978. *Political Elite in Bangladesh.* European University Studies Series XIX, vol. 4. Bern, Switzerland: Peter Lang.

"Bauls' Human Chain Protests at Rajbari Assaults," *New Age*, April 30, 2011, http://newagebd.com/newspaper1/metro/17148.html (accessed May 19, 2011).

Baxter, Craig. 1998. *Bangladesh: From a Nation to a State.* Boulder, CO: Westview Press.

Beit, Don. "The Coming Storm," *National Geographic Magazine*, June 2011, http://ngm.nationalgeographic.com/2011/05/bangladesh/belt-text (accessed May 18, 2011).

Bertocci, Peter. 2001. *The Politics of Community and Culture in Bangladesh.* Dhaka, Bangladesh: Centre for Social Studies, Dhaka University.

Bertrand, Jaques and André Laliberté, eds. 2010. Introduction to *Multination States in Asia: Accommodation or Resistance?* Cambridge: Cambridge University Press.

Bhardwaj, Sanjay K. 2011. "Contesting Identities in Bangladesh: A Study of the Secular and Islamist Frontiers." Unpublished working paper. Asia Research Centre, London School of Economics and Political Science.

Bhattacharya, Debapriya. 2005. *Delivering on the PRSP in Bangladesh: An Analysis of the Implementation Challenges.* Dhaka, Bangladesh: Centre for Policy Dialogue.

Bhattacharya, Deben. 1969. *Songs of the Bards of Bengal.* New York: Grove Press.

Bhuiyan, Abul Hossain Ahmed, Aminul Haque Faraizi and Jim McAllister. "Developmentalism as a Disciplinary Strategy in Bangladesh," *Modern Asian Studies* 39, no. 2 (2005): 349–68.

Blair, Harry. 1997. "Donors, Democratization and Civil Society: Relating Theory to Practice," in *Too Close for Comfort? NGOs, States and Donors,* ed. D. Hulme and M. Edwards. London: Macmillan, 23–42.

———. 2001. "Civil Society, Democratic Development and International Donors," in *Bangladesh: Promise and Performance,* ed. Rounaq Jahan. London: Zed Books, 181–218.

———. 2003. "Civil Society and Pro-poor Initiatives at the Local Level in Bangladesh: Finding a Workable Strategy." Paper presented at Staying Poor: Chronic Poverty and Development Policy Conference, University of Manchester, UK, April 7–9.

———. 2008. "Success and Failure in Rural Development: Bihar, Bangladesh and Maharashtra in the Late 1980s," in *Speaking of Peasants: Essays on Indian History and Politics in Honor of Walter Hauser,* ed. William R. Pinch. New Delhi: Manohar, 421–52.

Bode, Brigitta. 2002. "In Pursuit of Power: Local Elites and Union-Level Governance in Rural North-Western Bangladesh." Unpublished research report. Dhaka: CARE Bangladesh.

Bose, Sarmila. "Anatomy of Violence," *Economic and Political Weekly* 40, no. 41 (October 8, 2005): 4463–71.

Bose, Sugata and Ayesha Jalal. 2004. *Modern South Asia: History, Culture, Political Economy.* 2nd ed. New York and London: Routledge.

Boyce, James K. 1987. *Agrarian Impasse in Bengal: Constraints to Technological Change.* Oxford: Oxford University Press.

Bradnock, Robert W. 1984. *Agricultural Change in South Asia: Case Studies in the Developing World.* London: John Murray.

Bradnock, Robert W. and Patricia Saunders. 2002. "Rising Waters, Sinking Land? Environmental Change and Development in Bangladesh," in *South Asia in a Globalizing World: A Reconstructed Regional Geography,* ed. Robert W. Bradnock and Glyn Williams. Harlow, UK: Pearson Education, 51–77.

Brammer, Hugh. "Flood in Bangladesh (II): Flood Mitigation and Environmental Aspects," *The Geographical Journal* 156 (pt. 2) (1990): 158–65.

Brett, E. A. 2009. *Reconstructing Development Theory.* Basingstoke, UK: Palgrave Macmillan.

Buckland, Jerry. 2003. "Non-governmental Organizations and Civil Society in Bangladesh: Risks and Opportunities of Globalization," in *Globalization, Environmental Crisis and Social Change in Bangladesh,* ed. Matiur Rahman. Dhaka, Bangladesh: University Press, 141–62.

Carr, Marilyn and Sanae Ito. 2010. "Packaged to Perfection: The SPS Agreement and Aquaculture in Bangladesh," in *Trading Stories: Experiences with Gender and Trade*, ed. Marilyn Carr and Mariama Williams. London: Commonwealth Secretariat, 117–24.

Chandhoke, Neera. 2002. "The Limits of Global Civil Society," in *Global Civil Society 2002*, ed. M. Glasius, M. Kaldor and H. K. Anheier. Oxford: Oxford University Press, 35–54.

Chatterjee, Partha. 2004. *The Politics of the Governed: Reflections on Popular Politics in Most of the World*. New York: Columbia University Press.

Chatterji, Joya. 1994. *Bengal Divided: Hindu Communalism and Partition 1932–1947*. Cambridge: Cambridge University Press.

Chowdhury, Elora Halim. 2009. "Challenges for the Women's Movement in Bangladesh: Engaging Religion, Development and NGO Politics," in *Recreating the Commons? NGOs in Bangladesh*, ed. Farida Chowdhury Khan, Ahrar Ahmad and Munir Quddus. Dhaka, Bangladesh: University Press, 207–46.

Chowdhury, Zafrullah. 1995. *The Politics of Essential Drugs: The Makings of a Successful Health Strategy*. London: Zed Books.

Cockcroft, Anne, Neil Andersson, Deborah Milne, Md Zakir Hossain and Enamul Karim. 2007. "What Did the Public Think of Health Services Reform in Bangladesh? Three National Community-based Surveys 1999–2003," *Health Research Policy and Systems* 5, no. 1 (2007): 1–7.

Collier, Paul. 2007. *The Bottom Billion*. Oxford: Oxford University Press.

Cooper, Frederick. 2002. *Africa since 1940: The Past of the Present*. Cambridge: Cambridge University Press.

Corbridge, Stuart, Glyn Williams, Manoj Srivastana and Rene Veron. 2005. *Seeing the State: Governance and Governmentality in India*. Cambridge: Cambridge University Press.

Crook, Richard and James Manor. 1998. *Democracy and Decentralization in South Asia and West Africa: Participation, Accountability and Performance*. Cambridge: Cambridge University Press.

Crow, Ben with Alan Lindquist and David Wilson. 1995. *Sharing the Ganges: The Politics and Technology of River Development*. New Delhi: Sage.

Davis, Peter R. and J. Allister McGregor. "Civil Society, International Donors and Poverty in Bangladesh," *Commonwealth and Comparative Politics* 38, no. 1 (2000): 47–64.

Department for International Development (DFID). 2000. "Partners in Development: A Review of Big NGOs in Bangladesh." Dhaka, Bangladesh: UK DFID.

Devine, Joseph. 1998. "Empowerment and the Spiritual Economy of NGOs in Bangladesh." Paper to European Network of Bangladesh Studies, Fifth Workshop, University of Bath, April 16–18.

———. "Ethnography of a Policy Process: A Case Study of Land Redistribution in Bangladesh," *Public Administration and Development* 22 (2002): 403–14.

———. 2008. "Wellbeing and the Rotten Foundations of a Development Success." Briefing Paper 3/08. February. Economic and Social Research Council Research Group on Wellbeing in Developing Countries, University of Bath, UK, www.welldev.org.uk (accessed May 12, 2011).

De Vylder, Stefan. 1982. *Agriculture in Chains – Bangladesh: A Case Study in Contradictions and Constraints*. London: Zed Press.

Diamond, Jared. 2005. *Collapse: How Societies Choose to Fail or Survive.* London: Penguin.

Dorosh, Paul. 2000. "Foodgrain Production and Imports: Towards Self-sufficiency in Rice?" in *Out of the Shadow of Famine: Evolving Food Markets and Food Policy in Bangladesh,* ed. Rasiuddin Ahmed, Steven Haggblade and Tawfiq-e-Elahi Chowdhury. Baltimore, MD: Johns Hopkins University Press, 21–48.

Easterly, William. 2006. *The White Man's Burden: Why the West's Efforts to Aid the Rest Have Done So Much Ill and So Little Good.* Oxford: Oxford University Press.

Eaton, Richard. 1993. *The Rise of Islam and the Bengal Frontier, 1204–1760: Comparative Studies on Muslim Societies.* Berkeley: University of California Press.

Economist Intelligence Unit (EIU). 2009. Bangladesh Country Report, December, London: EIU.

Faaland, Just and J. R. Parkinson. 1976. *Bangladesh: The Test Case of Development.* London: C. Hurst and Company.

Farmer, B. H. 1983. *An Introduction to South Asia.* London: Methuen.

Fernando, Jude L. 2011. *The Political Economy of NGOs: State Formation in Sri Lanka and Bangladesh.* London: Pluto Press.

Food and Agriculture Organization of the United Nations (FAO). 2007. *Fishery Country Profile.* Rome: UN FAO.

Gardner, Katy. "'Londoni-gram': International Migration and the Village Context in Rural Bangladesh," *New Community* 18, no. 4 (1992): 579–90.

Gellner, Ernest. 1995. "The Importance of Being Modular," in *Civil Society: Theory, History, Comparison,* ed. John A. Hall. Cambridge: Polity Press, 32–55.

Glynn, Sarah. 2006. "The Spirit of '71: How the Bangladeshi War of Independence Has Haunted Tower Hamlets." Institute of Geography Online Paper Series, Paper GEO-020. School of Geosciences, University of Edinburgh.

Government of Bangladesh (GoB). 2005. *National HIV Serological Surveillance 2004–2005 Bangladesh: Sixth Round Technical Report.* Dhaka, Bangladesh: National AIDS/STD Programme, Ministry of Health and Family Welfare, GoB.

———. 2006. "The Role of Bangladesh in United Nations Peacekeeping Operations." United Nations Wing, Ministry of Foreign Affairs, Armed Forces Division, Dhaka.

Guhathakurta, Meghna. 2003. "Globalization, Class and Gender Relations: The Shrimp Industry in South Western Bangladesh," in *Globalization, Environmental Crisis and Social Change in Bangladesh,* ed. Matiur Rahman. Dhaka, Bangladesh: University Press, 295–308.

Haq, M. Enamul. 1975. *A History of Sufi-ism in Bengal.* Dhaka: Asiatic Society of Bangladesh.

Haq, M. Nurul. 1966. *Comilla Cooperative Experiment.* Comilla: Pakistan Academy for Rural Development.

Harriss-White, Barbara. 2003. *India Working: Essays on Economy and Society.* Cambridge: Cambridge University Press.

Hartmann, Betsy. 1995. *Reproductive Rights and Wrongs: The Global Politics of Population Control.* Cambridge, MN: South End Press.

———. "Rethinking Climate Refugees and Climate Conflict: Rhetoric, Reality and the Politics of Policy Discourse," *Journal of International Development* 22 (2010): 233–46.

Hartmann, Betsy and James Boyce. 1983. *A Quiet Violence: View from a Bangladesh Village.* London: Zed Books.

Hasan, Faruque. "Population Growth Rate Rising Again," *The Daily Star*, April 26, 2006, http://www.thedailystar.net/2006/04/26/d604261503127.htm (accessed May 16, 2011).

Hasan, Samiul. "Voluntarism and Rural Development in Bangladesh," *Asian Journal of Public Administration* 15, no. 1 (1993): 82–101.

Hashemi, S. M. 1995. "NGO Accountability in Bangladesh: NGOs, State and Donors," in *NGO Performance and Accountability: Beyond the Magic Bullet*, ed. M. Edwards and D. Hulme. London: Earthscan, 103–10.

Hashemi, S. M. and Hasan, Mirza. 1999. "Building NGO Legitimacy in Bangladesh: The Contested Domain," in *International Perspectives on Voluntary Action: Reshaping the Third Sector*, ed. D. Lewis. London: Earthscan, 124–31.

Hashmi, Taj ul-Islam. 1992. *Pakistan as a Peasant Utopia: The Communalization of Class Politics in East Bengal 1920–1947*. Boulder, CO: Westview Press.

Holloway, Richard. 1998. *Supporting Citizens' Initiatives: Bangladesh's NGOs and Civil Society*. Dhaka, Bangladesh: University Press.

Hoogvelt, Ankie. 2001. *Globalization and the Postcolonial World: The New Political Economy of Development*. 2nd ed. Basingstoke, UK: Palgrave Macmillan.

Hossain, Abul. 2008. "Dynamics of Khas Land Management and Settlement in Haor Basin of Bangladesh." Unpublished report. Power and Participation Research Centre, Dhaka, Bangladesh.

———. 2009. "The Institutional Landscape for Urban Service Delivery." Unpublished report. Power and Participation Research Centre, Dhaka, Bangladesh.

Hossain, Mahabub. 1990. "Bangladesh: Economic Performance and Prospects," *ODI Briefing Paper, November*. London: Overseas Development Institute.

Hossain, Maneeza. 2006. "The Rising Tide of Islamism in Bangladesh," in *Current Trends in Islamist Ideology*, ed. Hillel Fradkin, Husain Haqqani and Eric Brown, vol. 3. Washington, DC: Hudson Institute, 67–77.

Hossain, Mohammed Motaher. "Changing Consumption Patterns in Rural Bangladesh," *International Journal of Consumer Studies* 34, no. 3 (2010): 349–56.

Hossain, Naomi. 2004. "The Real-life Relationship between Donors and Recipients in Bangladesh: Exploratory Research into the Sociology of Aid Relations." Unpublished paper. Institute for Development Studies, University of Sussex.

———. 2005. *Elite Perceptions of Poverty in Bangladesh*. Dhaka, Bangladesh: University Press.

Howell, Judith and Jenny Pearce. 2001. *Civil Society and Development: A Critical Exploration*. London: Lynne Rienner.

Hulme, David. "Thinking 'Small' and the Understanding of Poverty: Maymana and Mofizul's Story," *Journal of Human Development* 5, no. 2 (2004): 161–5.

Huntington, Samuel P. "The Clash of Civilizations?" *Foreign Affairs* 72, no. 3 (1993): 22–49.

Huque, Mahmudul. 2002. "Foreign Policy of Bangladesh: Ideology and Internal Dynamics," in *Thirty Years of Bangladesh Politics: Essays in Memory of Dr. Mahfuzul Huq*, ed. Mahfuzul H. Chowdhury. Dhaka, Bangladesh: University Press, 203–16.

Hussain, Delwar. "Globalization, God and Galloway: The Islamization of Bangladeshi Communities in London," *Journal of Creative Communications* 2, nos. 1–2 (2007): 189–217.

International Crisis Group (ICG). 2008. *Restoring Democracy in Bangladesh*. Asia Report No. 151, April 28. Washington, DC: ICG.

Iqbal, Iftekhar. "Return of the Bhadralok: Ecology and Agrarian Relations in Eastern Bengal, c. 1905–1947," *Modern Asian Studies* 43 (2009): 1325–53.

Irish, Leon E. and Karla W. Simon. 2005. *NGOs in Bangladesh: Legal and Regulatory Environment.* Dhaka, Bangladesh: Local Consultative Group.

Islam, Nurul. 1977. *Development Planning in Bangladesh: A Study in Political Economy.* London: C. Hurst and Company.

_____. 2004. *Looking Outward: Bangladesh in the World Economy.* Dhaka, Bangladesh: University Press.

_____. 2005. *Making of a Nation – Bangladesh: An Economist's Tale.* 2nd ed. Dhaka, Bangladesh: University Press.

Islam, Syed Serajul. 2002. "Elections and Politics in the Last Decade of the Twentieth Century in Bangladesh," in *Thirty Years of Bangladesh Politics: Essays in Memory of Dr. Mahfuzul Huq,* ed. Mahfuzul H. Chowdhury. Dhaka, Bangladesh: University Press, 133–48.

Jahan, Rounaq. 1972. *Pakistan: Failure in National Integration.* New York: Columbia University Press.

Jahan Rounaq, ed. 2001. *Bangladesh: Promise and Performance.* London: Zed Books.

Jahangir, B. K. 1982. *Rural Society, Power Structure and Class Practice.* Dhaka, Bangladesh: Centre for Social Studies.

_____. 1986. *Problematics of Nationalism in Bangladesh.* Dhaka, Bangladesh: Centre for Social Studies.

Jalal, Ayesha. 1995. *Democracy and Authoritarianism in South Asia: A Comparative and Historical Perspective.* Cambridge: Cambridge University Press.

Jannuzi, F. T. and A. T. Peach. 1980. *The Agrarian Structure of Bangladesh: An Impediment to Development.* Boulder, CO: Westview.

Jansen, Eirik G. 1987. *Rural Bangladesh: Competition for Scarce Resources.* Dhaka, Bangladesh: University Press.

"JCD Vandalises at RU over VC Panel," *The Independent* (Dhaka), April 11, 2005.

Kabeer, Naila. 1994. *Reversed Realities: Gender Hierarchies in Development Thought.* London: Verso.

_____. 2000. *The Power to Choose: Bangladesh Women and Labour Market Decisions in London and Dhaka.* London: Verso.

Kabeer, Naila, ed. 2005. *Inclusive Citizenship: Meanings and Expressions.* London: Zed Books.

Kamal, Nahid. 2008. The Population Trajectories of Bangladesh and West Bengal during the Twentieth Century: A Comparative Study. Ph.D. diss., London School of Economics and Political Science.

Karim, Fariha and Ian Cobain. "WikiLeaks Cables: Bangladeshi 'Death Squad' Trained by UK Government," *The Guardian,* December 21, 2010, http://www.guardian.co.uk/world/2010/dec/21/wikileaks-cables-british-police-bangladesh-death-squad (accessed May 16, 2011).

Karim, Lamia. "Politics of the Poor? NGOs and Grassroots Political Mobilization in Bangladesh," *Political and Legal Anthropology Review* 24, no. 1 (2001): 92–107.

_____. 2009. "Democratising Bangladesh: State, NGOs and Militant Islam," in *Recreating the Commons? NGOs in Bangladesh,* ed. Farida Chowdhury Khan, Ahrar Ahmad and Munir Quddus. Dhaka, Bangladesh: University Press, 149–81.

Karlekar, Hiranmay. 2005. *Bangladesh: The Next Afghanistan?* New Delhi: Sage.

Khan, Azizur Rahman. 2006. "Rising Inequality in Bangladesh: An Analysis of Courses and Policies for Containment," in *Growth and Poverty: The Development Experience of Bangladesh*, ed. Sadiq Ahmed and Wahuiddin Mahmud. Dhaka, Bangladesh: University Press, 3–20.

Khan, Haider. 2008. "Challenges for Sustainable Development: Rapid Urbanization, Poverty and Capabilities in Bangladesh." Munich Personal RePEc Archive, MPRA Paper No. 9290, posted June 24, http://mpra.ub.uni-muenchen.de/9290/ (accessed May 12, 2011).

Khan, Mushtaq H. 2000. "Class, Clientelism and Communal Politics in Contemporary Bangladesh," in *The Making of History: Essays Presented to Irfan Habib*, ed. K. N. Panikkar, T. J. Byres and U. Patnaik. New Delhi: Tulika.

Khan, Shakeeb Adnan. 1989. *The State and Village Society: The Political Economy of Agricultural Development in Bangladesh*. Dhaka, Bangladesh: University Press.

Knights, Melanie. "Bangladeshi Immigrants in Italy: From Geopolitics to Micropolitics," *Transactions of the Institute of British Geographers*, New Series 21 (1996): 105–23.

Kochanek, Stanley. 1993. *Patron-Client Politics and Business in Bangladesh*. New Delhi: Sage.

———. 2001. "The Growing Commercialization of Power," in *Bangladesh: Promise and Performance*, ed. Rounaq Jahan. London: Zed Books, 149–80.

Lieven, Anatol. 2011. *Pakistan: A Hard Country*. London: Allen Lane.

Lewis, David. 1991. *Technologies and Transactions: A Study of the Interaction between New Technology and Agrarian Structure in Bangladesh*. Dhaka, Bangladesh: Centre for Social Studies, Dhaka University.

———. 1993. "Bangladesh Overview," in *NGOs and the State in Asia: Rethinking Roles in Sustainable Agricultural Development*, ed. J. Farrington and D. Lewis. London: Routledge, 47–58.

———. "On the Difficulty of Studying 'Civil Society': Reflections on NGOs, State and Democracy in Bangladesh," *Contributions to Indian Sociology* 38, no. 3 (2004): 299–322.

———. 2010. "Disciplined Activists, Unruly Brokers? Exploring the Boundaries between Non-governmental Organizations, Donors and State in Bangladesh," in *Varieties of Activist Experience: Civil Society in South Asia*, ed. David N. Gellner. New Delhi: Sage Publications, 159–80.

Lewis, David and Abul Hossain. 2008. *Understanding the Local Power Structure in Bangladesh*. Swedish International Development Cooperation Agency (Sida). Stockholm: Sida Studies No. 22.

Lewis, David and Nazneen Kanji. 2009. *Non-Governmental Organizations and Development*. London: Routledge.

Lifschultz, Laurence. 1979. *Bangladesh: The Unfinished Revolution*. London: Zed Press.

Liton, Shakhawat and Rashidul Hasan. "Beximco Top Defaulter," *The Daily Star*, July 6, 2009, http://www.thedailystar.net/newDesign/news-details.php?nid=95620 (accessed May 16, 2011).

Lovell, Catherine. 1992. *Breaking the Cycle of Poverty: The BRAC Strategy*. Hartford, CT: Kumarian Press.

Ludden, David. 1999. *An Agrarian History of South Asia: The New Cambridge History of India*, vol. 4. Cambridge: Cambridge University Press.

———. 2002. *India and South Asia: A Short History*. Oxford: Oneworld Publications.

Mahalanobis, Prasanta C. 1927. *Report on Rainfall and Floods in North Bengal 1870–1922*. Calcutta: Irrigation Department, GoB.

Mahbub ul Haq Human Development Centre (MHHDC). 2008. *Human Development in South Asia 2007: A Ten Year Review*. Islamabad, Pakistan: Oxford University Press.

Mahmud, Simeen. 2009. "Why Do Garment Workers in Bangladesh Fail to Mobilize?" *IDS Bulletin*, Brighton, UK: Institute of Development Studies.

Maksud, A. K. M. 2006. "Action Research for Human Development in Beday (River Gypsy) Community." Research report. Dhaka: Research Initiatives Bangladesh.

Mamdani, Masuma. 1992. "Early Initiatives in Essential Drugs Policy," in *Drugs Policy in Developing Countries*, ed. Najmi Kanji, Anita Hardon, Jan Willem Harnmeijer, Masuma Mamdani and Gill Walt. London: Zed Books, 1–23.

Mannan, Manzurul. 2005. "Rural Power Structures and Evolving Market Forces in Bangladesh," in *Civil Society and the Market Question: Dynamics of Rural Development and Popular Mobilization*, ed. K. B. Ghimire. Basingstoke, UK: Palgrave Macmillan, 271–98.

Mascarenhas, Anthony. 1986. *Bangladesh: A Legacy of Blood*. London: Hodder and Stoughton.

McGuire, John. 2009. "Globalization and Economic Change in Bangladesh," in *Trade, Labour and Transformation of Community in Asia*, ed. Michael Gillan and Bob Pokrant. Basingstoke, UK: Palgrave Macmillan, 24–35.

Metcalf, Barbara D. and Thomas R. Metcalf. 2002. *A Concise History of Modern India*. Cambridge: Cambridge University Press.

Migdal, Joel. 1988. *Strong Societies and Weak States: State-Society Relations in the Third World*. Princeton, NJ: Princeton University Press.

Ministry of Environment and Forests (MoEF). 2009. "Bangladesh Climate Change Strategy and Action Plan 2009," MoEF, GoB, Dhaka.

Ministry of Health and Family Welfare (MoHFW). 2005. "National AIDS/STD Programme. National HIV Serological Surveillance, 2004–2005: Bangladesh," 6th Round technical report. Directorate General of Health Services, MoHFW, GoB.

Mookherjee, Nananika. "Discussion: 'Research' on Bangladesh War, Part II," *Economic and Political Weekly* (December 15, 2007): 120–1.

Mosquera, Alexis and Noushi Rahman. "Arsenic in Paddy," *The Daily Star*, January 17, 2010, http://www.thedailystar.net/newDesign/news-details.php?nid=122135 (accessed May 16, 2011).

Mukherjee, Ramkrishna. 1971. *Six Villages of Bengal*. Bombay: Popular Press.

Muna, Lazeena, James L. Ross, Sandra L. Laston and Abbas Biuyan. 2002. "Failure to Comply? Anthropological Perspectives on Refusal of Emergency Obstetric Care in Rural Bangladesh," in *Contemporary Anthropology: Theory and Practice*, ed. S. M. Nurul Alam. Dhaka, Bangladesh: Jahangirnagar University/University Press, 325–48.

Murshid, K. A. S., Salma C. Zohir, Mansur Ahmed, Iqbal Zabid and A. T. M. S. Mehdi. 2009. "The Global Financial Crisis: Implications for Bangladesh." Working Paper No. 1. Policy Resource Programme, Dhaka: Bangladesh Institute of Development Studies (BIDS).

Naher, Ainoon 2002. "Rural-urban Migration in Bangladesh: An Anthropological Exploration," in *Contemporary Anthropology: Theory and Practice*, ed. S. M. Nurul Alam. Dhaka, Bangladesh: Jahangirnagar University/University Press, 283–301.

Nasrin, Taslima. 1994. *Lajja: Shame.* English ed., trans. from the Bengali by Tutul Gupta. New Delhi: Penguin Books India.

Novak, James J. 1993. *Bangladesh: Reflections on the Water.* Bloomington: Indiana University Press.

Osmani, S. R. 2005. "The Impact of Globalization on Poverty in Bangladesh." Working Paper No. 65. Geneva: Policy Integration Department, National Policy Group, International Labour Office.

―――. 2006. "Delivering Basic Health Services in Bangladesh: A View from the Human Rights Perspective," in *Growth and Poverty: The Development Experience of Bangladesh,* ed. Sadiq Ahmed and Wahuiddin Mahmud. Dhaka, Bangladesh: University Press, 193–218.

Parveen, Saila and I. M. Faisal. "People versus Power: The Geopolitics of Kaptai Dam in Bangladesh," *Water Resources Development* 18, no. 1 (2002): 197–208.

Putnam, Robert D. 1993. *Making Democracy Work: Civic Tradition in Modern Italy.* Princeton, NJ: Princeton University Press.

Quazi, Rahim. 2001. "Foreign Aid and Capital Flight," *Journal of the Asia Pacific Economy* 9, no. 3 (2001): 370–93.

Rahman, Atiur. "NGOs and Civil Society in Bangladesh," *Journal of Social Studies* 84 (1999): 23–45.

Rahman, Hossain Zillur. 2009. *Unbundling Governance.* Dhaka, Bangladesh: Power and Participation Research Centre.

Rahman, Mahbubar and Willem van Schendel. 2004. "'I am not a refugee': Rethinking Partition Migration," in *State, Society and Displaced People in South Asia,* ed. Imtiaz Ahmed, Abhijit Dasgupta and Kathinka Sinha-Kerkhoff. Dhaka, Bangladesh: University Press, 203–45.

Rahman, Matiur and Raymond Wiest. 2003. "Context and Trends of Globalization in Bangladesh: Towards a Critical Research Agenda," in *Globalization, Environmental Crisis and Social Change in Bangladesh,* ed. Matiur Rahman. Dhaka, Bangladesh: University Press, 3–32.

Rahman, Pk. Md. Motiur, Noriatsu Matsui and Yukio Ikemoto. 2009. *The Chronically Poor in Rural Bangladesh: Livelihood Constraints and Capabilities.* London: Routledge.

Rahmat Ali, Choudhary. 1933. "Now or Never: Are We to Live or Perish Forever?" pamphlet, full text available at http://www.columbia.edu/itc/mealac/pritchett/00islamlinks/txt_rahmatali_1933.html (accessed May 17, 2011).

Rashid, Haroun er. 2005. *Economic Geography of Bangladesh.* 2nd ed. Dhaka, Bangladesh: University Press.

Riaz, Ali. 2004. *God Willing: The Politics of Islamism in Bangladesh.* Oxford: Rowman and Littlefield.

Rogaly, Ben. "Micro-finance Evangelism, 'Destitute Women,' and the Hard Selling of a New Anti-poverty Formula," *Development in Practice* 6, no. 2 (1996): 100–12.

Rogaly, Ben, Barbara Harriss-White and Sugata Bose. 1999. "Introduction: Agricultural Growth and Agrarian Change in West Bengal and Bangladesh," in *Sonar Bangla? Agricultural Growth and Agrarian Change in West Bengal and Bangladesh,* ed. Ben Rogaly, Barbara Harriss-White and Sugata Bose. Dhaka, Bangladesh: University Press, 11–38.

Rosselli, John. Review of "The East Pakistan Tragedy," by L. F. Rushbrook Williams, *International Affairs* 48, no. 3 (1972): 525–7.

Rozario, Santi. 2002. "Gender Dimensions of Rural Change," in *Hands Not Land: How Livelihoods Are Changing in Rural Bangladesh*, ed. Kazi Ali Toufique and Cate Turton. Dhaka: BIDS, 121–30.

Rushbrook Williams, L. F. 1972. *The East Pakistan Tragedy*. London: Tom Stacey.

Saikia, Yasmin. "Beyond the Archive of Silence: Narratives of Violence of the 1971 Liberation War of Bangladesh," *History Workshop Journal* 58 (2004): 275–87.

Seabrook, Jeremy. 2001. *Freedom Unfinished: Fundamentalism and Popular Resistance in Bangladesh Today*. London: Zed Books.

Selim, Shahpar. 2008. Ecological Modernization Theory and Bangladesh: Lessons from the Environmental Compliance Upgrading Experiences of Bangladeshi Garments Firms. Ph.D. diss., London School of Economics and Political Science.

Sen, Amartya. 1981. *Poverty and Famines: An Essay on Entitlements and Deprivation*. Oxford: Oxford University Press.

———. "Quality of Life: India vs. China," *The New York Review* (May 12, 2011): 44–5.

Siddiqi, Dina M. 1998. "Taslima Nasrin and Others: The Conflict over Gender in Bangladesh," in *Women in Muslim Societies: Diversity within Unity*, ed. H. L. Bodman and Nayereh Tohidi. London: Lynne Rienner, 205–27.

Siddiqui, Kamal. 2000. *Jagatpur 1977–97: Poverty and Social Change in Rural Bangladesh*. Dhaka, Bangladesh: University Press.

Siddiqui, Kamal, Jamshed Ahmed, Kaniz Siddique, Sayeedul Huq, Abul Hossain, Shah Nazinud-Doula and Nahid Rezawana. 2010. *Social Formation in Dhaka 1985–2005*. Farnham, UK: Ashgate.

Sisson, Richard and Leo E. Rose. 1990. *War and Secession: Pakistan, India and the Creation of Bangladesh*. Berkeley: University of California Press.

Smillie, Ian. 1999. *Mastering the Machine Revisited*. London: Intermediate Technology Books.

———. 2009. *Freedom from Want: The Remarkable Success Story of BRAC, the Global Grassroots Organization That's Winning the Fight Against Poverty*. Stirling, VA: Kumarian Press.

Smillie, Ian and John Hailey. 2001. *Managing for Change: Leadership, Strategy and Management in Asian NGOs*. London: Earthscan.

Smith, Adam. 1776 (repr. 1970). *The Wealth of Nations*. Harmondsworth, UK: Penguin.

Sobhan, Rehman. 1982. *The Crisis of External Dependence: The Political Economy of Foreign Aid to Bangladesh*. Dhaka, Bangladesh: University Press.

———. 1993. *Bangladesh: Problems of Governance*. New Delhi: Konvark Publishers.

———. "Structural Dimensions of Malgovernance in Bangladesh," *Economic and Political Weekly* (September 4, 2004): 4101–8.

———. 2007. "Challenging the Injustice of Poverty: The Need for Structural Change in South Asia." Conference on Development Prospects of Bangladesh: Emerging Challenges, December 2–3, Dhaka, BIDS.

Sobhan, Zafar. "The Realpolitik of Fools," *The Daily Star*, March 19, 2010, http://www.thedailystar.net/newDesign/news-details.php?nid=130614 (accessed May 16, 2011).

Stephens, Ian. 1964. *Pakistan: Old Country/New Nation*. Harmondsworth, UK: Penguin.

Stiles, Kendall. "International Support for NGOs in Bangladesh: Some Unintended Consequences," *World Development* 30, no. 5 (2002): 835–46.

Streefland, Pieter H. "Mutual Support Arrangements among the Poor in South Asia," *Community Development Journal* 31, no. 4 (1996): 302–18.

Swedish International Development Cooperation Agency (Sida). 2010. *Health and Education Reality Check Report 2009*. Stockholm: Sida.

Tett, Gillian. "The Story of the Brics," *Financial Times Magazine*, January 15, 2010, http://www.ft.com/cms/s/2/112ca932-00ab-11df-ae8d-00144feabdc0.html#ixzz1MVjwjk4q(accessed May 16, 2011).

Thorner, Daniel. 1980. *The Shaping of Modern India*. Bombay: Allied Publishers.

Toufique, Kazi Ali and Cate Turton. 2002. *Hands Not Land: How Livelihoods Are Changing in Rural Bangladesh*. Dhaka, Bangladesh: BIDS.

Uddin, Shahzad. "Privatization in Bangladesh: The Emergence of 'Family Capitalism,'" *Development and Change* 36, no. 1 (2005): 157–82.

Uddin, Sufia M. 2006. *Constructing Bangladesh: Religion, Ethnicity and Language in an Islamic Nation*. Chapel Hill: University of North Carolina Press.

Van Schendel, Willem. 2001. "Bengalis, Bangladeshis and Others: Chakma Visions of a Pluralist Bangladesh," in *Bangladesh: Promise and Performance*, ed. Rounaq Jahan. London: Zed Books, 65–106.

———. 2005. *The Bengal Borderlands: Beyond State and Nation in South Asia*. London: Anthem Press.

———. 2009. *A History of Bangladesh*. Cambridge: Cambridge University Press.

White, Sarah. 1992. *Arguing with the Crocodile: Gender and Class in Bangladesh*. London: Zed Books.

———. "NGOs, Civil Society, and the State in Bangladesh: The Politics of Representing the Poor," *Development and Change* 30, no. 3 (1999): 307–26.

White, Sarah and Joe Devine. 2009. "Beyond the Paradox: Religion, Family and Modernity in Contemporary Bangladesh." Working Paper 32. Research Centre on Religion and Development, University of Birmingham, UK.

Williams, Ian. "In Bangladesh, Climate Change Is a Matter of Life and Death," National Broadcasting Company (NBC) Worldblog, December 7, 2009, http://worldblog.msnbc.msn.com/_news/2009/12/07/4376387-in-bangladesh-climate-change-is-a-matter-of-life-and-death (accessed May 16, 2011).

Wood, Geoffrey D. 1976. "Class Differentiation and Power in Bandakgram: The Minifundist Case," in *Exploitation and the Rural Poor*, ed. M. Ameerul Huq. Comilla, Pakistan: Bangladesh Academy for Rural Development.

———. "Rural Class Formation in Bangladesh 1940–1980." *Bulletin of Concerned Asian Scholars* 13 (October–December 1981): 2–15.

———. 1994. *Bangladesh: Whose Ideas, Whose Interests?* Dhaka, Bangladesh: University Press.

———. 1997. "States without Citizens: The Problem of the Franchise State," in *Too Close for Comfort: NGOs, States and Donors*, ed. D. Hulme and M. Edwards. London: Macmillan, 79–92.

———. 2009. "Clashing Values in Bangladesh: NGOs Secularism and the Umma," in *Recreating the Commons? NGOs in Bangladesh*, ed. Farida Chowdhury Khan, Ahrar Ahmad and Munir Quddus. Dhaka, Bangladesh: University Press, 43–78.

Wood, Geoffrey D. and Sarah Salway. "Introduction: Securing Livelihoods in Dhaka Slums," *Journal of International Development* 12 (2000): 669–88.

World Bank. 1996. *Pursuing Common Goals: Strengthening Relations between Government and NGOs in Bangladesh*. Dhaka, Bangladesh: University Press.

———. 2006a. *Bangladesh Country Assistance Strategy 2006–9.* Washington, DC: World Bank.

———. 2006b. *Economics and Governance of Nongovernmental Organizations in Bangladesh.* Bangladesh Development Series, Paper No. 11. Dhaka, Bangladesh: World Bank.

———. 2006c. *Social Safety Nets in Bangladesh: An Assessment.* Bangladesh Development Series, Paper No. 9. Dhaka, Bangladesh: World Bank.

———. 2008a. *Poverty Assessment for Bangladesh: Poverty Reduction, Economic Management Unit, Finance and Private Sector Development Sector Unit South Asia Region.* Report No 44321-BD. Washington, DC: World Bank.

———. 2008b. *Whispers to Voices: Gender and Social Transformation in Bangladesh.* Bangladesh Development Series, Paper No. 22. Washington, DC: World Bank.

———. 2009. *Problem-Driven Governance and Political Economy Analysis: Good Practice Framework.* Washington, DC: World Bank.

Yunus, Muhammad. 2010. *Building Social Business: The New Kind of Capitalism that Serves Humanity's Most Pressing Needs.* New York: Public Affairs.

Zaidi, S. M. H. 1970. *The Village Culture in Transition: A Study of East Pakistan Rural Society.* Honolulu: East West Centre Press.

Ziring, Laurence. 1992. *Bangladesh from Mujib to Ershad: An Interpretive Study.* Karachi, Pakistan: Oxford University Press.

# Index

Abed, Sir Fazle H., 5, 114
Adnan, Shapan, 173, 175
Afghans, 43–4
Aga Khan, 55
agrarian economy, 21, 50, 144
agrarian structuralism, 116
agricultural production, 15, 21, 80, 89, 146, 159, 175, 198, 201
Ahmadiyya, 29, 95
Ahmed, Dr. Fakhruddin, 76
aid industry. *See* foreign aid
*ajlaf*, 26, 99
Akbar, Emperor, 45
AL. *See* Awami League
Alavi, Hamza, 98
Ali, Chaudhury Muhammad, 65
Ali, Karamat, 52
Animist religions, 28
Anti-Corruption Commission (ACC), 96
Arab traders, 28, 43
Arakan, 28
army. *See* Bangladesh army
arsenic, 124, 138, 173
*ashraf*, 26, 99, 111, 204
Assam, 42, 185
Association of Development Agencies in Bangladesh (ADAB), 118
Association for Social Advancement (ASA), 117, 119
Aurangzeb, Emperor, 46
Awami League, 14, 77–81, 93, 97, 103, 112

Ayub. *See* Khan, Ayub
Azam, Golam, 92
Azam, Shafiul, 85

Babar, Emperor, 45
Babri Mosque, 92
BAKSAL (Bangladesh Peasants and Workers Awami League), 81
Banerjea, Surendranath, 53, 55
Bangladesh army, 14, 19, 73, 76, 80–2, 85, 91, 93–4, 96, 98, 184
Bangladesh Liberation War, 5, 14, 27, 35, 45, 70, 90, 145–8
Bangladesh Medical Association, 118
Bangladesh Nationalist Party, 16, 19, 29, 103, 132, 134, 146–7, 157, 200
Bangladesh Rifles (BDR), 99
Bangladesh Rural Development Board (BRDB), 121
Bangladesh University of Engineering and Technology, 173
banking, 63, 79, 115, 117, 146, 148
Bara Buiyan group (the twelve landlords), 45
basic democracies, 66–7
Bay of Bengal, 13, 17, 154, 171–2, 195
BBC News, 4
*bediya*, 28
Beel Dakatia, 175
Bengal famine (1943–4), 57
Bengali language (Bangla). *See* language movement

225

Bengali Muslim identity, 5
Bengali renaissance, 51
Bengal Legislative Council (1909), 56
Bengal Sultanate, 44
*bhadralok*, 16, 51
*bhasha andolon. See* language
    movement
Bhashani, Maulana Abdul Hamid
    Khan, 52, 64–5
Bhutto, Zulfiqur Ali, 69
Bihar, 27–8, 34, 42–3, 48, 52, 54–5,
    183
biodiversity, 171
Blair, Harry, 16, 34, 38, 80, 126, 129
blocked development, concept of
    (Brett), 102
BNP. *See* Bangladesh Nationalist Party
Bogra, Mohammad Ali, 64
Bombay presidency, 34
Bonnerjee, Woomesh Chandra, 53
Bose, Sarmila, 71
BRAC, 5, 24, 109, 114, 117
Brahmaputra, 13, 42, 168–9
Brammer, Hugh, 170
British colonial rule, 52–8
British East India Company, 45–51,
    107
Buddhism, 6, 28, 42–3
bureaucracy, 16, 38, 59, 72, 76–7, 80,
    84, 98, 101
Burma, 28, 45
Bush, George W., 5
Buxar, battle of (1764), 48

Canadian University Service Overseas,
    116
capital flight, 39, 166
caretaker government system, 19, 90,
    93–4, 134
cash-based transfer programmes, 188
Centre for Policy Dialogue (CPD), 25
Chakmas, 28, 30
child mortality, 5, 21, 165, 181, 190
China, 30–1, 35, 48, 98, 142, 150, 157,
    168, 171, 201
Chittagong, 70, 142, 147–8, 157, 160,
    162, 171, 184

Chittagong Hill Tracts (CHT), 28, 30,
    33, 160, 183–4
Chittagong Port, 96
Chowdhury, Dr. Zafrullah, 118
Christian missionaries, 111
Christians, 13, 25
CHT. *See* Chittagong Hill Tracts
CHT Land (Disputes Settlement)
    Commission Act (2001), 184
CHT Peace Accords (1997), 33, 94, 184
citizenship. *See* state
Civil Service of Bangladesh, 102, 107,
    132
Civil Service of Pakistan, 62, 70
civil society, 109–35
    citizenship and, 126–7
    as contested idea, 11, 110, 126,
        130–1
    corruption and, 124–5
    donors and, 126
    emergency relief and, 114
    globalisation and, 129
    language movement and, 112
    market and, 88, 124
    military and, 126
    nationalism and, 113
    NGO identity and, 127
    "old" and "new" civil-society idea,
        125, 127
    philanthropy and, 111–12, 117, 125
    professional associations and, 93
    religion and, 111, 131–3
    self-help and, 111–12, 114, 125
    state and, 11, 102
    "strong" vs. "weak" civil-society
        debates, 128
    student politics and, 114
    uncivil society and, 9, 134
class relations, 9, 14–15, 26, 49, 57, 67,
    100
climate change, 6, 40, 176–9, 198
Clinton, Hillary R., 5
Clive, Colonel Robert, 47–8
coal, 142, 148, 154–5
Coalition for the Urban Poor (CUP),
    164
Cold War, 30

Comilla, 45, 112, 141, 147, 188
Comilla cooperative model, 36, 112, 116, 119, 121
community clinics, 191
community development, 35, 111
Concert for Bangladesh (1971), 187
Congress. *See* Indian National Congress Party
Constitution of Bangladesh, 30, 81, 84, 193
 Eighth Amendment of (1988), 32
 Fifth Amendment of (1977), 83
 Thirteenth Amendment of (1996), 93
Cooper, Frederick, 10, 98, 202
Copenhagen climate change summit (2009), 177
Cornwallis, Lord, 49
corruption, 20, 24, 81, 86, 95, 100, 102, 104, 106, 137, 147, 154, 158
cotton, 49, 85, 179
Cox's Bazaar, 28, 178
credit. *See* microcredit
Curzon, Viceroy Lord, 54
cyclones, 6, 13, 68, 92, 113, 170–1, 176

Danone dairy company, 124
*darga*, 26
decentralisation, 75, 87, 104, 192
Delhi Sultanate, 43, 45
deltaic ecosystem, 13, 179
Department for International Development (DFID), 9, 177
developmentalism, 19, 36, 39, 110, 176
diaspora, 126, 182, 188
digital Bangladesh, 97
Dutch traders, 46

Eastern Frontier Rifles, 99
East Pakistan, 2, 12, 14, 27, 35, 49, 51, 57, 82, 97–9, 101, 119, 137, 183
economy, 136–66
 agriculture, 137–40
 energy sector, 142–3

energy, foreign investment in, 154–5
 exports, nontraditional, 148–52
 governance of, 145–8
 industry, 142
 infrastructure, 140–1
 poverty and economic change, 158–62
 remittances, 152–3
 role of foreign aid, 143–5
 urbanisation and, 162–5
education, 13, 24, 37, 108, 122, 182, 193–5
Education Watch, 194
*Ekush Dapha* (21 Points), 64
elites, 25–6, 33, 37–9, 50, 53–7, 66, 87, 131, 133, 162
 military, 14
 new business group, 16
 professional, 17
 rentier, 16
Ershad, Hussain Muhammad, 19, 31, 84–5, 88, 103
European Union (EU), 152
export-processing zone (EPZ), 147
exports, 1, 23, 37, 86, 136, 138, 148, 151–2, 155

*fakir*, 51, 111
famine of 1943/4, 57
Faraizi movement, 51–2
Farakka barrage, 174
Fazlul Haq, Abul Kasem, 56–7, 62, 64–5
Federation of Bangladesh Chambers of Commerce and Industry (FBCCI), 93
financial services, 16, 146
Five Year Plans (Bangladesh), 78–9, 148, 193
Five Year Plans (Pakistan), 35, 180
Flood Action Plan (FAP), 129, 175
flood control, 174–6
flood-control master plan (1964), 175
floods, 13, 19, 86, 89, 96, 138, 161, 168–70, 172, 175–7
food prices, 97

food production, 138, 143, 180
foreign aid, 4, 17, 24, 35–9, 68–9, 80,
  83–4, 115, 124, 143–5, 147, 155
  changing composition of, 144
  political role played by, 35, 37–8
  public attitudes to, 39
  role in defining Bangladesh, 7, 36, 38
foreign investment, 37, 82, 91, 146,
  153–4
formation of Bangladesh, 59–73
freedom fighters, 14, 72, 77
Freire, Paolo, 116

Gandhi, Indira, 30
Gandhi, M. K., 56–8
Ganges, 13, 31, 42, 169, 173, 214
Ganges Water Treaty (1996), 174
garments, 23, 33, 82, 148–50, 200
garment workers, 1, 24, 97, 150, 162
Garos, 28
gas, 33, 112, 142, 154–7, 163, 201
Gaur, 45
General Education Project (GEP), 193
genocide, 27
Ghaznavids, 43
Ghosh, Amitav, 170
global capitalist economy, 1, 4, 10, 24,
  33, 41, 50, 129, 166
global financial crisis (2008), 166, 201
globalisation, 33, 41, 129–30, 201
GO-NGO Consultative Council
  (GNCC), 121
*gono andolon*, 3, 89, 133
Gonoshasthya Kendra (GK), 87, 118
good governance, donor model of, 7,
  11, 24, 105, 110, 131
Government of India Act (1858), 52
Government of India Act (1909),
  55
*gram sarkar*, 83
gross domestic product (GDP), 20–1,
  83, 107, 110, 136–8, 151, 158, 165,
  188
Gupta dynasty, 42

Haji Shariatullah, 51
harassment (*hoirani*), 24

*hartal* politics, 89, 92, 97, 126
Hartmann, Betsy, 14, 178, 181
Hasina. *See* Wazed, Sheikh Hasina
Hastings, Warren, 48
health, 190–2
Health Education and Economic
  Development (HEED), 123
Health and Population Sector
  Programme (HPSP), 191
Hinduism
  caste, 43
  Hindu nationalism, 32, 57
  Hindu tradition, 6
  influence in Bengal, 43, 64, 204
  social organisation, 26
  traditions of charity, 111
HIV/AIDS epidemic, 190
human development index, 188
human rights, 24, 95–6, 110, 113, 131,
  184
Humayun, Emperor, 45
Hunter, W. W., 50
Huntingdon, Samuel, 5, 132

identity
  construction among diaspora
    communities, 188
  linguistic, 27
  and religion, 27
  state and, 103
illiberal democracy idea, 76, 97, 107
Ilyas Shahi dynasty, 44
immunisation, 192
India, 5, 12, 17, 32, 35, 62, 72, 81, 83,
  92, 94, 104, 123, 131, 139, 170, 201
  Bangladesh comparisons with, 33–4
  Bangladeshi migration to, 186
  Bangladesh relations with, 155–7
  border issues with Bangladesh, 17,
    156–7, 200
  intervention in Bangladesh
    Liberation War, 68
  water sharing, 31, 33, 173–4
Indian Councils Act (1861), 52
Indian National Congress Party, 53,
  56–7
indigo, 46

Indo-Bangladesh Friendship Treaty (1972), 30, 33
Indo-Soviet bloc, 30
industrial bourgeoisie, 16, 50
informality, 104–5
integrated rural development projects (IRDPs), 36
interest groups, 40, 73, 91, 101, 104, 126–7, 129–30, 133, 156
Inter-Governmental Panel on Climate Change (IPCC), Fourth Assessment Report of, 176
International Monetary Fund, 67, 155
Iran, 42
Islam, 180
    Bangladeshi nationalism and, 32
    conversion to in Bengal, 43, 64
    identity and, 31, 63, 85, 103
    Islamic tradition, 52, 111, 123, 132, 180, 187
    nationalism and, 27, 52, 59, 75, 204
    politics and, 29, 76, 157, 200
    traditions in Bangladesh, 25–6
Islami Oikya Jote Party, 95
Islamists, 27–8

Ja'amatul Mujaheedin Bangladesh (JMB), 29
Jafar, Mir, 47
Jahan, Rounaq, 3, 14, 19, 26, 213
Jainism, 42
Jalal, Ayesha, 49, 66–7, 70, 72, 80–1, 113
*jama'at*, 23
Jama'at-i-Islami (JI), 29, 90–2, 95, 97, 133, 187, 200
*jamdani* muslin, 46
Jamuna Bridge project, 94
Japan, 148–9, 170
Jatiya Party, 88, 91, 94–5
Jatiya Samajtantrik Dal (JSD), 82
JI. *See* Jama'at-i-Islami
Jinnah, Muhammad Ali, 56, 58
Johnson, Ural Alexis, 36
*jotedar*, 51
Jugunda party, 55
Jukto (United) Front, 64–5, 69

jute, 23, 49, 51, 62, 68, 78, 83, 85, 101, 137–8, 179

Kabeer, Naila, 82, 127, 142, 150, 199
*kabiraj* indigenous healers, 192
Kansat, 143, 154
Kaptai Dam, 183
Karnataka, 43
Khaleda Zia. *See* Zia, Begum Khaleda
Khaliji dynasty, 43
Khan, Ayub, 65–7, 69–70, 82
Khan, Dr. Akhtar Hameed, 36, 116
Khan, General Agha Muhammad Yahya, 67–9, 71
Khan, General Tikka, 70–2
Khan, Isa, 45
Khan, Liaquat Ali, 61
Khan, Mushtaq H., 100–3
Khan, Sir Syed Ahmad, 54–5
Khasis, 28
*khas* land, 87, 104, 122, 162
Kissinger, Henry, 36
Kochanek, Stanley, 23, 91–2, 99, 106, 127, 165
Kolkata, 46–8, 55
Krishak Proja Party (KPP), 56

labour market, 15, 149–50, 163
Lalbagh fort, 45
land fragmentation, 101
landlessness, 14, 58, 114, 117, 122, 127, 160, 162
landownership, 14, 50, 116, 161, 189
language movement, 63, 65, 74, 133
Larma, Manabendranath, 30
liberalisation, 32, 37–8, 84, 86, 102, 106, 136, 143, 145–9, 200, 202
Liberation. *See* Bangladesh Liberation War
livelihoods, 15, 23, 159, 179, 192
local government, 22, 40, 53, 66, 86, 91, 113, 187, 198
Lodhi dynasty, 43

*madrasa*, 29, 112, 193, 195, 204
Mahalanobis, Professor Prasanta C., 175

Maharashtra, 34
Malaysia, 181, 185
malnutrition, 190
Marmas, 28
Marxist theory, 9
*matbars*, 22, 100, 111
maternal health, 5
Mauryan Empire, 42
*mazar*, 26
media, 4, 6, 16, 125, 135, 178, 186, 197, 205
Meghna, 13, 168–9
Mennonite Central Committee, 116
microcredit, 114, 159–60
    achievements of, 119
    criticisms of, 29, 120
    donors and, 37
    government's role in, 121
    original Grameen Bank approach to, 115
    poverty reduction and, 159, 161
    rejection of by some NGOs, 117
middle classes, 16–17, 26, 33, 69, 101, 107, 114, 154, 195, 199
Middle East, 34, 152–3, 185
migration, 15, 17, 19, 33, 35, 156, 163, 178, 182–8
military-backed caretaker government, 96, 99, 133–4, 146, 153, 157
military coups, 3, 19, 48, 75, 81, 84–5, 91, 94
military fiscalism, 48
Millennium Development Goals (MDGs), 5, 20, 160, 202
minorities, 2, 27–9, 62, 71, 76, 83, 95
Minto, Viceroy Lord, 55
Mir, Titu, 51
Mirza, General Iskandar, 65
Mohammad, Ghulam, 61
Mohila Parishad (Women's Council), 112
Mughal period, 45–52
Mukherjee, Ramkrishna, 14
*mukhti bahini. See* freedom fighters
Multi-Donor Trust Fund (MDTF), 177

Multi-Fibre Arrangement (MFA), 149–50
Murshidabad, 45
Muslim League, 55–7, 59–61, 64–5, 82
*mustaan*, 16, 23, 133, 199
Mymensingh, 28–9, 45, 52, 139, 141, 179

Nasim, Staff General Abu Saleh Mohammad, 93
Nasrin, Taslima, 92
National Adaptation Plan of Action (NAPA), 177
National Education Policy (2010), 195
national elite, 26, 56
nationalism, 59
natural disasters, 13, 17, 57, 89, 112, 161, 165
natural resources and ecology, 168–71
Nazim-ud-Din, Khwaja, 61
Nepal, 4, 168
New Industrial Policy (NIP), 31, 82, 85
new universities, new private, 195
NGO. *See* nongovernmental organisation (NGO)
NGO Affairs Bureau, 121, 123
Nijera Kori, 117
Nirmul Committee, 187
nongovernmental organisations (NGOs), 24, 36, 87, 104, 113–25, 151, 162, 164, 190, 194, 198
    accountability and, 110
    achievements of, 121–2
    aid received by, 117
    critical views of, 118, 127
    numbers of, 109
    relations with government, 121–2

oil, 33, 185, 201
oil crisis (1973), 80
Operation Clean Heart, 95
opium, 48
Organization of the Islamic Conference (OIC), 31
Orissa, 28, 45, 48, 52, 54–5
Oxfam, 116

Pakistan, 58–69
  agrarian reform in, 60
  Bangladesh comparisons with, 5, 204
  Bangladesh relations with, 31
  break up of, 12, 26
  covert support to Indian dissidents,
    184
  creation of, 58–60
  disparities within, 67–8
  elite families of, 14, 77
  failure of governance in, 70
  failure of integration in, 97
  family planning efforts in, 180
  flood-control efforts, 175
  as foreign-aid recipient, 35
  government's failure to understand
    Bengali nationalist movement, 70
  hydroelectric power policies, 184
  idea of, 58
  imposition of martial law (1958), 66
  inequalities in, 69
  jute processing in, 23
  military-bureaucratic state, 84
  relative deprivation in, 62
Pakistan army, 2, 14, 69–72, 98
Pakistan People's Party, 67
Pala dynasty, 42
Palli Karma-Sahayak Foundation
  (PKSF), 121
Palli Mangal Samitis (Village Welfare
  Societies), 112
Panipat, battle of (1526), 45
Parbatya Chattagram Janasaghati
  Samity (PCJSS), 184
parent-teacher associations (PTAs), 194
Partition of 1905, 30, 54, 205
Partition of 1947, 12–13, 26, 50, 58–60,
  62, 73, 98, 183
patronage, 17, 23, 33, 48, 51, 57, 67, 77,
  85, 89, 92, 98, 101, 106, 112, 128,
  198
patron-client relationships, 22, 100
per capita income, 24
Permanent Settlement Act of 1793,
  50–1
Persia, 45
pharmaceutical industry, 16, 118

Plassey. *See* Polashi, battle of (1757)
Polashi, battle of (1757), 47–8
political economy, 9, 38, 161
political parties, 17, 19, 23, 30, 66,
  81–2, 93, 95, 100, 106, 122, 127–8,
  130, 133, 198
population, 2, 13, 20, 25, 59, 101, 162,
  173, 179–82, 189, 191
population-control programmes, 181
ports, 171, 195, 201
Portuguese traders, 45
poverty, 5, 15, 17, 19–20, 77–8, 106,
  113, 115–16, 119, 123, 131, 136,
  144, 163–4, 178, 188
poverty and economic change, 158–62
Poverty Reduction Strategy Paper
  (PRSP), 148, 152, 161
Power and Participation Research
  Centre (PPRC), 25
precolonial Bengal, 42–52
primary education, 5, 19, 21, 165, 181,
  193–4, 198
privatisation, 32, 37, 86, 102, 104, 110,
  145, 147, 194, 202
Proshika, 116, 119, 122, 125, 127
Public Safety Act (2000), 94
Punjabi bureaucracy, 14
*purdah*, 15

Rahman, Hossain Zillur, 105
Rahman, Sheikh Mujibur, 19–20, 38,
  75, 77–81, 84, 94, 100, 103, 113,
  116, 145, 193
Rahman, Ziaur, 19, 31, 37, 70, 81–3, 85,
  88, 103, 143, 145
Rahmat Ali, Choudhury, 58
railways, 156
*rakkhi bahini* (National Security Force),
  81
Rapid Action Battalion (RAB), 95
Rashid, Haroun er, 171
*razakars*, 71
Rebellion of 1857, 52
religion, 25–9
  and social life, 25
  and state, 83
  traditions of pluralism, 44

remittances, 4, 33, 144, 146, 152–3, 158, 166, 168, 182, 185, 188
rentier, 50–1
Revised Industrial Policy (RIP), 31
rice crop, 21, 57, 137
river systems, 13, 139, 162, 168–70, 172
Rohingyas (Arakani Muslims), 184
rural social movements, 101
*ryotwari* land tenure system, 34

*salish*, 22, 111
saltpetre, 46
*samaj*, 22, 111
Samarkand, 45
Samata, 117
Santals, 28
Saudi Arabia, 31, 35, 39, 153, 186, 204
Sayyid dynasty, 43
secularism, 5, 16, 28–30, 72, 83, 103, 112–13, 132, 156, 187, 193
Sena dynasty, 43
Sen, Amartya, 57
Shah, Ala al-Din Husayn, 44
Shanti Bahini, 184
Sheikh Hasina Wazed. *See* Wazed, Sheikh Hasina
Sheikh Mujibur Rahman. *See* Rahman, Sheikh Mujibur
*shia*, 44
shrimp, 4, 13, 86, 140, 151–2, 166, 170, 176, 200, 202
*shushil shamaj*, 131
Sida Reality Check Approach, 194
Singapore, 13, 57, 185
Six Point Programme, 69
Slave (or Mamluk) dynasty, 43
Smith, Adam, 9
smuggling, 17, 88, 99, 147, 156
Sobhan, Rehman, 7, 10, 37, 61, 69, 101, 133, 161–2
social protection, 188–9
society, 13–19, 100, 164
Sonargaon, 45
South Asian Association for Regional Cooperation (SAARC), 32

Southeast Asia, 17
South Korea, 1, 148–9, 181, 185
Soviet Union, 30, 32, 41, 67, 83
Sri Lanka, 4, 87
state, 75–108
  citizenship, 92, 105–6, 127, 134, 182–3, 199
  colonial, 98, 107
  the "everyday state," 104–5
  first government of Begum Khaleda Zia (1991–6), 90–3
  first government of Sheikh Hasina Wazed (1996–2001), 93–4
  governance and policy making, 105–7
  government of General H. M. Ershad (1982–90), 85–90
  government of General Ziaur Rahman (1976–81), 81–5
  government of Sheikh Mujibur Rahman (1971–5), 77–81
  and identities, 30, 102–3
  in the making, 40
  military-backed caretaker government (2007–8), 96
  military-bureaucratic, 84, 98
  patronage politics, 99–102, 104–5
  policy making, 105
  second government of Begum Khaleda Zia (2001–6), 94–6
  second government of Sheikh Hasina Wazed (2009–), 97
  secular nationalism, 75, 83
  state formation, 97–9
  weak vs. strong state arguments, 103–4, 110
Sufism, 6, 26, 45, 204
Suhrawardy, Huseyn Shaheed, 53, 56, 60, 64–6
*sundarbans*, 170, 179
Sunga dynasty, 42
*sunni*, 25, 44, 180
Suraj-ud-Daula, Nawab, 47
*swaraj* (self-rule), 55
Sylhet, 4, 59, 139, 154, 160, 168, 185, 188
Sylhetis, 185

Tagore, Rabindranath, 55, 204
Taiwan, 1, 185
Task Force on Primary and Mass
    Education, 193
taxation, 103–4, 147
tea, 48–9, 59
technology, 21, 140, 146–7, 154, 167,
    177
Teesta barrage, 174
terrorism, 5, 19, 95, 153, 156, 186, 199,
    203
textiles, 16, 46, 49
Thailand, 181
Tipaimukh hydroelectric dam project,
    174
trade unions, 113, 127, 199
Transparency International, 7, 20, 95,
    106
Tripura (Indian State), 28, 45
Tripuras, 28
Tughluq Sultanate, 44
Tukaroi, battle of (1576), 45
two nation theory, 54, 58, 73, 107

Union *parishad*, 22, 66, 122
United Nations, xiii, 20, 30, 32, 89, 162,
    165, 174
United States, 30, 32–4, 36, 39, 72, 91,
    148–9, 153, 157, 166, 185
universities, new private, 124
universities, public, 16, 124, 195
UN peacekeeping role, 33, 99, 153
*upazila parishad*, 86–7, 91
urbanisation, 15, 23, 162–5
Urdu language, 12, 26–7, 45, 61, 62–4,
    71, 183, 193
U.S. Agency for International
    Development (USAID), 37, 173,
    176

Van Schendel, Willem, 3, 6, 58–9, 77,
    183
vernacular elite, 14–15, 56, 78
Vikrampur, 43
Village Agricultural Industrial
    Development (V-AID), 35
village-level institutions, 21–3, 35–6,
    40, 83, 100, 111, 113
voluntary action, 24, 111, 113

Wahabi tradition, 51, 204
war criminals issue, 40, 103, 187–8
war on terror, discourse of, 5, 30, 186,
    200
Wazed, Sheikh Hasina, 20, 29, 32–3, 89,
    94, 97, 157, 174
West Bengal, 28, 30, 33, 42, 54, 59–60,
    65, 70, 77, 103, 156, 179
West Pakistan, 12, 14, 35, 50, 61–2, 66,
    68, 73, 78, 82, 98
Wikileaks, 96
women's empowerment, 29, 114, 150
women's status, 37
Wood, Geoffrey D., 7, 38, 50, 104, 110,
    132
World Bank, 9, 19–20, 37, 67, 79, 82,
    119, 131, 140, 145, 148, 155, 158,
    161, 165, 177
World Health Organization (WHO), 87

Yahya. *See* Khan, General Agha
    Muhammad Yahya
Yunus, Muhammad, 5, 115, 124, 140

*zakat*, 23, 111
zamindar, 50–1, 57, 59, 111
Zia. *See* Rahman, Ziaur
Zia, Begum Khaleda, 20, 29, 32–3,
    89–90, 93–5, 97, 194